# TREATED LIKE FAMILY

How an Entrepreneur
and His "Employee Family"
Built Sargento, a Billion-Dollar
Cheese Company

TOM FALEY

CENTER
STREET

NEW YORK   NASHVILLE

Center Street
Hachette Book Group
1290 Avenue of the Americas, New York, NY 10104
centerstreet.com
twitter.com/centerstreet

First edition: April 2018

Center Street is a division of Hachette Book Group, Inc. The Center Street name and logo are trademarks of Hachette Book Group, Inc.

The publisher is not responsible for websites (or their content) that are not owned by the publisher.

The Hachette Speakers Bureau provides a wide range of authors for speaking events. To find out more, go to www.HachetteSpeakersBureau.com or call (866) 376-6591.

Library of Congress Cataloging-in-Publication Data

Names: Faley, Tom, author.
Title: Treated Like family : how an entrepreneur and his "employee family" built Sargento, a billion-dollar cheese company / Tom Faley.
Description: First edition. | New York : Center Street, [2018]
Identifiers: LCCN 2017046550| ISBN 9781478992868 (hardcover) | ISBN 9781549168123 (audio download) | ISBN 9781478992882 (ebook)
Subjects: LCSH: Gentine, Leonard, 1914–1996. | Sargento Foods Inc.—Biography. | Sargento Foods Inc.—History. | Cheese industry—United States—Biography. | Cheese industry—United States—History.
Classification: LCC HD9280.U62 F35 2018 | DDC 338.7/6373092 [B] —dc23
LC record available at https://lccn.loc.gov/2017046550

ISBNs: 978-1-4789-9286-8 (hardcover), 978-1-4789-9288-2 (ebook)

Printed in Canada

FRI

10  9  8  7  6  5  4  3  2  1

For my parents, Francis and Maxine Faley, who taught me the value of family.

Your legacy lives in your children and grandchildren.

# CONTENTS

# CONTENTS

TREATED LIKE FAMILY

# Prologue

## Chavannes-les-Grands, France
## March 1892

JOSEPH GENTINE PLANNED to commit the ultimate act against his family—against his father, his grandfather, and the many generations before them.

Standing among rows of grapevines in the predawn morning, he paid no heed to the weather or his discomfort as mist speckled his face and wind drove the cold drizzle deep into his clothing. His stomach tightened. His breathing labored. His shoulders tensed.

*This is it*, he thought. *This is the last day.* The thought rang with a somber finality, and he felt the rats of guilt gnawing at the edges of his conviction. Today, he and his family would pack the wagon, hitch the horses, and leave this province of France: Alsace, his birthplace, the birthplace of generations of his family before him. The Gentine family, for as far back as he could remember, had always lived in this small town of Chavannes-les-Grands.

His grapes grew from French soil. His family was French, but they no longer lived in that once ennobled country. Germany stole the land—Alsace-Lorraine, along with his family's vineyard—after the

The Gentine family:
Back row: Thomas and Leo
Middle row: Josephine, Jules, Louis, and Joseph
Front row: Joseph Jr.

Franco-Prussian War. Kaiser Wilhelm II spurned the people of Alsace, and in return, the Alsatians shared the same contempt for the kaiser.

Joseph had brooded over his options during the prior winter. In the end, he and his wife, Josephine, grew to accept a distasteful solution: leave Chavannes-les-Grands with their five sons, and start their life over elsewhere. As the winter winds howled in the evenings, they plotted.

There were friends—German friends he had come to know—that had left behind their homes, forsaken their family's past, and found a new life in a German community in the United States west of a city called Milwaukee. Just months earlier, in the fall, he had sent a letter to them. Late winter, their response reached him. "Come," they wrote. They would house his family until land could be purchased for their farm.

That would be their destiny, he and Josephine agreed. Unlike their intolerable life in Chavannes-les-Grands, they would begin a new life in America, a country that—unlike Germany or France—respected its citizens, a country that found no value in prejudice and hate, a country free from onerous taxes. With them, they would bring their valued possessions, their French traditions, and their family history. Just as important, they would bring cuttings from the family's vineyard, securing their sons' future.

Mentally, Joseph calculated the number of cuttings needed from their vines to reestablish a sizable vineyard at the end of their journey. With determination, he plodded through the mud, toward the oldest vines—those closest to the house. These he valued above all. They symbolized the roots of the generations before him, the history of their family.

He bundled the clippings in a damp cloth, tucked them into a lidded wooden box, and entered the house. The room, lit only by the flickering flames of the fireplace, caused his family's shadows to jump and dart furtively along the walls.

"I'm all set, Jo," he said. "All the vine cuttings are wrapped and loaded in the wagon. Have you packed everything we need?"

As Josephine turned toward him, the orange-copper glow from the fire revealed only part of her face, leaving the rest in shadow. A tear tracked silently over the crest of her cheek. She didn't answer. Just nodded.

He studied her as Josephine took a slow look around, as if she were etching details of her home in her mind. Pulling her into him, he wrapped his arms around her, giving a long, reassuring hug.

She had borne him a family of six children: five boys and one girl. The oppressive weight of melancholy nearly crushed her years ago when Marie passed away as an infant. Josephine's emotional wound healed as she reconnected with her family once again. But the scar remained, along with a residue of sadness at the corners of her eyes.

Josephine took a long, shuddering breath in his arms as if she once again recalled the reality of her sacrifices. Of the family she was leaving behind and the only life she had known for forty years. Of her daughter and the small grave she was abandoning, to be left unattended, overgrown with weeds and forgotten by generations that would follow.

They stood embracing in the middle of the room. "Are you OK, Jo?" he whispered in her ear.

"I'm fine," she said, pushing away from him. "We must do this for the children..." Then, meeting his eyes, she repeated, "I'll be fine."

They stood in silence until a loud rap on the door trespassed the moment. The door eased open and the toothy smile of their neighbor poked in.

"Just me, Joseph. Would have been here earlier, but roads are getting muddy."

Joseph raised his hand in welcome. "Your timing is perfect. We were just loading the wagon."

As his three oldest sons gathered their baggage, Joseph snuffed the flames in the fireplace with water and a poker. The house grew dark. A rectangle of early-morning light seeped through the open front door— a light leading them away. He grabbed his wife's hand and together they closed the door behind them for the last time.

With an air of solemnity, the family piled into the wagon, slick from the morning mist. Their neighbor would accompany them as far as Belfort before returning with the horses and wagon to the Gentine homestead. Joseph sighed. The *former* Gentine homestead. They no longer owned the horses and wagon, and it was no longer his vineyard. All was sold. Everything.

With the house slowly receding behind them, a lump rising in his throat, Joseph glanced at his wife and children huddled in blankets against the damp weather. His future, the future of his entire family, suddenly shrank to twelve pieces of baggage and approximately three hundred vine cuttings bound in a ragged cloth. They were all he had now, but they were all he would ever need.

He turned toward the road ahead, his back to the home he had always known. The wagon moaned as it rocked over the uneven road. Ahead, the two horses thumped along, snorting small vapor clouds into the cold morning air, their leather harnesses squeaking as they strained against the weight they pulled.

Unseen by others, tears welled up and blurred his vision. He remained head bent, facing forward. Joseph no longer wanted to see the sacrifice he was making.

# 1

# Out of the Blue
## 1933

Leonard Gentine's high school photo

SEVEN SECONDS. In the same amount of time it took nineteen-year-old Leonard Gentine to comb his hair as he prepared to leave the house, fate jolted his life, leaving behind a palpable air of uncertainty and unease.

Much the same as any other Saturday morning, he had arranged to spend the day with Dolores Becker, a woman five years his senior, who lived with her parents in Milwaukee. Navigating over lightly traveled roads, his thoughts had wandered, forsaking careful attention to his driving.

It was 1933, a time when President Franklin Delano Roosevelt introduced the New Deal, a time when the nation still reeled under the weight of the Great Depression, a time when the anemic economy and paltry wages made the purchase of gasoline a luxury. Families often relegated their cars to garages in deference to public transportation.

The car Leonard drove—an older vehicle with an annoying rattle, a stiff steering wheel, and doors that groaned when swung on their hinges—belonged to his parents, Louis and Anna Gentine. Their agreement had been simple. If he paid for the gas from his wages working at an industrial equipment manufacturer, they allowed him the use of their car.

Driving that morning, Leonard thrust his hand out the window, feeling the pressure of the air as he sped down the streets. Two men, sitting on a porch, had turned their heads as he rattled by. Leonard had barely noticed them. Absorbed in thought, he automatically turned right, spinning quickly around a corner.

It was then that fate played its card, waiting for this exact moment. From the midst of reverie, Leonard suddenly grew aware of the slow-moving vehicle—one that appeared to have dropped out of the blue—directly in front of him.

Seven seconds compressed into a single stroke of time. He stomped on the brake pedal. Tires squealed. He spun the steering wheel hard to the right.

Then, as if in slow motion, his car stuttered across loose gravel on an irrevocable path into the rear of the vehicle ahead.

The crash, so sudden, so startling, threw Leonard into the unforgiving rim of the steering wheel. A cacophony of senses consumed him: pressure on his lungs, impact to the head, crunching of metal, shattering of glass.

An odd stillness followed. The world had stopped, briefly, giving him time to collect his wits. With his long fingers barely looped over the top of the steering wheel, Leonard squeezed out his breath.

He surveyed for injuries: His ribs hurt. His left shoulder ached. His forehead sported a small lump. He could see no traces of blood. OK. He breathed easier. *I'm fine*, he remembered thinking. *Just a few bumps.* The car had suffered the brunt of the collision.

Then panic gripped him. His parents' car!

Leonard's knuckles whitened as he gripped the steering wheel. Ahead, the door slowly yawned open, and a finely polished shoe stepped onto the running board followed by its wearer, a sturdy, balding man in his mid-thirties. The man, freed from his vehicle, strode back to the point of impact.

Creaking open the door of his car, Leonard stepped out to offer his apologies and to study the damage. There was no anger, no shouting. The man, dressed in a somber suit and tie, examined the crumpled black metal and frowned. He then looked squarely into Leonard's face. "Son, you're going to have to pay for this."

Leonard's stomach clenched. He hadn't considered the expense of the other vehicle. Where would he find the money for that? Not from his parents. He knew they couldn't afford it. Leonard met the man's eyes and merely nodded agreement.

Then an image of the crash—just moments before the impact—flashed back to him. Could that be right? Leonard inched backward to gain a better perspective of the other vehicle. Yes, it was true. That's exactly what he had seen.

Now, standing mid-street, his mind racing, he made a quick assessment and chose the only recourse he could imagine.

# 2

# The Obligation
## 1933

LEONARD WORRIED. The agreement, hesitantly accepted at the scene of the accident, might pale in comparison to this pending conversation with Dolores. He was uncertain of her reaction, how his agreed-upon undertaking might bruise their relationship.

Arriving later than he had promised, he took a deep breath as he approached the Becker home.

From her parents' porch, Dolores watched as he parked by the curb. Concern painted her face and grew even more pronounced as she hurried down the steps to greet him.

"Oh, Len!" Dolores gaped in shock. "You were in a car accident?"

"It wasn't just another car I hit," he explained. "One instant the road was clear. Then—*wham!*—out of the blue, there's this hearse in front of me! A hearse!"

Leonard shoved his hand into his pants pocket. "I have the name of the man driving it." Fishing out the note, he unfolded the paper. "Hobart Brigden," he said, carefully pronouncing the name. "He owns the Brigden Funeral Home over on West Lloyd Street. Gave me his phone number and address."

The sound of movement from the porch drew Leonard's attention. Dolores's younger sister, Margie, clung to the porch railing. He flashed a quick smile and a wave, and then returned his attention to Dolores.

"He told me I had to pay for the damage," Leonard continued, "and I panicked. I don't have that kind of money. But when I stepped back and saw it was a hearse, it gave me the idea. At first, Mr. Brigden hesitated, but after I explained my situation . . . well, he agreed to let me work off the debt."

As Dolores listened, she ran her hand over the dented car fender, her fingers probing the sharp creases in the metal and ridges left by the chipped paint.

"He'll let me know the total cost I need to work off. Next Saturday I might even drive the hearse—if there's a funeral. Said he'd pay me four dollars a day."

Dolores scrunched her brow. "You ran into this man's hearse and now he's going to let you to drive it? By any chance, did Mr. Brigden also suffer a bump on the head?" She touched his forehead. Leonard winced.

"Well . . . I think I kinda talked him into it." Then he quickly added, "Of course, driving the hearse may not be something I do all the time. I let him know that whatever else needs to be done, I'd do that, too."

Dolores studied Leonard's face. Despite the gravity of the situation, she grinned. "Well, aren't you quite the charmer, Mr. Gentine. Who else could crash into a man one minute and, in the next minute, be offered a job?"

Leonard returned the smile, grateful for the implied understanding and hopeful this would be only a short-lived obligation and minor inconvenience for the two of them.

The following Saturday, at the Brigden Funeral Home, in his best suit, Leonard trimmed hedges. His list of responsibilities was unexpected. Mr. Brigden unabashedly assigned him any job not requiring a mortuary degree: washing windows, mowing the lawn, cleaning up after embalmment, and occasionally driving the hearse.

At first, Leonard stood tentatively in the shadows, watching Hobart prepare the bodies for their funeral. The process was unfamiliar, slightly uncomfortable. Surprisingly, as his exposure increased, Leonard grew more intrigued and less reluctant.

"What we do here is not for the benefit of the dead," Hobart said, "but for the comfort of the living. Focus your emotions on the needs of those left behind. Allowing the family to see their loved one at peace is an important responsibility."

As weeks passed, when Brigden met with a grieving family, when a funeral needed greeters at the door, or when a body required prepping, Leonard eagerly volunteered, witnessing firsthand the inner workings of the funeral business. Each week, he routinely peppered his new boss with questions.

As a friendship grew, Hobart shared the nettlesome financial side of his business as well—the continuous stream of bills, the slow payments from those still struggling with the economy.

"To bring in a little extra money," Hobart confided, "I tinker with inventions. Here's something that I've sold to a few people. Some of the local stores offer it, too." Hobart pulled out what appeared to be a small test tube—a pointed tip at the bottom with a rubber stopper at the top. "I hope to patent it someday. You stick it in the ground by the roots and it automatically fertilizes the tree."

Leonard studied the small tube. How many of these things would Hobart need to sell to pay just one of the bills on his desk? he wondered. And the damage to the hearse, since Leonard's free labor wasn't paying any bills. Hobart didn't replace anybody at the funeral home nor did he cut another employee's hours. He allowed Leonard to work off his debt, an arrangement that probably helped Leonard more than it repaid the damage.

Why would he do that when his funeral business could use the money? Why not insist Leonard pay his debt outright from his earnings at the Falk Corporation—the full-time job he held during the week?

It seemed illogical. Is that how a business is run? He didn't think so. Still, Hobart's empathy, his sense of caring, the unorthodox way he treated his staff—as if they were considered more than employees—changed how Leonard viewed his time spent at the funeral home. He found himself arriving earlier each week and leaving well after his promised time, a way for him to convey an unspoken appreciation.

As Leonard suspected, the increased hours at the funeral home made a social life with Dolores difficult. Occasionally, they attended a dance or a movie. More affordably, their dates revolved around family events and meals.

In a blur of emotions, late one Sunday morning, Leonard drove Dolores to Brookfield, Wisconsin. His grandparents' vineyard was a part of his past—a chapter in his life—that had shaped his boyhood. On the farm, he learned the value of hard work, and the satisfaction that followed a long day's labor.

There his grandfather taught him balance—not the careful footing while tending grapes on a steep slope, although there was skill in doing that. It was the lesson of keeping work in perspective. Leisure—hunting, fishing, or just playing cards well past a boy's bedtime—needed to counterbalance the arduous demands of the farm.

And while he felt the joy of sharing this part of his life with Dolores, he remained guarded. He had yet to share with her his hopes of one day owning his grandparents' farm, of carrying forward the Gentine tradition of growing grapes, a tradition that skipped over his uncles' and his father's generation.

Dolores was a city girl, unaccustomed to life constrained by the limitations of a farm. *What if she doesn't find the vineyard appealing?* he'd wondered. They were early in their dating. It might be too soon, their relationship still too fragile to discuss such long-term plans.

Turning the car onto the plank road that led to the farmhouse, Leonard pointed out the vines on their left. "My grampa told me those grapevines came from France."

Leonard searched Dolores's face for the slightest hint of excitement as she poked her head around him to gain a better view. Rows of vines with their leathery leaves nodded in the breeze. To her right, on her side of the road, stood two more rows of vines—short rows but well-groomed. Stout tree branches trellised the gnarled vines.

Gentine farm in Brookfield, Wisconsin, circa 1933

The farm, now maintained by his uncles, remained in fair condition. Some of the house clapboards, surrendering to the weather, allowed the rain and ice to chisel away portions of their paint and permitted the summer sun to gray its wood. A few listing fence posts, long abandoned by their railings, stood as ineffective sentinels to the property. Shingles on the south end of the barn curled and pulled away from the roof.

"Before my grampa died, he used to rent this land for hunting," Leonard explained as he stepped from the car and scurried to open the door on the other side. As Dolores slid from the car, Leonard threw a hand above his eyes to block the sun and scanned the property. "It's about forty acres. The owner of the Pabst Brewing Company, he's hunted here. He and other owners of big companies have been out with their hunting dogs."

The slam of a screen door drew their attention. Josephine, with her wooden cane, stuttered down the porch steps one at a time. Leonard rushed the short distance to hug her.

Turning back toward the direction of the car, with his arm around his grandmother's shoulder, he smiled. "Dolores, this is my gramma Gentine—Josephine. Taught me many things about life. Just don't let her friendly face fool you. She's ruthless at cards."

Josephine affectionately patted Leonard's chest.

With that cursory introduction and a promise to return for lunch, Leonard escorted his grandmother back to the house and toured Dolores around the hilly property. Steep inclines—perfect for growing grapes—plunged so dramatically that they slowed their pace to keep from tripping and rolling down.

They poked in and out of the barn, toolshed, smokehouse, and gazebo. Sweeping away thick ropes of cobwebs, they explored the rustic cabin—long deserted—that languished at the far edge of the property.

Midday, Josephine prepared a light lunch, and after the meal, they drifted out to the porch to relax, talk, and escape the heat mounting inside the house. Each angled a chair to best capture the occasional breeze that slid over the crest of the land. Josephine chose the stiff-back chair closest to the window and propped her cane against the sill.

Josephine and Leonard Gentine

"Think we could have a small glass of wine as we sit out here?" Leonard asked his grandmother following a few minutes of silence. Turning to Dolores, he asked, "Would you care for some? Just a taste maybe?"

With a shrug of her shoulders and a reserved smile, Dolores politely nodded.

Josephine reached for her cane. "I'll see what we have," she offered, her voice colored by a faint French accent.

"No, no, you stay where you're at, Gramma. I know where it is." Then, throwing his words in Dolores's direction, he said, "I'll be right back." Leonard reentered the kitchen, allowing the screen door to bang behind him.

A few minutes later he returned with two partially filled glasses, handing one to each of the ladies. Josephine waved off the glass. "No, I don't want one, Len. You take that one."

Leonard beamed as he took a sip from his glass and joined Dolores. "Another one of my childhood memories."

"Your parents let you drink wine when you were young?" Dolores questioned. "My dad liked his beer, but my mom frowned on the habit. She wasn't a big advocate of prohibition or anything like that but to her the law was the law. 'Course, my dad would always protest, saying it was legal to drink at home, but she didn't even want the appearance of sneaking alcohol around."

Noticing she'd mostly talked about how her parents felt on the subject and not her own opinion, Leonard proceeded with caution. "Um, well...I would drink just a sip. Once in a while. But only just a sip of wine...or sometimes brandy. I'm not sure my mother totally approved, either," he added, "but my dad never saw any harm in just a small taste every now and then. After all"—he smiled at Josephine—"that's our heritage. Right, Gramma? We made wine."

"You made this wine?" Dolores asked, raising her eyebrow at Josephine.

"Well, I'm not sure Gramma still makes wine," Leonard quickly interjected before Josephine had the chance to respond. Then, unsure, he looked at his grandmother. "Do you?"

Josephine shook her head as she pressed her lips into a tight line.

"Probably my uncle Leo does that now," Leonard suggested. "All the vines we saw today? They ferment the juice. Sometimes, they'd store ten or twelve full barrels of wine in the root cellar."

His grandmother leaned forward in her chair as if to share a closely held secret. "I would put a sign out by the road that read *Eggs for Sale*. That sign let the neighbors know that we had barrels of wine ready if they wanted to stop by."

Leonard cringed. Would Dolores now think they were some sort of bootlegging operation, or would she think they were just being neighborly? He watched for a reaction but couldn't read her expression.

"Gramma"—Leonard gestured toward Josephine—"and my grampa, of course, used to live in France. My uncles—my father, too—were born there. They owned a large vineyard—but things didn't turn out as my grampa hoped. The vineyard was in the family for generations. I think he was hesitant to leave it. A sacrifice he made, he told me."

"We all have an obligation to family," Josephine murmured more to herself than to her guests.

Leonard paused, cast a sympathetic smile at his grandmother, and abruptly changed the direction of the conversation. Looking over at Dolores, he said, "All of my cousins would sit right there, on the edge of this long porch. Our legs dangling over the edge. Gramma, most times Grampa, would tell us about France and the war and the grapes and the farm. I remember all the stories."

Josephine stirred uneasily in her chair. Turning a knitted brow to Leonard, she said, "You've had this poor girl hopping around since you got here. Just let her enjoy herself. No need dredging up old stories." Then to Dolores, she asked, "Why don't you tell me a bit about your family?"

Dolores shifted in Josephine's direction. "Well," she began, "I'm the second oldest of eight children. Peter and Anna Becker are my parents. With a name like Becker, I would guess you would know my ancestors are from Germany. Trier, Germany, actually."

Leonard rolled back into his chair, finishing the last sips of wine as he listened. Dolores looked his way, flashing him a grin in midsentence, and he felt his apprehension dissipate. *Perhaps*, he thought, *Dolores would enjoy life on this farm.* They would talk about it in the months ahead.

One thing he knew for certain: No matter what his calling might be, no matter where life led him, he wanted it to be with Dolores at his side.

# 3

# Gentine Funeral Service
# 1937

"WE NEED TO dump the body out of this casket," Bob Merkel grumbled. "It's too heavy!"

Attempting to avoid any gouges to the door frame, the casket, or—just as important—his knuckles, Leonard lofted his end of the coffin over his head. He issued a muffled groan. There was no body in the casket, but even empty caskets were not light, Leonard had to agree.

"C'mon, old man!" Leonard razzed. "This is the last of them. Get this one downstairs and you can take your mandatory afternoon nap."

Weekends with Hobart Brigden encouraged Leonard to consider operating his own funeral home. "There's good money in that business," he had told Dolores. Once he'd met his debt to Hobart, with Dolores's nod of approval, Leonard enrolled in school.

During his studies at the Wisconsin Institute of Mortuary Science, he met Bob and his quirky humor. A friendship blossomed—late nights studying together, prepping for tests. As graduation neared, Leonard suggested they continue to work together—for a limited time—as Leonard opened his funeral home in Plymouth, Wisconsin.

Back and arm muscles aching, the two men lowered the casket to

Bob Merkel and Leonard Gentine

the floor. Leonard had selected this area of the basement for the sale of caskets—far from the walled-off section they earmarked for embalming. Easy access down the stairs from the back door, Dolores had pointed out. Plenty of good lighting. The main floor could be reserved for visitations and the top floor for living quarters.

He remembered Dolores's smile the day they toured the house. The view overlooked the millpond, a small body of water seated at the base of a sloping blanket of grass. Resting on more land than other properties they considered, the imposing home at 728 Eastern Avenue—the former residence of the town's first mayor—projected an air of respectability.

As they walked through the house that day, Dolores even mentioned how one of the smaller bedrooms might prove ideal as a nursery—a comment that left him without a response.

Over the past year, the two of them had talked of marriage in comfortable conversations. Yet both were well aware of the hurdles. Neither of them had saved enough money as they struggled through the Depression.

To secure the Plymouth house, Leonard's parents provided the funding. The needed mortuary equipment Leonard either rented or borrowed. In time, he believed, the business would provide the income to repay those debts and support a wife.

A source of income aside, another obstacle impeded the marriage. Her father refused to allow his daughters to wed out of faith. That Leonard dismissed as well. If that was the prerequisite, he would convert to Catholicism. Once he fully settled in Plymouth, he would befriend the priest and later surprise Dolores—and her father—with the news.

In a way, he mused, it was the Catholic faith that brought them to Plymouth, Wisconsin. Looking for a suitable location for their funeral home, they ventured fifty miles north to this small town of four thousand residents. Prospects looked promising. The town had only one funeral home, and it wasn't Catholic. As they assimilated into the community, they planned to convert the large number of Catholic families to their funeral home.

Before any of that could occur, the house and the business had to be put in order. As Bob gathered scraps of cardboard and packing material, Leonard dragged several caskets closer along the wall. In the small room to the side, he uncrated tools, arranging them in a haphazard fashion, and then tugged the embalming table closer to the sink. A faint smell of formaldehyde already hung in the air.

Out of breath, Leonard paused, straightened, and let out a large puff of air. *Slow down*, he lectured himself as he tapped out a Philip Morris. *Think.* Blowing out the match flame from the corner of his mouth, he eased into the larger room. Leonard mentally arranged the caskets and display materials. Then mentally arranged them again.

"Tell you what," said Leonard, pushing away his thoughts. "No mandatory nap as I suggested"—he curled up the corners of his mouth at Bob—"but I'll buy you a cup of coffee upstairs in the kitchen. We can come back down and do the rearranging and cleaning after we rest."

On the top floor of the home, Leonard dragged the metal dining room chair across the linoleum floor and eased into the seat to finish his cigarette with his coffee. Bob claimed a spot at the table adjacent to him. As cigarette smoke curled from the ashtray, Leonard stretched his long legs and slid down, his head resting on the back of his chair. "Did I ever tell you about Joseph, my grampa?"

"The one that came from someplace in France?" Bob took a draw from his cigarette and blew a stream of smoke to the side. "Yeah, you said he grew grapes, made wine."

"OK, so I told you." Leonard rested in silence for a few minutes. "Joseph's grampa, Jean Pierre Gentine, fought for France, you know. For Napoleon. Like my grampa, he was proud of his French heritage. Proud of his country."

Bob shrugged and then reached across the table and tapped an ash into the ashtray. "Yeah, lots of immigrants came over here, Len. They all made sacrifices. You don't think others were proud of the countries they left?"

Leonard sat up and took another swallow of coffee. "I keep thinking about my grampa's decision. Imagine leaving behind a business your father—and his father and his father's father—left for you to run? He must have felt he let them down." Leonard took a draw on his cigarette. "He never said that, of course. And I don't think he ever went back to France. Maybe the grapevines are still growing over there. Maybe they're not. I remember asking him once if he would do it again if he had the chance."

"What'd he say?"

Leonard snuffed out the end of his cigarette. "He never really answered me. But I keep thinking that if he would have stayed—you know, Germany eventually gave that land back to France—if he had stayed, my dad would have owned the vineyard—or part of it anyway—and then it would have been passed down to me and my cousins.

"My gramma, to this day, reminds me it was all for the good of the family. Family is the priority. He forfeited his family's heritage to give his sons a better life. The vines he brought with him..." Leonard lowered his head. "No one cares about them anymore. Not my dad. Not my uncles. It's as if what was important to my grandfather is being lost."

Leonard drained the last of his coffee, pulled himself up from the table, and stretched, arching his back. "That's why I want this business so bad. Something to pass down to my family someday. Maybe rebuild a little bit of what my grampa had to leave behind. What he lost. Maybe make enough money to buy that vineyard. Bring it back. For my grampa. For my family."

He shoved the chair back under the table. "Speaking of which, let's get crackin'. We have lots of boxes to unpack, caskets to arrange." Throwing a glance at the kitchen clock, he added, "I have only three more hours before I head back to Milwaukee."

Leonard worked third shift at the Falk Corporation. Logic told him to keep that Milwaukee job. With Bob at the Gentine Funeral Service, Leonard could put in his hours, drive the fifty miles back to Plymouth, work with Bob, and then scrape together a few hours of sleep. It shouldn't be too challenging, he thought. He'd rest on weekends.

Once his funeral home started making a steady profit, he'd propose to Dolores. Bob could leave to start his own funeral business. She would move out of her parents' house, and the two of them would run their little business together. That was the plan.

Leonard frowned, looking down at Bob, who remained in his chair. "Are you coming, old man?"

Bob stubbed out his cigarette in the ashtray and dragged himself from his chair. "What's the rush? We have plenty of days to organize. I don't recall you mentioning any funerals you've booked yet."

*No, no funerals yet*, Leonard thought. They would come. It would just take time. Small towns thrive on symbiotic relationships. Tightly knit communities prefer to do business with those they have known for years—those who are friends of the family or friends of their friends.

To offset that tendency, he would remain patient while at the same time immersing himself in civic organizations—becoming "one of them" through visible community involvement. Plymouth would grow to love their twenty-three-year-old mortician from Milwaukee, he believed.

It would just take time. He hoped he was right.

# 4

# A High School Teacher's Plea
## 1941

Leonard and Dolores Gentine

LIFE DIDN'T FALL together the way Leonard imagined. It wasn't as if they had foolishly jumped into this without thought. He and Dolores had had a plan.

"Our funeral home will be our own little family business," he remembered telling Dolores. "We'll save our money. Enjoy a little freedom. Then start a family."

Leonard stood before the mirror, tucking his brown tie under his collar, forming two lengths into a Windsor knot. He'd be twenty-seven years old this year, he thought. Twenty-seven, married for two years.

Holding his third-shift job at the Falk Corporation in Milwaukee during the first two years he operated the funeral home in Plymouth had driven him near the brink of total exhaustion. But he did it. It had been a test of his will and he had passed. Or maybe, more accurately, he'd survived.

Grabbing his beige suit coat from the hanger, he slid his arms into the sleeves as he descended the stairs to the funeral home office on the main floor. He'd seen Dolores slip back there after breakfast.

Approaching the rear of the house, he slowed and then stood, unnoticed, in the hallway, studying his wife at work, hunched over a mound of paperwork. A rush of love, gratitude, and awe filled him, and he considered with admiration the pencil she had tucked behind her ear. Dolores was not only a like-minded life partner, but also an equally suited business partner, providing him the freedom to pursue his ambitions.

Although they dreamed of the day they would build a home of their own, separate from his business, Dolores never voiced distaste for their current arrangement: living above rooms filled with caskets, an embalming table, and an occasional corpse. How many women would consider that!

Standing unobtrusively in the hallway, basking in her dedication to their life together, he drew a small smile on his face. But the moment faded. As if sensing his presence, she glanced up and cast a questioning look.

"Working at the desk early this morning?" Leonard asked as he walked into the office and slid into the chair next to her.

Dolores thumbed a small pile of envelopes. "Some of these bills are past due. Now that the business is picking up a bit, I was hoping to pay a few of them."

"Yeah. It's been a couple of good months, and yesterday I scheduled another funeral for Thursday afternoon. Oh, by the way, I talked with Bob Merkel. He's doing good and said anytime I needed help, he'd be glad to come over and lend—"

The desk phone rang, startling the two of them. He shrugged as he reached for the phone. "Maybe it's another funeral?"

"Hello? Well, nice to meet you too, Margaret." He listened, his head bent.

"That's really nice of you to—" Leonard clutched the phone, attentive to the caller on the other end. "Yes, of course, but you see—" He pinched the bridge of his nose and squeezed his eyes shut as he allowed Margaret to continue.

"Well, at the moment, we aren't in a position to hire any additional help. Perhaps in the future we—" He sighed and patiently waited his turn. "Yes, of course. Yes, I agree. That's understandable, Margar—"

"Well, perhaps in the future," he began again, "we'll have a need for some extra help around here. Right now, our budgets are tight and we seem to be doing fine but should that change, I—"

He let out a sigh, giving up. "OK. Sure. That'd be fine. Here tomorrow. I'm making no promises. Just to talk. All right? Yes...yes, that'd be great." After a pause, he added, "OK then, we'll see you tomorrow."

He hung up the phone. Dolores tipped her head in his direction.

"That was Margaret Wernecke, one of the teachers in Plymouth. She has a high school graduate that she'd like us to hire."

"Hire! You're looking to hire someone? Where will we get the money for that?"

He held up both hands in response. "Of course I'm not going to hire him. And I tried to explain that to her. But she's very insistent.

"This student," he continued, "had a grandfather that was an under-taker, and he wants to get involved with the business. Actually, think-ing about it, I see this as a positive sign. Plymouth may be starting to consider us as a growing part of the community and less of an outsider's business. Feeling more comfortable reaching out to us. Margaret said they'd be stopping by tomorrow afternoon."

"The teacher and the student?"

"Yep. Both. It's just to share my thoughts on the business and to give a tour of our place. Nothing more."

Dolores shot a glance at the wall calendar. "Well, I promised Katie O'Connell I would do something with her tomorrow afternoon, but I'm sure you can handle Margaret and the young man just fine."

The next day, at the scheduled hour, Leonard answered a knock at the front door. On the other side stood a prim bespectacled woman who introduced herself as Margaret Wernecke. Beside her, very businesslike in appearance, stood a young man, seemingly uneasy with this arrangement.

"This is Chuck Strobel—the young man I was telling you about on the phone." Margaret grinned at her former student and paused, but Chuck added nothing further to the introduction.

"Chuck," said Leonard, offering a handshake. "Nice meeting you." Then he waved them in. "I have some chairs in the next room. We can sit in there and talk."

"I don't know if I told you," Margaret began as she settled into her seat. "I teach high school English and Latin at Plymouth High. Chuck was in one of my classes, and until he graduated, I tutored him after school."

"Yeah. I believe you mentioned that." Leonard dragged a chair closer, forming a tighter circle.

Then, as if driving home a few of her selling points, she launched the conversation. "He's a quick learner, industrious, a young man with great personal values. And he's very bright."

"I'm sure he is." Leonard turned in Chuck's direction. The young man sat, posture erect, offering no conversation but plenty of polite facial gestures.

"So, Chuck, why do you think you want to become a funeral director?" Though Leonard had learned the story from Margaret, he preferred to hear it from Chuck.

Chuck Strobel's high school photo

"It's just something that interests me, I guess. My grandfather ran a funeral home. I live right next door to the Wittkopp Funeral Home so I did ask them if they would hire me. They said they didn't have any openings at the moment."

Leonard nodded in understanding.

"So I applied at the Kraft plant and they gave me a job." Chuck leaned forward in his chair. "They put me on the production floor."

"That's why we're here," Margaret jumped in. "Working for a cheese company! He has so much more potential than that. I asked him if he didn't have higher aspirations and that's when he mentioned that he wanted to someday own a funeral business."

Margaret smiled at Chuck. "So I told him, let's talk to Leonard at the Gentine Funeral Service. They might be more interested in teaching the business."

"Well, I think I may have mentioned this already…" Leonard reinforced the idea one more time. "Maybe sometime in the future we might have—"

"I know you're not hiring, Leonard," she assured him. "You mentioned that on the phone, I believe." A long pause followed and then Margaret suggested, "Maybe you could show us around?"

The Gentine funeral home offered few unusual characteristics, but Leonard dutifully provided them an overview of his business, similar to the cursory tour Hobart Brigden provided Leonard on his first day. As they strolled the main floor, he pointed out the two viewing rooms, the entryway from the canopied parking area, the smoking room in the back, as well as the funeral home office.

It seemed to Leonard that, for every point of interest mentioned, Margaret interjected one of Chuck's enviable attributes: his intelligence, his physical strength, his experience at handling repairs, his ability at recordkeeping. Chuck, for his part, offered little conversation, just the occasional nod or a brief burst of acknowledgment as Leonard

Mantel in the Gentine funeral home

described the unremarkable rooms on the main floor of the funeral home—sections of a funeral home seen by anyone attending a visitation for a friend or family member.

Leonard suggested they next view the embalmment room. As they descended the back stairs to the basement, Margaret grew noticeably taciturn, falling several steps behind the two men, preferring to listen from a distance. In contrast, Chuck drew closer to the equipment, bubbling up streams of questions.

Moving into the casket room—the room displaying burial options for customers—Leonard noticed Margaret's return to her loquacious personality, questioning the weight of each casket and underscoring her student's prowess in wrestling in high school. Leonard sighed and then led his tour up the front stairs, returning them near the front door.

Gentine funeral home

"I was just thinking," Margaret pushed onward, "that Chuck could probably do some of the routine work for you and that would give him a chance to observe your business firsthand. He's very athletic. Besides wresting, he was the star player on the football team in high school. He also played basketball. Why, I bet Chuck could handle any chore you'd have."

"Margaret," Leonard protested. "Business is slow at the moment and it's really not a good time to hire someone. There's no room in the budget for another person. As I've been saying, maybe at some time in the future, we could—"

Margaret shot up her palm to stop Leonard from continuing. "Leonard, I'm not asking you to hire Chuck. In fact, I don't think you should, actually."

Silence hung in the air as Leonard blinked in momentary confusion. "But I thought you were—"

"I completely understand what you are saying," Margaret interrupted. "You need to stay within your budget."

Chuck threw a puzzled glimpse in the direction of his former teacher.

"What I'm saying"—Margaret expanded her thought—"is that Chuck would be more than happy to help out around here. That would give him a chance to experience the business that appeals to him. He's not asking to be paid. Learning the business would be payment enough."

Leonard's brow tightened as he thought. Maybe he had misread her intentions all along. "I see. Sorry, I...I misunderstood, but see what you're saying." Then with a sigh he added, "Well, I just don't feel right about Chuck working and me not paying him."

Leonard turned in Chuck's direction, but the young man remained reticent. In fact, he appeared as bewildered at the turn of the conversation as Leonard felt.

"No, I don't like that arrangement at all," Leonard repeated.

"I completely understand, Leonard." Margaret hesitated and then added, "Well...you could think of it as if he were an apprentice. Some businesses don't pay an apprentice at all. Others only offer a stipend because they are providing valuable training. Teaching a trade. If you feel uncomfortable not paying, you could compensate him with token wages and then, when you have need for another hand around here, you could bring him on your payroll. How much do you think you could afford right now?"

Leonard let Margaret's question hang in the air.

He studied the young man before him and remembered his experience—still fresh in his mind—working for Hobart Brigden. He had reported to work each week, eagerly anticipating the day's responsibilities. He earned no money. He merely fulfilled an obligation. The reward fell to him in other, intangible ways. Perhaps it was the joy of learning a new trade. Or the sense he was part of a small family business. Or that Hobart sincerely appreciated his ideas and efforts. He was never quite sure of the reason that job appealed to him.

Chuck's situation was different. He had no debt to repay. If Leonard offered the same experiences Hobart provided, he believed Chuck should be compensated—even if it proved to be a modest amount.

"OK," Leonard finally said, "we can do that. But here are my conditions. Give me two months before you start. You'll need to keep your schedule flexible and be available when needed. In this business, we don't choose our hours." As he ticked off his requirements, he looked directly at Chuck.

Leonard paused, staring in thought. "If you are in agreement..." He shifted uneasily, mentally searching for the right number. He didn't need a reputation in the community for being cheap, but—when it came right down to it—he couldn't afford any amount greater than zero. "I can pay you...twelve dollars a week. That's it." He threw both hands up to emphasize that he could offer no more. "Twelve dollars a week."

Leonard hooked an eyebrow at the young man. "You want to think about it, Chuck?"

Before Chuck could answer, Margaret chimed in. "Well, now, I think that's more than fair, don't you, Chuck? You can learn the funeral business and at the same time get paid."

Chuck shrugged. "Sure. I guess...that sounds fine."

"Very well." Leonard, eager not to get any deeper into this than he already found himself, opened the front door. "I'll see you two months from today." Then he added hopefully, "Let me know if you change your mind."

"OK, thanks, Mr. Gentine." Chuck extended his hand and the two shook on the arrangement.

"You can call me Leonard, Chuck."

"OK…thanks…Leonard."

With little more than that, Margaret took Chuck in tow, whisking him from the house with a sense of *veni, vidi, vici*. The high school Latin teacher came, saw, and conquered.

From his doorway, Leonard watched them climb into Margaret's car. Although not his initial intent, he felt an unexplained pride in this decision. Still, he wondered three things: How did he lose control of the conversation? How in the world would he find twelve dollars a week to pay that young man?

Above all, how was he going to break this news to Dolores?

# 5

# Catalysts of Change
## 1941

CHUCK STROBEL'S AMBITION was surpassed only by Dolores's patience.

Given the circumstances, she accepted the new apprentice idea reasonably well, Leonard had to admit. She called it a noble gesture. Just bad timing.

Chuck's energy and drive even exceeded Margaret's lofty promises. Unless Leonard made specific requests, Chuck launched into one enterprise after another, trimming the hedges, watering the lawn, and washing the storm windows. He scraped sun blisters from the side of the funeral home and applied a fresh coat of paint. The Packard gleamed in the sun thanks to the layers of wax Chuck rubbed into its pores.

"It's Saturday," Leonard said one weekend as he approached Chuck pushing the lawn mower. "Finish up the front section of the yard so it doesn't look half-mowed and then take the day off. Spend some time with your friends and family."

Chuck untied the shirt from his waist and mopped away the beads of sweat collecting on his forehead. Squinting to block the early-fall sun, he looked toward the back of the house. "I was hoping to get this mowed today. Next week, if the weather holds, I was thinking of putting on the storm windows.

"That is," he added, "unless you have a funeral you need me for?"

Leonard felt the pangs of personal disappointment in the inquiry and masked it with a small grin. "We won't be undertaking any undertaking for a while. And that's good news for Plymouth. I'll let you know if that changes.

"There're plenty of things to do around here. That old carriage house in the back needs a lot of help. I can get any supplies you need: wood, nails, you name it. But for now, finish the front yard and go home. You earned it."

Leonard watched as Chuck returned to the mower, its metal reel blades unfurling a misty carpet of grass clippings at his feet, and wondered how long he could afford Chuck as an apprentice-employee.

There had been an uptick in the business, but he needed it to grow just a bit faster, produce a little more income. Often, he would lie awake at night thinking, tossing the same thoughts over in his mind, hoping to uncover an idea that would increase his earnings. After four years as a funeral director in the community, he struggled to make inroads against his only competitor. Most of the business still flowed to the Wittkopp Funeral Home.

How he tired of well-meaning friends' hackneyed appraisals of his sporadic business. "Looks like the funeral business is a little dead." He would return a polite smile. They'd bellow at their own wit. Or they would quip, "Looks like no one is dying to use your funeral home, Leonard." How many times had he heard that one?

At times, he felt indebted to everyone in town. An absurd feeling. Of course, it wasn't true. Money was tight. Local retailers extended him credit. Barker Lumber ran a tab. Other necessities—food, gasoline, clothing—were sometimes tied to handshake agreements with friends or verbal promises to pay later. Bills accumulated. Although he longed for a connection with the community, undue financial obligations chafed at his conscience.

Not everybody paid their funeral bills on time, making it impossible to rely on a monthly income. After a funeral, some asked him to carry an IOU or presented him with a horse or a cow instead of cash. Until they could depend on a steady income, he and Dolores agreed not to start a family.

*Everything will be fine*, he lectured himself. Thanks to Dolores and her skill at handling the books, they were making ends meet. Still, as months lapsed, he questioned if there might be a short-term path— another temporary business he should consider—to bring in extra money. Despite the comments, despite the doubters, despite the slow growth, he still believed.

During those months when the weight of debt rose, so did his determination.

"Thanks, Cletus," Leonard enthused into the phone. "I'll let you know in a week or so. Dolores and I are still working out the details. But I thank you for the offer."

Renewed energy bubbled up inside as he replaced the handset on the desk phone. *This could be an answer to our sluggish income*, he thought. He crossed the driveway to the carriage house so quickly, it was as if the distance between the two buildings shrank to two of his long strides. Early that morning, he had seen Chuck enter the building—a sure indication that he would be working there.

Leonard entered through the nearby door, and found Chuck prying a cracked and sagging tread from the stringers of the inside stairway.

Chuck looked up. "Good morning, Leonard. Need me for something?"

The carriage house behind the funeral home

"No. Just thought we could talk...if you have a moment." Leonard took in the full measure of the stairway under reconstruction and then dragged an old paint-splattered sawhorse closer for his seat. "Just curious about your thoughts on something."

Chuck set his hammer and crowbar aside and sat on one of the repaired stair treads.

"I believe I've mentioned—even when you and Margaret Wernecke came to the house—that business is slow. Now, you've seen firsthand the truth of the matter."

Leonard leaned forward on the makeshift chair. "We already have an ambulance service to help offset some of our costs. But I've been thinking: What else is there we could do?"

"Like another service for the funeral home?" Chuck suggested.

"Maybe. Or maybe a totally new business. Something small. Easy

40

to do. Something we could handle on a flexible schedule. A whole new little business that you could help me run."

Chuck narrowed his eyes in thought as Leonard sat back upright, broadened his frame, and pushed forward his idea.

"There are a few folks," Leonard said, "some in a couple of the men's organizations that I've joined, that are raising mink. I've looked into it. Read a couple magazine articles. It would be easy to build up an inventory. The gestation period for mink is only thirty-nine days."

Carefully studying Chuck's face, he continued, "I wanted your opinion. If we were to start a business like that, do you think you could manage it?"

"I'd sure try. I never raised mink before, but I probably could do it. You thinking of putting them in here?"

Leonard gazed around the room. "I considered that but one of the guys I know, Cletus Wieser, owns a large tract of land north of here. He just told me he'd let me use a portion of his property to raise them." He paused and then said, "Think about it."

Leonard leaned forward as if to prevent anyone in the empty carriage house from hearing. "Don't mention anything to Dolores, though. She's not too keen on the idea yet."

Then, pushing up from the sawhorse, Leonard said, "It's almost noon. C'mon, let's get something to eat."

"I have news!" Dolores said over lunch. "Margie's coming to visit."

With a quizzical expression, Chuck first looked at Dolores and then at Leonard.

Leonard helped clarify. "Margie is Dolores's little sister. They shared a bedroom growing up."

Chuck nodded as if all was now clear.

"Since we've been married, it's been hard on her," Dolores explained. "Growing up, we were close even though there's a difference of fifteen years between us. She writes regularly, so we keep in touch that way. But with school closed for the holiday, she thought she would take the train from Milwaukee tomorrow to visit."

"I'll check the time schedule at the depot and pick her up," said Leonard.

"I mentioned that, but she said not to bother. She'll have just a small suitcase and prefers to walk since it's not far." Dolores brightened. "This morning, I got the spare bedroom all set for her."

The next afternoon, Dolores habitually consulted the clock. "She must have arrived by now. It's past when they said the train would pull in."

Leonard took a seat on the couch and picked up the newspaper. "Let's give her a few more minutes and then I'll go look for her."

Moments later, the door downstairs opened and slammed shut. Up the stairs scrambled Margie, suitcase in hand and in full blush.

"Margie!" Dolores threw her arms around her sister as she reached the top of the stairs. "How was the trip?"

"Fine." She glanced between Dolores and Leonard. "I just met the man you hired."

"Chuck? Did something happen? You all right?"

"Why didn't you tell me he was so good looking?" she gushed.

In the days to follow—despite Chuck's dedication to his work—coy glances and poignant moments of brief conversations fostered what appeared to Leonard as a nascent romance between Chuck and Margie. With increasing frequency, Dolores's sister visited Plymouth, becoming a regular guest in the Gentine household.

That Thanksgiving, Leonard remained optimistic as he looked ahead to 1942. Repeatedly, he told Dolores—and Chuck—that change was in the air. The funeral business would stabilize, and all their persistence over the years would finally pay off.

Leonard proved to be partially right. Things did change. For the worse.

On December 7, President Roosevelt declared war in response to the bombing of Pearl Harbor. Even for an undertaker, war offered no rewards—only uncertainty.

Of that, Leonard already had plenty.

# 6

# Responsibilities
# 1943

DEATH IS NO friend to the undertaker.

Plymouth, like the nation, worried as its young men and women left to fight in Europe and in the Pacific. A disquieting shroud hung over the town of Plymouth as families prayed their children would return alive.

On a dreary November day following a late-afternoon funeral, Leonard accompanied Chuck to the mink farm to make quick work of their obligation before the sun set. Dolores had acquiesced to the mink-raising idea. Since then, either Chuck or Leonard fed them daily and changed the bedding—tasks that always threw them in harm's way.

The business venture was not without its initial setbacks. With an interest in expanding the type of pelts offered, Leonard purchased a pair of nutria, South American beavers that resembled plump, furry rats. For months, he encouraged the two animals with little luck. Frustrated, he asked the advice of the local vet: "How can I encourage them to mate?"

The vet examined both animals. "'Fraid it ain't gonna happen, Leonard." Casting a sideways look, the animal doctor added, "They're both the same sex."

In stride, Leonard took the brunt of the humor as the story passed from one businessman to the next. After purchasing one more South American beaver, the population of both mink and nutria expanded on the small parcel of land on Cletus Wieser's farm.

Leonard drove onto a small dirt path leading to the animal pens as tangles of dark clouds dragged across the sky, harbingers of the rain forecast that evening.

Chuck slid from the Packard as Leonard opened the back and grabbed two metal buckets of mink feed. A gust of wind stirred a small stream of dried leaves along the side of the road, rustling them past their feet as they hurried to the cages.

Setting his bucket next to one of the pens, Chuck stared as if assessing his ability to safely reach inside. With one fluid motion, he yanked opened the door and shoved his hand in the direction of the food tray.

"Ahhhhhh!" he screamed, quickly withdrawing and slamming the door shut. One of the mink skulking off to the side, in an act of territorial protection, had lunged at Chuck's hand.

"These things are nasty. Just outright mean."

He tugged off the glove to inspect the injury. The gash on the back of his finger bled but it was a small bite. "I've got one more wound to add to the collection of scars on my hand," he said wryly.

"Wear your gloves," Leonard chastised. "At least they give some protection."

"I am. They're biting clear through them!"

Chuck watched the animal angrily charge the cage wall. "Only an iron glove would slow down those sharp teeth."

With more care and cunning, he freed the feeding dish on his second try.

Leonard fared no better than Chuck. With a cigarette pinched in the corner of his mouth, Leonard attempted to wrest a feeding bowl that had migrated to the center of the pen. Poking a stick through the cage, he planned to snag the rim and drag it to the edge where he could quickly snatch it.

One of the animals clamped down on the end of the stick, pulling it in the opposite direction. A tug of war: man versus mink. Leonard reached into the cage, only to be rewarded with a swift claw from a neighboring mink, raking his forearm.

Neither Leonard nor Chuck anticipated the animals' temperament. Quite often Chuck returned to the funeral home—scratched and bit—in need of minor medical attention. Not only were the animals aggressive, Chuck learned mink and nutria often bit the hand that tried to feed them.

As they both slid back into the car, Leonard inspected his arm and Chuck toyed with the gash on his finger. "We're a sorry pair," Leonard said. "We always leave this place looking as if we stepped out of the middle of a war zone. Dolores tells me one day she's going to find me eaten alive."

Chuck suddenly grew pensive. "I'm sure the war zone is much worse in Europe. They might welcome a heated skirmish with mink instead."

Rubbing the wound on his finger, he rode the next few miles in silence.

Leonard glanced in his direction. "Something on your mind, Chuck?"

Casting his eyes downward, he nodded. "It seems like all my friends are enlisting. They're going off to fight the war against the Germans and the Japs. I know neither of us are required to enlist because of our jobs. But it just seems like...well, like I should be joining my friends."

"You're providing a critical public need right here," Leonard assured him as he turned his attention from the road. "Families are losing their sons and daughters to this war. We're here to comfort and care for those left behind. To honor those that have passed away. To serve and support our community during these emotional times.

"The draft board recognizes the value of our service. Truth is, everyone needs to play a role in this thing. And it doesn't take a gun or a hand grenade."

Chuck stared in thought as tiny drops of rain freckled the windshield. "I know. I know. It just doesn't feel right to me, that's all. I feel like I'm evading some sort of responsibility."

On the way back to Plymouth, as the storm gathered momentum, Chuck listened as Leonard outlined some of the pros and cons of enlisting. The wipers arced back and forth, clearing the windshield. Then, Leonard ticked off some of the advantages of serving in the mortuary business. Water racing down from the car roof blurred their vision as they slowed in traffic.

Pulling into the driveway of the funeral home, Chuck turned and watched a young tree arching against the punishing wind and rain. Clouds, releasing their payload, pummeled the carport, drumming the canopy as the two men lingered in the car to finish their conversation, voices rising above the din.

"Chuck, you need to do what you think is right. If you really feel strongly about enlisting, you should go. But give it some thought. Don't rush into this."

Chuck nodded, silently massaging his injured finger.

Then, abruptly, the rain stopped.

By early 1942, the funeral business showed signs of strength again, and that small momentum of business growth pushed its way into the following year. Leonard, hoping that the leanest years lay behind him, began to breathe easier.

Brighter business prospects offered Leonard and Dolores renewed hope and a new direction. On May 11, 1943, she gave birth to a son: Leonard Alvin Gentine Jr.—a healthy child with bright eyes and a thick clump of dark hair. Leonard's responsibility to the next generation could not have been made more apparent.

Neither could Leonard quash his pride—a son, bearing his name, to one day walk in his footsteps. He refrained from calling him Junior. Their neighbor, Irish O'Connell, began calling him Butch in jest. The name stuck.

During his free time, he and Butch were inseparable. Leonard walked him about town, played with him in the backyard, and lavished him with a level of attention aptly given to firstborns.

As his contribution to the war effort, Leonard volunteered his free time at the munitions factory—the PIP building, one block from the funeral home. Each night, he returned home, cleaned off the dirt and soot that had accumulated from the factory, and then began the highlight of his day—playing with Butch before putting him to bed.

"You might want to take a job at the munitions factory, too," Leonard suggested to Chuck. "I'm sure they could use the extra help."

Chuck thanked Leonard for the suggestion, but said that type of job would fail to assuage his need to fight in the war. Not long thereafter, Chuck made up his mind. "I thought about it, Leonard. I'm going to enlist."

Leonard weighed Chuck's words in silence before responding. "I guessed this would be the choice you would make. You realize, no one knows what'll happen at the end of the war. Business could slow again. I can't guarantee you'll have a job here when you come back."

He watched as Chuck nodded in understanding. Then, the look of conviction transformed his face. "This is something I need to do. So . . . I guess I'll take that chance."

As one of his last responsibilities in November, Chuck installed the storm windows to the funeral home. Then he reported to the medical corps at the Naval Station Great Lakes.

Leonard had grown accustomed to his sounding board, partner, and friend. Now, he remained behind to oversee the funeral home and spar alone with the mink at the farm. All too familiar with death and the rising shipments of casualties returning from the war, leaving families to grieve in their wake, Leonard, for the first time, felt death's shadow eclipse his community and wondered if this might be the last time he saw Chuck alive.

He was surprised by how much he already missed the boy he never wanted to hire in the first place.

# 7

# The Family Expands
## 1946

OVER A FEBRUARY evening in 1946, a winter storm howled, frosting the funeral home and raking knee-high windrows of snow across the driveway. While Leonard attacked the deep snow the next day, Dolores tugged three-year-old Butch on his wooden sled, its metal runners pressing parallel tracks in its wake.

"Leonard?" The voice at his back, familiar but unexpected, surprised him. Turning, he peered into a friendly bearded face.

"Chuck?" His words formed a wispy cloud of vapor before drifting away. Then a smile stretched across his face. "Marge told us the Navy discharged you, and with the war long over, we were sure we'd hear from you any day now. How long have you been back?"

"Just a couple of days. I wanted to spend time with my mom and family. I immediately called Marge, of course, but I haven't gone to Milwaukee to see her yet. Sorry I didn't stop by sooner."

"Don't be, we completely understand. We're just glad you're home," Dolores said as she extended her arms and hugged him.

Chuck bent down, peering into a crimsoned face, drubbed by the wind. "So this little guy is...Butch?"

Dolores beamed. "That's Butch."

"He's grown since I've been gone!" Then Chuck looked up at Leonard and abruptly changed the topic. "Do you suppose you would have a few minutes to talk? I just need to ask your thoughts on something."

With a friendly push on their shoulders, Dolores said, "You two go on in and talk. Butch and I'll be out here for just a little longer."

"Once I cleared the driveway," said Leonard, "I was gonna see if Joe, across the street, needed help. But I could stand to be warmed up a bit. C'mon, let's go inside."

"Someone move into that place over there?" Chuck asked, nodding in the direction of the house on the other side of the road.

"Not too long ago. His name's Joe Sartori. His father is part owner of the S&R cheese company in town, and it sounds like Joe's hoping to take over the company someday. Great guy. I'll introduce you. Dolores and I've gone out to dinner with him and Marie—that's his wife—a dozen times or so. Or sometimes we'll play bridge together. We got lucky. They're good people, great neighbors."

Stomping the snow from their boots, the two entered the house, dragging the cold air into the hallway with them.

"Take off that coat and have a seat," said Leonard as he tugged a chair from the corner of the room and waved Chuck into one adjacent to it.

"Your son is getting big," Chuck said as he settled into his seat.

"Yes, he's growing fast." Then with a knowing, fatherly nod, he added, "He learned how to charm us real fast. Even when he's doing something he knows he shouldn't, he makes it hard to stay upset with him. And I don't know if you noticed but Butch has got a little brother or sister on the way. The family is growing, Chuck!"

Then, remembering Chuck's desire to talk privately, Leonard shifted the conversation. "What're your plans now that you're home? Have you had time to give any thought to that?"

"Actually, that's one of the reasons I stopped by. To see you…and Dolores, of course…and to see if I might have my old job back. The Navy gave me some hands-on medical training over the past couple of years."

Chuck threw his leg over his knee. "I would only be able to work here for a couple of months. While I was at sea, I got to thinking. With the G.I. Bill, the government'll pay for part of my education. So I'm seriously thinking of getting my mortuary degree."

"Well, good for you." Chuck, as a licensed mortician, would be beneficial, thought Leonard. Although the business couldn't support that type of salary, it would take him two years to earn his degree. Things just might improve by then.

Leonard compressed his lips tight before responding. "You know, since I met you, that's what you've wanted to do. Going to school is a smart decision, Chuck."

"Well, I wouldn't start school until this fall. So I'd have some time. I could help out around here if you could use me. But there's another reason I wanted to talk with you." Chuck took in a full breath and squeezed out the air before he continued. "I'm going to ask Marge to marry me, but I feel I need to ask her father's permission first. What was it like when you told Peter Becker you wanted to marry Dolores?"

"Peter? He's a good man." Leonard carefully chose his words—staid and serious, but painting hints of the man's character. "Protective of his daughters, but a good man. He's been nothing but good to me and Dolores. Built the kitchen cabinets for us upstairs. You treat him right, he'll be fair to you."

The front door clicked opened and slammed shut. Both men craned their necks down the hallway. Dolores coaxed a reluctant Butch into the house, shaking snow from his cap and coat, collecting his mittens.

"Oh, I almost forgot," Chuck said. "While I was stationed on Bora Bora, I bought a grass skirt and sent it to Marge." Then, with seemingly newfound, roguish humor, he said, "I would have got one for you, but didn't know how often Dolores would let you wear it."

Leonard offered a smirk in response.

"I got you this instead." Reaching into the inside pocket of his coat, Chuck pulled out a brass cylinder. "It's a shell casing and it's just about the right size for a nice pencil holder."

Leonard turned the casing over in his hand. "Very nice. Thanks, Chuck. I'll put it right here on the corner of my desk."

"Well, I best be going." Chuck straightened up from his chair. "I promised Marge I would drive down this afternoon. The roads should be clear, but driving always takes a little more time in the winter."

"Give her our best. And about working here... We'll talk when you get back." As he watched Chuck leave, Leonard had an odd feeling he'd experienced this all before.

How would he ever afford to rehire Chuck? This time around, he couldn't get by with an offer of twelve dollars a week.

In May, Dolores gave birth to a second son: Lawrence John Gentine. And once again, a newborn's cries filled the upstairs of the funeral home.

For the occasional scheduled funerals, Dolores attempted to keep both children quiet, often with limited success. No door separated the upstairs from the main floor. Larry's crying easily drifted down the stairs. The thudding of Butch's feet beat a tattoo on the ceiling below. Keeping children quiet for the length of a funeral was an art.

By June, Leonard received the painful news. His grandmother, Josephine—already struggling with poor health—had passed away. Her loss left a large void, but it also placed his life into sharp perspective. At this point in time, he had expected to have owned a profitable funeral home and to have shared that achievement with her.

Larry, Leonard, Dolores, and Butch Gentine

During one of his visits the previous year, Leonard had shared his interest in purchasing the farm should the family consider selling it in the years ahead. If the funeral business failed to achieve his vision, Leonard thought, perhaps he would pass the vineyard and winery into the hands of his children. That the original Gentine legacy should carry on seemed to be a form of poetic justice.

But now his grandmother was gone. The funeral business—nine years since he'd opened its doors—offered only marginal success.

As he drove to the Brookfield farm, he had two objectives in mind:

to officiate his grandmother's funeral and to reiterate his interest in purchasing the family vineyard.

Around the kitchen table sat his dad and uncles reviewing their mother's estate. Leonard offered his recommendations for the funeral arrangements. Then, he restated his intentions to purchase his grandparents' property.

The brothers exchanged glances. "You have that kind of money, Leonard? You'd be able to pay cash for the land?"

"Well, not exactly," Leonard admitted. "I'd be willing to take over the property and make payments to all of you until I met your selling price."

Those at the table looked askance at Leonard. His father jerked his head in the direction of the adjacent room, inviting his son, out of earshot, into a brief conversation.

"I don't think your offer is gonna fly." Wrinkling his brow, his dad spoke in hushed words. "A couple of my brothers could use the money right away. They have bills. Some of them pretty big bills. If you can't make a hefty down payment or the full price"—his dad shrugged—"they'll sell the property as quickly as they can to bring in some money. Sorry. That's just the way things are."

Leonard had arrived in Brookfield with a vision for his grandparents' farm. He left with disappointment. Months later, he watched in dismay as the farm sold for a fraction of its value—everyone, including his father, it seemed, in a hell-bent push to land a quick sale.

*Had I been able to accumulate profits over the past nine years with my funeral home,* Leonard grumbled in thought, *I might have been able to buy that farm!* Now, the homestead, the vines, the land—everything was sold. All that remained of the once-proud French family legacy was memories. A hollowness opened inside him, an unsettling void. Everything forever lost. The money from the sale, he was sure, had been quickly spent with little to show for it.

"Let it go, Len," Joe Sartori said, consoling him. "There's nothing you could have done. Put your attention toward your business, toward your family, and move on."

After a few weeks of regretting the lost opportunity, Leonard took his friend's advice and shoved the pangs of regret behind him, choosing to focus on the future and a more joyous occasion: a wedding. Dolores's sister had accepted Chuck's proposal and the two quickly prepared marriage plans. They would live as a couple before Chuck left for school.

Chuck Strobel—the young man Margaret Wernecke brought to Leonard's front door five years earlier—was now...Leonard's brother-in-law. Odd how life unfolded.

And life continued to evolve with mixed blessings. The next year—the early summer of 1947—Leonard's father fell ill. At first, the family thought it was little more than the flu or a bad cold. But his father grew worse.

As he visited his dad in Milwaukee, Leonard pulled his mother, Anna, aside. "Why don't you and Dad think about moving to Plymouth? I've already mentioned this to my neighbor, Irish O'Connell. He has an apartment—actually a portion of the house he lives in—that you and Dad could rent. With him that close, we'd help you take care of him. Let's move him while he's still able to travel."

But she decided to stay in Milwaukee.

One of the family's bittersweet moments neared: Louis's sixty-fifth birthday on June 26. As that day approached, Anna planned to celebrate the occasion at his bedside. Nothing spectacular. No cake with glowing candles to extinguish. Just family surrounding his bed, telling him that they loved him. There was hope that perhaps—just perhaps—a miracle would allow Louis brief consciousness, an ability to see his family, hear his grandchildren.

Louis, Anna, and Butch Gentine

The week prior to the celebration, Leonard browsed through the card section at the dime store. He thoughtfully wrote a message in a card. Words from his heart, son to father. If his father remained unconscious, he planned to read it to him.

On June 25, exactly one year to the day that his mother passed away, Louis went to live eternally with her and his father. Plans for the family gathering were abandoned, as Louis died one day short of the birthday celebration.

Unwilling to pile more grief on his mother and without a better alternative, Leonard tossed the sealed birthday card in the wastebasket. Alone in his office for an undetermined amount of time, he stared at the card in the trash, his message unshared, grief washing over him. A catch formed in the back of his throat. His eyes watered.

As the days passed, the sorrow weighed heavily until, once again, his neighbor Joe stood at his side, taking time away from his duties at his cheese company to console his friend. They spent time together as Joe allowed Leonard to come to terms with the string of personal losses: his grandmother, the farm, and now his father.

Life is a scale ever in motion, always seeking balance. As the pan on the scale dips downward, the pan on the other side counteracts, rocking back and forth until life balances once more.

December 18, offsetting losses, was a day of joy: Dolores, nearing the end of her third pregnancy, was quickly driven to the hospital. Leonard's mother, following her husband's death, had taken Leonard's advice and moved next door to the funeral home. As Dolores traveled to the hospital, Anna took residence and charge of the Gentine household.

At the hospital, Leonard chain-smoked, pacing in the small "father's room." With his wife in labor, Leonard tried everything to distract himself from his worry for Dolores.

The hands on the wall clock inched along so slowly that Leonard wondered if there were moments when they stopped unnoticed. At long last, the door to the father's room opened. "You have another son, Leonard. Mother and baby are fine."

"When can I see my wife?"

"It will be a little longer. We've wheeled her out of the delivery room. She's resting. Give her a little bit of time."

As the doctor left, Leonard stubbed out the remaining length of cigarette in the marble ashtray. Then, without thought, he grabbed his pack of cigarettes and lit another one.

He turned and gazed out the window. It was snowing. Large fluffy flakes peacefully, silently drifted down from the heavens, like legions of feathery angels.

Light wisps of snow. He watched as they began to accumulate outside at the base of the window. In unpredictable directions, they fell as random as events in life, he thought. A father lost. A son gained. How proud his father had been of Butch and Larry. He felt certain his father would have been equally proud today, especially knowing the name he and Dolores had chosen: Louis Peter Gentine.

From behind, he heard the door reopen. Leonard turned and faced the doctor wearing a thin, weary smile. It was time for Leonard to hug his wife and meet his new son—Lou.

# 8

# The Turning Point at Long Last
## 1949

LEONARD GLANCED AT his watch. Almost two. The men would be arriving soon.

Dolores poked her head into the funeral home office and then turned, throwing her voice behind her in Leonard's direction. "I believe all we have left is this room. While you straighten up in here, I'll go up to the kitchen and start making the food."

With that, she was gone.

The two of them spent the morning cleaning the house, shuffling the children's toys from the playroom, then shoehorning a table and several chairs back into that room. A cramped but suitable spot for poker and camaraderie. At times like these, he longed for more living space than the funeral home provided.

These men were his boyhood friends—those years living in his old Milwaukee neighborhood near Thirty-fifth and Wisconsin. Most of them now owned or managed large profitable businesses.

Before the cards were dealt, he planned a tour of his house. Just a quick view of the business, one that would showcase his small operation.

Scores of papers and envelopes smothered the top of the office desk.

He considered arranging them in a way that portrayed an active, but organized, funeral home. Drudging through the clutter of invoices, industry magazines, and papers branded with crescent coffee stains, he sifted the items into discrete piles. Then, he thought better of that idea.

In a quick change of direction, raking the papers into one large stack to stuff out of sight in a desk drawer, the corner of a misaligned envelope struck the pencil holder, knocking it off balance. He threw his hand out to catch the teetering collection of pens and pencils, only to watch it topple, roll from the desk, and land on the linoleum floor with a dull metallic thud.

With a sigh, Leonard circled the desk to retrieve it. The impact spewed its contents in such a jumble that it bore the resemblance of the children's game of Pick-Up Sticks.

Scooping the pens and pencils from the floor and dropping them back into the holder, he brushed the shell casing with his sleeve, returning it to its rightful place on the desk. He had received that gift on a day similar to this blustery March Saturday. Chuck had brimmed with excitement and a clear plan. He would marry Marge, earn a mortuary degree, and rejoin Leonard in the business. All that happened but one.

The previous year, eager to launch his career, Chuck had announced—with a freshly printed mortician license in hand—his interest in returning to the Gentine funeral home. This time with the full authority of a funeral director. Excitedly, Chuck outlined how the two of them—two brothers-in-law!—would unite and build the business to even greater dominance in the community.

Leonard had pinched his lips as he listened, attempting to hold back what he was about to say—what he had to say. With his revenues fluctuating in erratic swings, barely covering his own expenses at times, the business could not support the salary of a second licensed mortician. He regretted the direction of the conversation, but it was not a reflection of Chuck. It was a business decision.

*Let's talk about this*, Leonard had said.

Crushed, Chuck nodded in reluctant understanding as Leonard explained. Weeks later, under thinly veiled optimism, Marge and Chuck packed their belongings and relocated to a funeral home in Janesville, Wisconsin, where he would serve as the assistant funeral director.

Leonard looked at the shell casing on the desk. Chuck and Marge were family—his family. For the past year, he felt as if he had let them down, sent them packing. But if the business couldn't support another person, he was right in his decision. Wasn't he? Dolores told him she understood, but in her eyes, he read disappointment.

He shoved the papers into the drawer and shoved his thoughts of Chuck behind him.

Within the hour, the house boomed with his friends' voices as they ambled through the funeral home and then settled into the fine art of poker. Cards shuffled. Chips clacked. The men overwhelmed the small room with cigarette smoke and bravado. It was debatable as to which of the two was the thickest.

Friendly jabs and barbs yielded to anecdotal accounts of the past holiday—inoperable tree lights, standing-room-only Mass, the sweaters they received but would never wear.

"Speaking of gifts," one of the men interjected, "I always try to find an employee gift everyone can use. Last year, I gave a tin of mixed nuts. The year before a fruitcake." Seeing the grins, he shook his head. "Yeah, no one really wanted that one. I struggle for something unique. A little more interesting. It occurred to me that maybe a gift box of cheese might do the trick."

Counting four chips and pushing them to the center of the table, he continued, "Leonard, you're living in the Cheese Capital of the World. Do you think you might be able to find me a cheese company that would sell me about a hundred gift boxes in November?"

Leonard matched the bid and tossed two more chips to the center.

"You bet! There's over twenty cheese companies around here. There will be several that could do that. I'll just ask around."

Many of the cheese company executives belonged to one or more of the same service clubs as Leonard. He imagined the ease in leveraging his relationships to uncover several gift-box options. After all, it seemed logical that one or more of those companies already produced them each holiday.

Over the following weeks, Leonard sat in numerous company lobbies. He spoke with key individuals of nearly every cheese company in the county, all with no luck.

"Don't you ever receive requests for cheese gift boxes?" Leonard had asked one of the business owners.

"Sure we do. All the time," he replied. "We just deep-six those letters." Looting the wastebasket near the secretary in the outer office, he grabbed a few as proof.

"I couldn't believe it!" Leonard mentioned to Dolores several days later. "Almost every company gets mail requests but all of their letters are going unanswered. Those companies sell their cheese by the truckload to large operators, not by the ounce to individual households."

As Dolores listened, she served breakfast to the children, pouring syrup over pancakes and sectioning the food into small bites for the two younger boys.

"So I called my friend back," Leonard continued. "Said I couldn't find a single company willing to make a hundred gift boxes for him."

He watched as his son ate his syrup-soaked pancake and then reached across the table to reposition the glass of milk sitting dangerously close to Butch's animated elbow. "And then I asked if he would trust me to make the cheese boxes myself. He said, 'Fine.' Whatever I wanted to do. So"—Leonard locked on Dolores's face to catch her expression—"possibly . . . we'll go into the cheese business."

He saw her jaw tighten before she bent out of view, below the table, to retrieve an errant bite of pancake that had found its way to the floor. As she surfaced, she said—her words spoken as a sigh—"Well, here we go…again!"

Leonard lowered his head and nodded agreement. Dolores reached over and placed her hand on his arm. "I know how hard you are trying, and I'm not asking you to give up on what you believe in. From the first day I met you, you dreamed of a family business, talked about a family business, and drove yourself to build a family business."

She paused and held her head down as if to collect her thoughts. "Len, besides the funeral home, you have a mink farm and an ambulance service—well, I guess that's part of the funeral business…Now cheese? Of all the men I know, I'm betting my life that you will achieve whatever you set out to do. I just worry that you are spreading yourself too thin. Just choose something and go after it."

Leonard shook his head in thought. "I understand. Let me talk to a few people before I fully jump into this thing."

The next day, he networked. He then talked to Joe Sartori.

"It could be done," assured Joe. "If you can stir up repeat business throughout the year, it could be a nice little business." Joe paused in thought and then said, "I'll help you if I can. We can provide some of the cheese from S&R. You can pay us after you've been paid."

With the cooperation of a few businessmen—lending credit, providing materials—Leonard considered assembling the boxes in the rustic building behind the funeral home. It lacked heat. He could fix that.

With a plan in mind, he talked to Dolores again. "What do you think? It wouldn't cost us much up-front money to give it a try. My mom might even be willing to help assemble them. I can ask our neighbors…a few of our friends."

Dolores studied his face. "Do it if you think it's what you need to do. But can you promise me one thing? Will you promise me you'll get rid of the mink?"

With the population of the mink exceeding three hundred head—and with a proportionate increase in bites, scratches, and festering wounds—it was a bargain he willingly accepted. He sold the livestock and plowed the cash from the sale into the purchase and installation of a previously owned cooler.

For weeks, he designed, and redesigned, the size and contents of the gift box. To determine an optimal size and weight, he spoke to his friends at the post office. The local grocer carried wheels of cheddar and blocks of Swiss so he included those two varieties in the gift box.

"I don't know anything about cheese...other than I like to eat it," Leonard confided to Joe.

Joe suggested three cheeses not normally found in homes: mozzarella, provolone, and Parmesan. "S&R can provide them. But a lot of homemakers may not know how to cook with one or more of those Italian cheeses," Joe cautioned. "A few may. You can always put a small flier in the box with suggestions for eating and cooking."

Satisfied with the assortment and the container, Leonard wax-coated small blocks of each of the five cheese varieties, made an appointment, and drove to Milwaukee to present his suggestion.

Tucking the sample gift box under his arm, he followed a secretary as she escorted him to a small conference room. Leonard walked in.

His eyes narrowed and his mouth dropped slightly. A feeling of disorientation engulfed him. His mind muddled. *Did the secretary usher me into the wrong conference room, causing me to interrupt a meeting in progress?* Thinking she might redirect him, he turned and saw her smiling.

Several of his friends—friends from the poker party he had hosted in March, friends that also owned businesses in the Milwaukee area—sat around the table. One of them served as the spokesman.

"Leonard, we all know how challenging this will be. This is asking you to make an investment that may result in only a small amount of profit. So we're all here to order gift boxes for our companies, too. A little more money for your efforts."

Leonard was speechless.

He tried to estimate the quantity needed. Although he had difficulty responding, his mind ticked through the logistics: sourcing cheese and shipping materials, finding labor, constructing an assembly line, and scheduling time.

Leonard left that gift box approval meeting with an agreement on the contents of the box. Of greater significance, it was clear he would now be producing more than four times the number of boxes than he had originally anticipated.

As he drove to Plymouth, he began to wonder if Joe had been right. Could this be a larger opportunity? Other companies might possibly have an interest in gift boxes, too. Perhaps he could sell enough of them to pay some of the year-end bills that always haunted him.

At his desk, on a sheet of paper, he drew up a list of potential Milwaukee companies. Perhaps he could sell a thousand boxes, he speculated. Was that possible? Maybe two thousand? Perhaps two thousand was too optimistic.

Leonard tossed the pencil into the pencil holder, listening to it rattle back at him as it found a resting spot.

He thought once more of Chuck and Marge, the pangs of his conscience renewed. When he was a boy, his grandparents and his parents stressed the importance of people. In all matters, they had preached that people and the respect of others always took precedent. Always.

Had he been true to those beliefs? Or had he somehow wandered, taking a divergent path?

Leonard leaned back in his desk chair, staring vacantly, allowing the events of his recent past to replay before him like a spliced newsreel, recapping the highlights. There was a nagging sense of some insight—a lesson perhaps—that he had yet to grasp. As if it were lodged in the far reaches of his mind, he struggled to bring the nettlesome idea forward.

A family business. That's what he wanted, had always wanted, never wavering. And it seemed clear to him, a family business should be anchored by its value to…the family. If his family saw no value, it would die when he died. Isn't that what had happened to his grand-parents' vineyard? None of their sons saw any value in producing wine, and so the farm vanished.

For twelve years, Leonard struggled to build his funeral home large enough to support him and Dolores. The day it was profitable to do so, he planned to put others on the payroll.

But his funeral business languished, never offering a profit more than "just enough"—or occasionally slightly more than "just enough." And still they had debt to accompany those twelve years of moderate success. Never had he saved enough to live beyond the next unforeseen crisis, let alone set aside enough money to buy the house he had always promised Dolores.

Their growth felt stunted, as if a translucent lid covered him. If extra help was needed, he asked neighbors for their free labor, relying on their generosity, or he and Dolores merely doubled their efforts. The latter, he had to admit, was generally the case.

Leonard cast a glance at the pencil holder once more. Perhaps he was approaching this all wrong.

Instead of building a profitable business and then, later, inviting others into it, perhaps it was the opposite. Perhaps a family doesn't grow *into* an existing business. Perhaps, the business grows as a *result* of a family's invested efforts. What if the process was to first involve others in the business and then build the business *around* them? Was that possible?

Leonard looked down at the scribbled estimates on the pad of paper. If it were possible to sell a thousand boxes—a number so outlandish!—but...if it *were* possible, who would he want at his side to help build that business?

Leonard grabbed the handset of the desk phone, dialed the lengthy sequence of numbers, and waited. "Chuck?" he said. "How's business in Janesville?"

Leonard paused, eyes closed, listening intently. "That's great. And Marge and the kids? They're fine?"

Another pause as he listened. "You'll never believe what's been happening here." Leonard summarized the opportunity and what he thought could happen. Then, without waiting for a reaction, he took the conversation in hand.

"Well...I'm just going to ask. I want your honest answer." He took a deep breath and launched his question. "My funeral business here is turning around." *Not entirely true*, he thought. "Well, I got to thinking, I'm going to be in need of a man to help me with funerals and this cheese thing I got started. Would you be interested in working for me again?"

Silence filled the funeral home office as he listened to the voice at the other end. Leonard smiled.

Several days following that conversation, Chuck, Marge, and their family packed their car. After a little more than a year in Janesville, they were coming home.

# 9

# Plymouth Cheese Counter
## 1949

"CHUCK, C'MON IN." Leonard opened the front door wide. "I've got coffee in the office. Pour yourself a cup before we go."

Faint wisps of steam swirled and rose from the cup as Chuck cautiously pressed the hot liquid against his lips. It was his second cup this morning.

Leonard checked his watch and then beckoned with his hand as he grabbed his suit coat. "Bring the coffee along. We need to get on the road."

Following Chuck and Marge's return to Plymouth, Leonard's earlier regrets were replaced by—he struggled for the feeling—not quite elation, he thought, but close to that. A sort of inner contentment knowing that, regardless of any resulting consequences, his choice—his decision—was the right thing to do.

As darkness drained from the sky, they climbed into Leonard's car with the intent to reach their first destination before the morning rush hour. Leonard had called early in the week, making three gift box appointments.

"I think when you see all there is to this," Leonard said, "you'll be able to do this yourself. Don't think of it as selling gift boxes. We're not doing that at all. We're just telling 'em that other companies are ordering these for their employees and we want to let them in on it, too, if they like."

As he drove on, he glanced sidewise at Chuck in the early-morning shadows. "I know you said you'd help with this gift box idea. You should know, I'm also thinking of using part of the carriage house for a related business.

"One of Dolores's best friends, Leonore Meltz, you know, Lou's god-mother? She agreed to loan us fifteen hundred dollars so we could start a small retail cheese shop. I'm working on the details of that right now."

Chuck, continuing to nurse his cup of coffee, nodded and said, "Interesting idea."

"The truth is that I don't know where all this is leading me. I've been working for twelve years to make the funeral home a success, but some-times Dolores and I have still been forced to live hand to mouth. I've been thinking that maybe Plymouth just isn't big enough to need two funeral homes. A big part of me doesn't want to believe that, though.

"Then—out of the blue—this gift box idea comes along." He paused, reliving the moment. "I tried to get a cheese company to just make a hundred boxes. A hundred boxes! But nobody would bite, so I said, what the hell, I'll just do it myself. Now, this cheese shop idea comes up. With all these things happening, I need some help, so... would you be willing to come along for the ride?"

"If it helps pay my wages, I'm glad to help, Leonard. I've never done anything like this before, but sure, I'll try. You know I will."

Leonard drove on in silence, thinking. The landscape brightened as morning broke. As they approached Milwaukee, large expanses of empty land fell behind them. Houses crowded one another; billboards and business signs conspired to hide what little open land remained.

"I know your heart has always been with the mortuary business,

Chuck. Mine as well. When we talked on the phone, before you decided to return to Plymouth, I mentioned my need for your help with these cheese ideas. If they produce a steadier income than the funeral home, I may…"

Leonard thought in silence, unwilling to finish the thought. "If you help me out with this and later you want to stay in the funeral business—if that's what happens here—I'll set you up with"—he drew in a long gulp of air—"whoever takes over the Gentine funeral home."

Chuck set his empty cup on the floor of the car. "Leonard, I was excited to earn my funeral director's license. I was. And yes, that has been something I've always wanted to do. But as I worked the year in Janesville, I realized that my excitement that day was only partially due to my degree. It took me a long time to come to the truth that I was far more excited that you and I would be working together. When that didn't happen…When you said there was no way the funeral home could afford me…"

Before he could continue, Chuck swallowed and took a breath. "Well, that was emotional for me—and Marge. Especially Marge. But by then, I didn't know how we could ever return if your business continued to make as little as it had for years. Then you called. It was if my prayers—our prayers—had been answered. If shipping gift boxes of cheese means I get to work with you, if operating a cheese shop does that…if being bitten by a thousand mink is what it takes, well, then I—"

"Well, there's no mink to battle anymore," said Leonard, "and the South American beavers will be sold someday soon."

Chuck laughed. "Not that I'll cry about that. Anyway, what I'm trying to say—I just want to work with you. Marge sure loves living closer to Dolores. She's so much happier since we moved back. Tell me what you want me to do, and I'll do it. But I'll probably share my thoughts now and then. I'm not one to just take orders."

Leonard turned and blew out a burst of air as he squeezed out half a laugh. "Share every idea you can think of. I'd like that. I can use all the ideas I can get."

Leonard replaced the phone on its cradle and scribbled a note on his calendar. Two funerals scheduled in the last ten days. Not that that meant much. His funeral business, known for its long cycles of feast and famine, always taunted him, keeping him hopeful that the business was finally building trust in the community.

Shoving the calendar aside, he tugged open the top desk drawer. Out of sheer curiosity, he slid out the ledger used to track the number of presold gift boxes. He flipped to the dog-eared page. Eight hundred ninety-five!

"Eight hundred ninety-five!" He repeated the number, this time aloud. The quantity was hard to grasp. Only a hundred and five more and they would hit the thousand-box threshold—a number he could never have imagined possible at the start. Yet now it seemed more than probable they would be shipping that many boxes by the end of the year. Or perhaps more.

The thought both excited and worried him. The pending sale of a thousand boxes promised a welcome profit. It also signaled the potential that these cheese gift boxes might be a long-term business opportunity. He could use a steady stream of profit each year to offset the vagaries of his funeral business.

But at the same time, a very real concern nagged him, and anxiety intensified as the preorder total increased. Leonard massaged the back of his neck.

With permission from the local cheese companies, he and Chuck stopped regularly to pick up letters received from people requesting product shipped to their homes. His mother and her friend, Tillie Mayer, would comfortably slice a small section of cheese, dip it in a preserving wax, and pack it for shipment. It was time-consuming, but easy enough when they shipped only four or five boxes a week.

The end-of-the-year orders would be different—much different. Each business would expect their employee gift boxes delivered within a short period—the exact timing that every other business wanted their gift boxes delivered. Within those few weeks, how could they hope to assemble a thousand gift boxes? Certainly, they could cut and wax ahead of time, then store the small chunks of cheese in refrigeration. But if they were to do that, he would be required to purchase some of that bulk cheese well in advance of when their customers would pay them.

No, he reasoned, they needed to find a method of mass-producing small chunks of waxed cheese. He knew of no cheese company using equipment to do that. If he had any chance at success, he would first need to build the equipment required to speed that part of the assembly.

A series of raps at the back door disturbed his thoughts. Three additional knocks followed. Leonard tucked the ledger back in the drawer and pushed away from the desk.

He opened the door, and Irish O'Connell stood before him.

"Hope this is a good time, Leonard," his neighbor said. "You said I could stop by and see what you're working on in your carriage house. I figured since it's Saturday and there are no cars pulled in for a funeral, I'd—"

"Your timing couldn't be better." Leonard disappeared for a second and returned with a book. "Let's go over there. I'd like your thoughts on an idea."

"It's not quite finished in here," Leonard said, entering the building. "I'm calling it the Plymouth Cheese Counter."

Irish ran his hand over the long counter. "You build this yourself?"

"Well, I helped. Actually, Chuck and I built it together, and then we put that linoleum on the top."

Leonard placed the book he brought from the house on the corner of the counter. "That's a color book of the different cheeses from around the world," he said as he patted the cover.

"A whole book? That thick?" Irish's eyes narrowed as if in thought. "All I've seen in the grocery store is Swiss and cheddar and, uh..."

"American."

"Oh yeah, American. How many more kinds are there?"

"That's where this place is gonna shine," said Leonard. "There are so many different kinds other than those in the stores, and we're offering them right here at the Cheese Counter. Out here"—Leonard pointed to the room in which they were standing—"I'll have shelves with syrup and other Wisconsin products. Right along the counter will be a couple of wooden barrels that I'll fill with hard candy and nuts.

"But this," he said, moving to a door at the side of the counter, "this will be the main attraction. A walk-in cooler. First of its kind in the state of Wisconsin. First I know of at least. Come inside. Brace yourself, though—it's chilly."

As they entered, Leonard watched as Irish studied the shelves on both sides, his face a picture of amazement. Each shelf displayed an assortment of cheese—English cheddar, Gorgonzola, provolone, Romano, Parmesan, and a smattering of other unfamiliar-sounding cheese names such as Colby, Gouda, and Monterey Jack.

"Over here will be my cheese-from-around-the-world shelves. Cheese from Italy, France, England, and Germany."

"This is amazing, Leonard."

"So my idea is this." Leonard picked up a knife from the shelf and lopped off a small chunk of Parmesan. "Shoppers can walk through this cooler and sample any cheese they like. Just like this." He handed the chunk of white cheese to Irish. "No obligation to buy. None whatsoever. They can browse through the cheese book I just put on the counter and read how to serve or use the different cheeses. Or they can ask one of the Cheese Counter's staff."

Leonard waited until Irish finished sampling. "So what do ya think?"

"Family-sized packages of cheese sold in the Cheese Capital of the World." Irish chuckled. "I like it, Leonard. And I like the cheese!"

"My mom will help me run the shop. And you're welcome to stop by—or work here—anytime you want. Here"—Leonard pulled a small waxed block of mozzarella from the shelf—"take this home. Tell Katie to use this instead of Velveeta when she makes a casserole."

"OK, I will. Thanks."

As Irish left, Leonard called out to him, "Tell your wife to stop by sometime. I'll give her some provolone, too. You can tell me what your boys think of it."

Leonard turned and looked about the empty cheese shop, his thoughts returning to the challenge of cutting and waxing cheese in some form of a production line.

There was a man, Bill Linstedt, he remembered—a retired employee of Kraft who loved to build things in a small shop behind his house. Leonard strode back to his desk in the funeral home. He would give Bill a call.

In the weeks to follow, Bill Linstedt and Leonard tinkered with different ways to convert bulk cheese into small waxed packages.

Leonard and Chuck continued to post additional gift box presales into the ledger. As orders inched near two thousand, a knot formed in Leonard's stomach, causing him to increase the hours spent with Bill.

Gift box assembly line

Drawing on his knowledge from his former job at the Falk Corporation—where he learned the mechanics of machinery—Leonard collaborated with Bill to fabricate the cutting and waxing stations. Their development path, which was anything but straightforward, resulted in two crude but reliable pieces of equipment. They were so simply designed, even those lacking mechanical experience could operate them.

As fall approached, Leonard and Chuck shifted from selling to production. Leonard's mother convinced neighboring housewives to help in exchange for a little added household income. Through November, the carriage house buzzed with chatter as the crew hand-packed the boxes and stacked them for delivery. By the first week of December, every gift box request had been filled.

Including the boxes shipped as part of their year-round, mail-order business, Leonard, his family, and his neighbors shipped more than five thousand boxes from that building behind the funeral home. An unbelievable number!

Even more than the accomplishment of shipping that many boxes, it was the first time Leonard earned a sizable profit from any of his businesses.

# 10

# Genstrupp
## 1951

*IT MUST HAVE been the custard stand*, Leonard thought.

The previous year, when Elkhart Lake—the small town to the north of Plymouth—announced their intent to sponsor an open-road car race, drawing a crowd of over fifty thousand tourists, his mother insisted on opening a drive-in at the edge of Plymouth.

"There's not a custard stand anywhere about in this county," Anna said, her eyes burning with excitement. "And you think of the people driving along Highway 23 and 57 for that big race. Hot. Hungry. We'd be doing them a service, offering something for them and their families."

Leonard threw a dismissive hand in the air. "Mother, we don't know a thing about ice cream. And besides, who'd run it? We're busy enough with what we have."

"Tillie Mayer and her husband once owned a restaurant and she said she would help me." Anna looked at her son from the corners of her eyes, waiting for his response.

"I was hoping you'd still run the Cheese Counter this year," he said.

He watched the enthusiasm empty from his mother's face. "OK. Tell you what. Let me think about it."

Day after day, with single-minded determination, Anna continued to persuade her son on the wisdom of her idea. Leonard, no longer able to diffuse his mother's enthusiasm, reluctantly agreed to the business.

One day he threw a large sign over the building with the name Plymouth Cheese Counter—the same name as his cheese shop behind the funeral home—and later suggested they also sell chunks of cheese at that drive-in. "Those carhops on skates could deliver more than cones and sundaes," he reasoned.

Anna peered out the drive-in service window. Girls were delivering trays of food. Cars with teenage boys were flirting with the carhops. She frowned and shook her head. "We can try selling cheese, but I don't think it'll be popular. I'll tell you what I'd like to add instead. Hamburgers, hot dogs, and grilled cheese sandwiches. Tillie's sure she could handle a few burgers and hot dogs on a grill."

Marge Strobel in front of the custard stand

"Hamburgers! Hot dogs?" Leonard had trouble imagining that. "That makes no sense at all. Who the hell would want to eat a hamburger in their car?"

"They're offering hamburgers and other food in drive-ins around Milwaukee," she countered.

Leonard puffed out a burst of air in frustration. He did *not* want to argue with his mother. "Fine. If that's what you believe, give it a try. But we'll add wedges of cheese to the menu, too."

As he strode out the back door of the building, he turned and said, "I'm telling you right here and now, despite what Milwaukee drive-ins have on their menus, selling hamburgers is a short-lived fad, not a viable idea for a drive-in."

The custard stand proved to be a popular attraction in Plymouth, drawing a constant stream of cars and a great deal of local attention. Conversations with people Leonard knew always seemed to include a reference to "that custard stand" at the edge of town. So it must have been the thing, Leonard decided, that tipped the scales with the men in Plymouth.

Suddenly, talk of Leonard's business acumen spread in wider circles. Leonard was earning a reputation, not as a premier undertaker, but as a savvy entrepreneur, owning a portfolio of different enterprises: a funeral home, an ambulance service, a gift box business, a cheese shop, and... "that custard stand."

In the past, men had approached him with an occasional get-rich-quick idea. Now, an incoming tide of "opportunities" washed over him. As if believing Leonard possessed the business equivalent of the Midas touch—prospering in every venture he pursued—ambitious men and dreamers shared their bright visions. Some worth considering. Most completely outlandish. Each man hoped Leonard would endow them with his managerial talent and a large cash investment.

June "JC" Tupper, who had worked at Kraft, was one of those men. But it was Chuck, not JC, who first presented the opportunity to Leonard.

At the carriage house, as Chuck and Leonard unloaded a delivery of cheese—a replenishment order from their supplier, the Milwaukee Cheese Company—Chuck opened the discussion. "Some of these international cheeses are starting to sell pretty good. That got me to thinking what other cheese we could stock."

Leonard wrapped his long arms around a case and dragged it to the front of the truck bed, waiting to hear Chuck's idea.

Chuck took advantage of the moment. "I was talking to my brother-in-law over the weekend. Since they closed the Kraft plant in Plymouth, JC's been commuting every day to their plant in Green Bay. He hates the drive. I think it's wearing on his wife, too. Virginia would like to have him traveling less."

Too vividly, Leonard remembered his own daily commute to Milwaukee years ago as he worked at the Falk Corporation on third shift while Bob Merkel oversaw the funeral home. "Has he thought of finding a job at another cheese company here in Plymouth? He's a cheese scientist. I'd bet he could find another company in town that could use him."

"Perhaps," Chuck offered as he propped an elbow up on the edge of the truck. "I don't think he's really interested in working for another big cheese company. He's saved a bit of money over the years and…well, he's been thinking of using it to start his own little cheese company."

Leonard remembered JC talking about a couple of projects while he worked in the Kraft plant. He was reformulating Velveeta. There was also a cheese spread that he had been testing, something he said Kraft was thinking about calling Cheez Whiz or Cheese Whip. He wasn't sure. He just remembered the name sounded odd.

"What kinda cheese is he thinking of making?"

"Kraft said they had no interest in one of the cheese ideas he was working on. He could make it and sell it if he wanted. Something called Koch Kaese." Chuck crisply enunciated the foreign words. "That's German for 'cooked cheese.' "

"Cooked cheese? I thought all cheese was cooked, or am I wrong about that?"

"I asked him that, too. If I'm getting this right, he takes curds of cheese, cooks them, and blends them into a paste or...some kinda spread. A limburger spread. A pimento cheese spread. People put it on crackers or bread."

Then Chuck added, "He has samples. I can have him bring some over. JC's got most of the money to fund the company, but he's looking for business partners. He's a scientist with no experience running a company."

With the gift box business in its second year and with increased traffic shopping at the Plymouth Cheese Counter, a trickle of money was flowing into the coffers. For once, Leonard was paying down his bills. Not enough left over to launch another business, he thought. Not even close.

He was already in unfamiliar territory with two cheese businesses, although he was learning as fast as he could. Cooked cheese? Instead of converting cheese from big blocks to small chunks, they would be manufacturing products. That was a whole different ball game.

Following weeks of deliberation, Leonard phoned Chuck at his home. "OK, tell JC we should meet here at the funeral home some night to talk about this."

Before that meeting, seeking an expert's opinion, Leonard met Joe Sartori for lunch. Joe listened impassively and then offered his cautionary advice.

"Not a lot of people are going to be interested in that," he said. "Cooked cheese probably appeals most to those with German heritage. A lot of Germans settled in Wisconsin, so you could find people interested in the product. If you're thinking of just a small business...it might work, who knows? It would be a risk."

*Not exactly a glowing recommendation*, thought Leonard. Yet there was a certain appeal. With JC's background in cheese science, perhaps there would be an opportunity to augment the product line and get into new and unique products. Maybe expand into a much larger company over time.

As the three men met, discussing the mechanics of making the products and what would be required in the partnership, they reached an agreement. At Leonard's suggestion, they selected a small portion of the carriage house as the company's start-up location.

"I've been giving some thought to the name of the company," said Leonard one morning. "Since all three of us threw equal amounts of money into the pot, and each of us has equal responsibilities, I thought we could name the business after all three of us. If we take the *Gen* from Gentine, *str* from Strobel, and *upp* from Tupper—it forms the German-sounding name of *Genstrupp*."

With agreement on the company name, Chuck's wife, Marge, designed the logo: a globe of the world with Plymouth, Wisconsin, at its nucleus.

They cobbled together and pressed into service a jar-filling unit similar in design to the one JC remembered using at Kraft. Responsibility for the remaining equipment fell to Leonard and Bill Linstedt, the local machinist.

Conserving funds, choosing not to buy or design new equipment, they jury-rigged machinery from odd parts. Instead of an expensive extruder, they purchased a used meat grinder from the A&P in town and welded it below the drain of a washtub. Instead of traditional cheese-curing equipment, they chose a metal garden rake, a watering can, and a hand-held Mixmaster.

In similar fashion, Leonard and Bill modified an industrial ice cream maker to serve as their cheese cooker. Purchased from the ice cream factory near the S&R Cheese factory in town, they modified the machine to heat rather than freeze. The unit stirred and pasteurized, providing 100 pounds of creamy cooked cheese. Unfortunately, it took trial and error to overcome the inordinate amount of time required for the cooker to heat the cheese curds. In addition, to everyone's frustration, the cheese sauce occasionally contained lumps during those early trials.

Yet by the end of the year—the carriage house offering limited space—Leonard found himself standing with Chuck in a rented building—the back half of 405 East Mill Street—watching jars of cooked cheese travel down a conveyor belt.

Leonard snagged one of the jars from the line before JC's daughter, Carol, could pack it in a carton. Cocking his head, he studied it as if seeing it for the first time.

"Chuck, none of this is gonna amount to anything unless we find ways of getting it into more stores."

His words belied his intended meaning. As part of the management team, Chuck had volunteered to oversee sales. Leonard saw his brother-in-law's face take on the appearance of a chastised child.

"No. No, Chuck," Leonard said, clarifying his meaning. "You're doing all you can, but there's too much going on. How can you sell this product into stores when you also have funeral home responsibilities? When you're also in charge of the Plymouth Cheese Counter? Both locations?

"We need to find a better way to do this. You know Ken Wondergem? The delivery guy from the Milwaukee Cheese Company? I asked him if he could sell our products off his truck. He's checking with the company owners and will let me know next Wednesday."

The following week, Ken Wondergem leapt from the cab of his truck in an obvious display of excitement to greet Leonard and share the good news. "I showed them your products, Leonard. They're interested! Asked me to tell you to call them to set up an appointment."

Encouraged, Leonard immediately phoned, made an appointment, and a few days later, Leonard and Chuck drove to Milwaukee to meet with the company owners. A week following that meeting, they reached a handshake agreement, which quickly evolved into an eagerly signed contract.

Unfortunately, their good fortune at finding representation quickly soured, and Leonard soon regretted their distributor partnership.

"I meant this to be a celebratory dinner," Leonard said as he and Dolores met Joe and Marie Sartori one night for dinner. "Well, it is, I guess. I sold my custard stand this week. Verland and Dorothy Kasten will take over the business in May. Sold them all of the equipment inside, too, as part of the deal. A lot of work went into selling that place. I didn't think I'd ever find a buyer."

Joe picked up the bread basket and passed it to his wife. "That place was always busy last summer. Too bad you couldn't have made a go of it. But selling it does let you focus more on your other businesses."

Joe and Marie Sartori with Dolores and Leonard Gentine

"That place!" Marie shook her head. "Nothing but noisy cars, loud radios, and high schoolers. Honest to Pete, it seemed like each time I drove by there, I heard that Fats Domino guy singing his crazy song from one of the car radios. It was Plymouth's teenage hangout."

"Naw, that didn't bother me," Leonard said. "It was the expenses. Even when it's closed in the winter, and I'm not making a dime from it, I have mortgage payments, electricity and heating bills—each month. I'm just glad to be done with it."

"So...it is a celebratory dinner then," offered Joe.

"Yeah, sorta."

He didn't want to have the evening turn into a gripe session. But he hoped for Joe's thoughts on his cooked cheese business. Having difficulty sleeping for the past few months—unable to stop thinking about the problems—he needed to find a way to put Genstrupp back on track.

"I'm rid of the custard business but now Genstrupp is giving me headaches. Ever since we signed on with our distributor, they keep raising the price of our products to the retailers. That makes the retailers raise their price in the store. And I don't think they give us a spit of attention."

Leonard could feel the emotions well up inside. "Their salesmen put more effort behind all of the other products they represent. Never the Genstrupp products."

Dolores looked at him and then turned to Marie. "Honestly, I keep thinking that they bit off too much too quickly. I think Len was happier when he came home from the mink farm all chewed up. Even though I hated that business," she hastily added.

Leonard leaned back and slapped his hands on his thighs. "The thing is I'm always at odds with the distributor. They're not very good business partners, and when I call them, I—"

"Walk away," Joe interrupted. "Just walk away. Get a different distributor. Or a food broker instead of a distributor. I could recommend a broker. One that I trust."

Leonard pushed out a deep and long burst of air. "Unfortunately, at the outset, Milwaukee Cheese insisted on exclusivity. Their name appears on each of our jars. We were so excited to have a distributor, we didn't give it the thought we should have. I guess we trusted they'd be working in our best interest. Watching out for us."

"Walk away," Joe repeated. "If Genstrupp is legally contracted to use them as their distributor, you can always shut the business down. It's early in the game. Start a new company. Different name. Different types of products." Joe cast a sideways glance and an angled grin. "You have plenty of experience starting new companies, Len. That should be a piece of cake for you."

Tapping his finger on the table, Leonard weighed Joe's comments as the waitress took their orders. When Joe mentioned different types of products, he knew just the items they could consider.

Leonard sipped his coffee. As the waitress walked away, he set the cup down by his plate. Thinking of a way to introduce his thought, he chose to begin by referencing a familiar topic.

"I've been tracking the sales over at the Plymouth Cheese Counter," he said to Joe. "Your Italian cheeses are strong sellers. Chuck'll need to place another order for mozzarella and provolone. We may even need more Parmesan soon."

"Just send the order my way, Len, I'll take care of it."

Leonard gazed in thought. "It seems we sell more of those items than we do Swiss or cheddar. Well, maybe not cheddar," he corrected himself. "But I would guess some weeks that might be the case."

It was then that Leonard decided to float his latest idea. "I've been wondering if we couldn't sell wax-coated blocks of cheese in grocery stores. You know, the size we sell in our gift boxes." He held up both index fingers to indicate the size of the cheese. "They're probably— what?—five or six inches in length.

"Is it possible," Leonard asked Joe, "that a grocery store would have an interest in selling individual chunks of cheese that size? All I've ever seen them carry are blocks of cheddar and wheels of Swiss. And the clerk has to cut it, weigh it, and wrap it. What if a company did all that cutting and wrapping for them?"

"Perhaps," Joe reflected. "You know you could test the idea in a few A&P stores. I'm sure they'd let you do that. Just a few items. Their refrigerated cases don't have much room." Joe mulled it over and then added, "No harm in trying it. You're already waxing cheese at the Cheese Counter. Offer to put them in a few stores. See what they say."

Head bent in thought, Leonard absently nodded as he watched the waitress deliver their food. *Enough business talk*, he thought. It was a night out with their wives. Time to change the subject.

# 11

# A Bigger Idea
## 1953

"AT WHAT POINT would you consider getting out of the funeral business?"

Leonard permitted Joe's question to hang in the air, unanswered, until the lunch chatter at the Mitchell Hotel restaurant overtook it. Instead, Leonard swirled his water glass, watching the ice race around the inside edge. Truth was, he had no answer to that question.

It was not his nature to give up. He'd struggled for so long to make the funeral home a success that the effort had become part of him. Something vital he couldn't—or maybe refused to—abandon. Whatever it took, whatever life demanded of him, he always believed he was smart enough, resourceful enough, and determined enough to tackle anything head-on and eventually overcome.

Had he gone this far, only to go this far?

As if reading his thoughts, Joe arched an eyebrow. "Some dreams do die. And there is pain in allowing them to die. Sometimes," Joe ventured, "it's a choice. The disappointment in giving up on a dream. Or the regret of missing out on something better."

Leonard Gentine

Joe paused, tested his chowder, and decided to let it cool.

"You've owned and managed the funeral business for, what, sixteen years now?" Joe pointed out. "And over that time, it doesn't appear to have grown significantly. What it does do is drain your attention and time from what you could be accomplishing.

"You should consider shedding some of your businesses. Take them down to the one that offers the greatest potential. I suspect it's not the funeral business. Is it the Cheese Counter? Genstrupp?"

*Genstrupp? No, not Genstrupp*, Leonard thought. Realistically, he probably should not have agreed to get into that business from the start. As for the Cheese Counter, it was profitable. Yet Leonard was unsure it would offer a long-term income, despite the annual gift box program he was developing. On the other hand, he had to admit that his heart was not as heavily invested in the funeral business as it had been in 1937.

Leonard set the water glass back on the table. "I wouldn't bet all my chips on Genstrupp. You know my view on that. Distributor issues. The limited product line and an inability to expand into other products. That's the biggest monkey on my back."

Joe threw both hands in the air as if to say he'd heard this all before. Leonard just needed to make a decision on that company.

Leonard had made up his mind on Genstrupp, but he would need to approach that solution tactfully. The eventual outcome had to include options that provided a source of income for JC. After all, JC was a distant member of his family, and Leonard felt he owed him that much.

But taking all his businesses down to just one? That forced a decision on his funeral business. Perhaps there is wisdom in knowing when to stop, to take another path in life. To see the past efforts as learning and use that knowledge to be successful on the next attempt. Where was that tipping point on the fulcrum when it became clear it was time to cut the losses and move on?

Leonard spooned his clam chowder. He had an idea, and he wanted Joe's thoughts before they went their separate ways. "I hope you have the time. I want to run an idea past you."

Taking a sip from his glass, Joe eyed Leonard. Clanking the glass back to the table, he slapped his pocket, looking for his lighter. "What's your idea?" he asked. From his other pocket, he plucked a cigar and disrobed it of its cellophane wrapper, waiting for Leonard's response.

"This is old ground, I know," he said as he rested his elbows on the table. "I'm getting out of Genstrupp. Not because of the business, not because of JC or Chuck. I feel we are hamstrung by the distributor, and it will only get worse. I don't see another way out."

Joe didn't respond, but remained impassive, as if waiting to hear the full thought.

"There are things we could make and sell," said Leonard, "and JC has made it very clear that he doesn't want to expand much beyond cooked cheese. Not now anyway. Or maybe not ever. He doesn't want Genstrupp to get too large.

"I don't seem to be able to change Genstrupp, the distributor, or the products. I've suggested we shut down the business and start fresh with a new company. Nope. Not a direction to be considered. So it looks like my options are limited."

Leonard pulled himself up to his full height in his chair, his fist clenched, his determination ramrodding his spine. "I'm starting a new company—on my own. I'm gonna take the same wax-coated items I'm selling in the gift boxes, the same wax-coated Italian cheeses I'm selling in the Cheese Counter, and see how they sell in A&P stores."

"Good for you," Joe said as he offered a slight nod.

"Bill Linstedt and I are designing machinery that would allow us to do that—mass-produce those blocks of cheese faster. Unfortunately, I don't have the financial wherewithal to start that type of business. I've been calculating all the costs for a building, equipment, cheese, employees, packaging and shipping. The expense to start a business like that... It's a big number.

"So... I was wondering if you might... if you would have an interest in investing in the business and also allow me to purchase cheese from S&R on credit."

Joe's face became rigid, serious, staring hard at his friend. "Have you given any thought to how much money you would need? How big is that number, do you think?"

Leonard, making direct eye contact, took a minute or so before responding. "My best guess would be around fifteen thousand dollars."

"Fifteen grand!" Joe blew out his breath. "That's a lot. You can buy a house for that price." Silence hung heavily between them. Then Joe said, "As a friend, I could see what I could afford. Perhaps I could help you find another investor. How much are you contributing?"

Leonard steepled his hands and exhaled into them. "I'll scrape together all I can. Definitely, I'll contribute at least what I have invested in Genstrupp. I'm going to ask JC to buy out my shares in the company.

I'll use that money to help fund this. And I'll ask Chuck if he would have an interest in going in with me."

Joe looked at his watch and then up at Leonard. "I need time to think about this. Why don't we talk about this later? Let's just enjoy our lunch."

Leonard nodded. But his thoughts drifted elsewhere.

# 12

# It Begins
# October 23, 1953

DARK PANELING HUGGED the room, underscoring the somber transactions commonly discussed around the bulky conference table. A scattering of books—bound in tan hardcover bindings and gilded letters—claimed temporary residence at the table's far corner.

At the opposite end, Leonard awaited the arrival of Joe Sartori, his thoughts carrying him back over the past several weeks. His conversations with JC. His failed efforts to redirect Genstrupp.

"There are a few new products I'd like us to consider for Genstrupp," he had mentioned to JC one day over a cup of coffee. "I'm able to mass-produce wax-coated cheese—the same cheese I sell in the Plymouth Cheese Counter. A&P'll stock 'em in a few of their stores. Adding your products to those, stores could pick 'n' choose the ones they think would sell the best."

JC remained in momentary silence as if weighing his thoughts. "Seems to me—if we did that—we'd be moving too fast with too many items," JC had said at last. "If we get too big too fast, it's gonna be hard to manage. And how would we afford all the equipment we would need? Another bank loan? Let's just take it slow for a while. Sell what we have. Maybe down the road…perhaps it may be possible…" JC's voice trailed off as he shrugged.

Leonard had expected that response. Yet he had been hopeful. Perhaps if he brought over a few samples, he might be more convincing. A few days later, he tried that with no better results.

Leonard changed tactics. "Had you given any more thought to the distributor? Joe believes there's a way to sever our relationships with them. Move on to other options. I think he's right, but—since we all own equal shares—we all have to be in agreement."

JC looked up from the lab table where he was testing that day's vat of cheese. "I know you aren't happy with Milwaukee Cheese. Their intentions are good. I'm convinced of it. Seems to me, all of this will even out over time. It's all just learning how to work with them. That's all. We might be overreacting, given our limited experience."

"But even Joe with his experience thinks—" Leonard began in defense and then, in resignation, refused to push the argument further. It was clear JC was content with the way things were.

Long evenings stretched before Leonard as he had sat in silence, alone in his thoughts, cigarette in hand, in search of an answer. He imagined the ripple of his choices in the past. The crests and troughs of his early funeral home decisions affected only him and Dolores, much the same way his grandfather's decisions with the vineyard affected only his family. But now, Leonard's ripple arced outward, reaching farther than those of his grandfather, sending more distant members of his family bobbing.

JC counted on Leonard as a business partner. Now, with a growing contention between him and the distributor, Leonard wrestled with his decision. With the partnership less than a year old, Leonard considered stepping out of the business, leaving JC to bear the additional role of business manager along with his responsibilities overseeing the manufacturing.

*Is a business decision just a business decision, nothing to be taken person-*
*ally? Is that how companies are to be run? A wary eye only on the ledger,*
*not on its people? Surely, business is not just about the money, the profits*
*garnered at the end of each year.* The thought caused him to wince. The
memory of his earlier decision with Chuck was still fresh.

Leonard reached a verdict in the end. It demanded soul-searching,
numerous days alone with his thoughts, and more cups of coffee than he
cared to admit. Still, Leonard believed his departure was the right choice.

The door to the conference room clicked open as Joe entered, dis-
rupting Leonard's thoughts.

"I brought two separate checks," Joe said as he took a seat near
Leonard. "One written from the S&R account and the other from my
personal account. Five thousand apiece. If you brought a check for five,
we should be set."

"It's right here," Leonard said, pulling an envelope from the inside of
his suit coat.

Over the past several weeks, Joe not only agreed to serve as the primary cheese supplier for Leonard's latest business venture, but also
agreed—in exchange for fifty shares—to invest $5,000 of his own
money and an equal amount of S&R funds in the undertaking. Leonard's $5,000 rounded out the full initial investment.

Reaching into another pocket of his suit coat, Leonard grabbed his
pack of cigarettes as he simultaneously stretched across the conference
table for the ashtray. As he did so, the door reopened. The attorney
entered and took the empty seat facing them.

So quickly had the lawyer snatched the documents from the secretary's typewriter that the paperwork needed sorting and organizing.
Removing the carbon paper, the attorney separated the originals from
the copies, placing a completed set in front of Joe and Leonard.

"I have listed," the attorney began, "the company's name as Sargento. S-A-R-G-E-N-T-O. Is that correct? I just want to verify that."

"That's right," affirmed Leonard. "*Sar* from Sartori, *Gent* from Gentine, and an *o* at the end to give the company an Italian feel."

The attorney offered a practiced smile.

Leonard instinctively grabbed the pen from the table in anticipation as the attorney methodically walked through the language of the agreement. Stoically, Joe weighed the importance of each word read aloud, evaluating its accurate interpretation of their verbal understanding.

As the attorney summarized each document, he allowed brief pauses for questions. Few were voiced. In the end, when neither party raised any further inquiries, he slid the agreement, first to Leonard for his signature and then to Joe, who signed, first, as himself and then as S&R Cheese Corporation. In turn, each fully executed document circled back to the lawyer for his notary seal.

Validation of funding completed the exercise. Stock certificates, to be issued several days later, would be drawn and recorded.

Following the signing of the documents, Leonard and Joe shook hands—a more meaningful compact between the two men as far as Leonard was concerned. That was it. No celebratory drink.

*How different it feels*, thought Leonard, *than the buoyed emotions I felt the day I started the Plymouth Cheese Counter.* Joe returned to S&R to finish his day. Leonard, after some thought, drove to Genstrupp.

Still concerned about many of the foreseeable hurdles with the Genstrupp business, Leonard again approached JC. "Just signed the paperwork with Joe this morning. It's official. I'll start selling wax-coated cheese chunks to stores in the next couple of weeks." Leonard brought his head down in thought and then added, "I really hoped that you would throw in with me, JC. It's still possible, you know."

JC gave the appearance of possibly accepting Leonard's offer and then said, "I'm better off staying right here. If it's all right with you." JC paused. "I'm going to change the name to Tupper Cheese. Keep Milwaukee Cheese as the distributor but change the name."

Leonard waved off JC's concern. "I would probably do the same if it were me."

Privately, outside of the building, Leonard asked Chuck if he had an interest in investing in Sargento as well. Chuck gave it serious consideration and then decided against it. Given the demands of his growing family, he would wait. Eventually, in the years ahead, he would make an investment.

Chuck glanced at the building. "Just as soon as I feel JC is financially stable enough to operate his company on his own, I will ask him to buy out my share, too. Then, if I could, I'd like to help you at Sargento."

Leonard offered a broad smile. "Chuck, I could think of no better man I'd want in my corner. You've always been my right-hand man. In every business I've owned, you were there with great ideas. And you've always kept things in perspective for me. But most of all, you and I seem to share the same vision."

A dubious expression crawled across Chuck's face. "Both of us are trained as funeral directors. I'm not likely to be your best choice to help you run a cheese company. I've learned some at the Cheese Counter. But you might be better off with a real cheese person as your second in command."

"Chuck," said Leonard, "you are exactly the type of person I need. Building relationships is a key part of the funeral business. The same holds true at the Plymouth Cheese Counter and in the gift box business. You're good at that. I don't need someone good at making cheese. I need someone good at making friends."

"Give me about a month, Leonard. Just to make sure JC is doing OK. Then I'll join you. If you need me to help in between, I will."

Leonard rubbed his chin in thought. "I am asking around, looking for a few people to help. If you know of anyone, send 'em my way. We'll be working out of the carriage house. I'm squeezing Sargento in on the other side of the Plymouth Cheese Counter. For now, it will need to share space in the gift box portion of the building.

"I don't think I told you," Leonard went on, "about a month ago, I talked to Bob Griese. He said it'd be OK to test a few Sargento products in some of the local stores. If they showed promise, he would suggest making them available in every A&P store across the country. And that's coming from the president of the A&P Dairy Division.

"Just think. The number-one grocery chain in America carrying Sargento cheese! It's all about personal connections, Chuck. Honest, sincere connections. And you are one of the best at that."

Chuck's jaw dropped slightly as if he were attempting to imagine the number of stores that would have one or two Sargento products in their cooler case. "That's . . . that's a lot of stores. A lot of packages of cheese. Good for you! I hope that works out." Then nodding at the Genstrupp building, he said, "I best get back inside. I promised JC that I would help him load the truck coming today. We have over two hundred cases of product to move up from the basement and into that truck. It will take us a while even with the conveyor belt."

Leonard watched Chuck climb the stairs and enter the building.

The reality of his new venture struck him. The burden of the company's success now fell solidly on his shoulders. Joe would help in what way he could, of course. However, Joe's primary responsibility was S&R Cheese. Leonard's responsibility, on the other hand, was to reward Joe's faith in him by making Sargento a success.

Despite his experience in starting other companies, launching Sargento felt more ponderous. Although Joe never gave voice to that potential, Leonard knew he could be displaced if the situation warranted. Outvoted on any decision. Joe was a good friend, but this was business. To build and maintain confidence, Leonard—and soon Chuck—would need to be ever-vigilant in their relationship with Joe.

Setting up regular meetings—Saturday mornings might be the best time for Joe—would give everyone a time to identify problems, share ideas, and foster camaraderie.

Of all that had come before, Sargento, Leonard knew, was his largest gamble.

"As you and Bill Linstedt were working on the equipment," Chuck shared with Leonard weeks later, "I asked Marge to provide some drawings for the Sargento logo and package labels. The past couple of mornings, she was up before me, sitting at the kitchen table using our daughter's back-lit toy makeup mirror to help her draw Italian symbols.

Marge Strobel

"I'll bring them over. But she drew one where the Sargento name is lying on top of the Leaning Tower of Pisa. You can look at them all, but I think you'll like that one."

The next day, Chuck tossed a handful of drawings on Leonard's desk. Leonard studied them, taking the time to absorb each option. Taping the Leaning Tower drawing to the wall, he stepped back, narrowed his eyes, and stared in silence. There was no doubt that people would recognize the building, he thought. And he liked the old-world feel to the lettering, especially the *S*.

"You're right," Leonard said at last. "This one's the best. I can picture it on our packages." He stared in silence once more. "Yeah, let's use this one. Tell Marge thanks."

"Dad?" In the doorway of the office stood Leonard's five-year-old son. "The pedal on my bike is loose. Can you fix it?"

"Lou, Uncle Chuck is showing me something. Can I take a look at it in a minute?"

"OK." And Lou turned to walk down the hall toward the rear of the house.

Leonard leaned over to get a better view of his son. "Lou, I don't think you said hi to your uncle."

Lou turned his chin over his shoulder and said, "Hi, Uncle Chuck." With that, he bounded out the back door.

# 13

# The Sartori-Gentine-O'Connell Gang
# 1953

LOU GENTINE PULLED the tricycle out of the carriage house while he waited. It had been Larry's bike, but at five-going-on-six years of age, Lou had grown into it. Larry owned a two-wheeler now.

As he waited for his dad to fix his pedal, Lou rode around the driveway in loopy circles, giving thought to what they might do today. With school closed for the summer, each day was an adventure.

Sometimes his little sister, Ann, played with them if they stayed in the yard. She was three and a half, so his mom wanted her to be closer to home. Of course, she could always play with his brother, Lee, thought Lou. He was a one-year-old, but he loved to play with toys.

Many times, it was just the boys—Butch, Larry, Lou, and Paul Sartori from across the street. Jim and Jack O'Connell, on the other side of the driveway, rounded out the gang.

Lou jumped from his tricycle as Butch and Larry sprang from the back door. As his two older brothers ran down the driveway, Lou followed. "We're going to Paul's house. See what he wants to do today," Larry said over his shoulder.

"Larry! Lou's your responsibility," Dolores called out the back door.

"Wait for him so you can cross the street together." Larry stopped, making his body limp in silent protest, waiting for Lou to catch up.

Paul was a year older than Larry, and many times they complained that they wanted to do things older boys did—without Lou. And sometimes they did slip away on adventures, taking them farther from home. That usually happened when Dolores had lined up activities and chores to keep Lou occupied.

Most of the fun happened outdoors: baseball games with makeshift cardboard bases and lazy hours spent as Huck Finn wannabes, their fishing lines dangling from the town bridge. But when the weather didn't cooperate, they found a secret pleasure in playing in the funeral parlor with its ample covert cubbyholes, corners, and concealments for hide-and-seek.

The basement was off-limits. "Under no circumstances do I want to find any of you boys playing in the casket room," their dad lectured.

"No, Dad," Larry would assure him, trying to look sincere. "We'll just play hide-and-seek up here."

When their dad left for work, the boys would furtively drift to the lower level—the tempting, forbidden area. Although Lou cringed at the thought, Larry thought it fun to crawl into empty caskets to hide, knowing it would deter the others from looking there.

The forbidden area had its risks. Beyond the occasional nightmares that visited Lou in the evenings, all three boys knew that serious consequences would follow if they were caught.

On the top floor of 728 Eastern Avenue, where the Gentine family lived, hung a razor strop in the bathroom. Many mornings, Lou watched his father sharpen his razor on that strip of leather before he shaved. His father regularly pointed out the other use for that strop if he learned any of his children misbehaved. Just the sight of that leather hanging near the sink was a fearful reminder.

When the weather cooperated, they preferred the outdoors. Away from the watchful eyes of parents, they found a lot more things that interested them. And Lou particularly liked it when his brother Butch joined them. His oldest brother was ten. *And when you're that old*, he thought, *something exciting happens every day.*

Like the time Butch suggested they pick vegetables. From the carriage house, they would grab rakes, take them over to the corner across the street from their house, and wait.

Open-bed trucks, slugging past their homes with fresh-picked beans or peas, became targets. Daringly, like undersized pillagers of Sherwood Forest, they plotted to rake their ill-gotten gain of green vegetables as the vehicle rounded that corner toward the cannery. Even Lou was known to dart out brandishing his rake, leaping and swiping at the vegetables hanging precariously near the back end of the truck. Many a windfall of peas and beans found their way home, where Dolores—thinking they were a gift from a neighbor—cooked them for dinner.

"What're we gonna do today, Butch?" Lou asked once they reached Paul's house.

Butch's face brightened. "I know. You wanna ride our bikes and see the Ferris wheel?"

"Lou's too little," Paul shot back. "He can't ride his bike that far."

"Can too," protested Lou.

Butch looked at his youngest brother. "It's OK. We'll take the path. On the way, we'll grab some candy."

Recrossing the street, Butch waved at Jim and Jack O'Connell to join them as he tugged open the door to the Cheese Counter. The six boys tumbled in. As Gramma Gentine talked to a customer, the boys scuttled over to the hard-candy barrel.

"What are you boys up to?" she asked, interrupting her conversation.

"We just want some candy, Gramma," Lou said as he grabbed a fistful.

Larry, Butch, and Lou Gentine

"No. No, just one piece each," she told them. "Those are for our customers."

Lou reluctantly put all but one back. When his gramma turned, each grabbed more.

"This your grandma?" asked the man at the counter.

"Yep," said Larry with pride. "She's our gramma Gentine."

"She's *our* gramma," Lou pointed out, "not Paul's or Jim's or Jack's."

Anna arched an eyebrow. "You're right, Lou, but I can be their grandma, too, if they like. Can't have too many grandmas, right?"

Anna smiled at the neighbor boys and they grinned in return.

"Most people just call me Gramma Gentine now," she told the stranger. "I'd bet half the town does—adults and children. It's nice. I've grown to like it."

Quickly she spun in the direction of the boys. "Hey, Butch. I saw you just take another piece of candy. Now, put it back and out the door with all of you. Go on now. It's nice outside. Go."

With that, the six left, sucking on pieces of candy with one or two furtively tucked in their pockets.

Mr. Linstedt's home—a distance of five blocks from the funeral home—remained a common destination. Taking the route along the edge of the pond, they stopped every now and then, picked up a stone, and challenged one another to rock-skipping contests. Lou tried to match Butch's skill. He really did, but all of his attempts ended in a single deadening plunk.

Their well-worn path led them to the bottom of the ski jump, and they raced up the hill as weeds slapped against their trousers. At the top and straight ahead sat the county fairgrounds. "This is where they held the German prisoners during the war," said Butch with an air of authority. "World War II prisoners marched through town from here to work at the canning company."

Lou clawed his fingers into the chain-link fence. *Not much of a prison*, he thought. Even he could climb this fence if he had to. He tried to imagine prisoners inside, turned to ask a question, and found he was alone. The others had moved on.

"Lou!" Butch called. "Let's go find the Ferris wheel. We'll see if you're brave enough to go by yourself to the top."

Lou found it difficult to swallow. He'd never ridden to the top of the Ferris wheel alone. He'd never been in Mr. Linstedt's Ferris wheel at all. But then neither had the others. It was never working, and usually it lay in scattered pieces on the ground.

As they approached the yellow clapboard house, they could already see the large gazing ball Mrs. Linstedt planted in front as a lawn ornament. "I think that's where Mrs. Linstedt looks to see the future," Jim said. "Want your fortune told, Paul?"

"Nooo," Paul responded as Jim pushed him forward.

"Go knock on the door," suggested Larry. "See if Mr. Linstedt's home. It's OK. He's a friend of our dad. They make stuff together all the time."

"Listen!" said Butch as everyone drew silent. An intermittent pounding echoed from behind the building. As they rounded the corner, they found Mr. Linstedt completely engrossed in a tangle of metal pipes and tubes—the frame of a go-cart!

Looking up, Mr. Linstedt smiled at the boys standing in the distance. He straightened his tall frame and waved them over.

"You building a go-cart?" Larry asked.

"Well, I'm fixing one for Mr. Mienk—one of the cars he uses on the race track behind the custard stand. Have any of you seen that place?"

"I have!" said Butch, puffing out his chest and pushing to the front. "And I drove one before, too. You got one here we can ride?"

Mr. Linstedt rubbed his chin. "No. I would need your parents' permission even if I did. There's one over by that tree. No motor. But you can climb in and pretend if you like."

The boys sprinted in that direction, their interest in seeing the Ferris wheel completely forgotten. Each attempted to clamber into the car at once. Mr. Linstedt strolled over, allowing them, one by one, to have a turn behind the wheel.

With short attention spans, the boys soon grew bored and left. "Hey, this is Friday," Larry remembered. "Gramma Gentine will be doing a fish fry tonight."

Retracing their route back, they arrived at the Gentine house and Lou watched as his father pulled his car into the driveway and then stepped out.

His father smiled and wiggled his finger at them as they trudged in his direction. "You boys want me to put the wings out on this car and make 'er fly?"

Breaking into a run, the boys scrambled into the car. Butch and

Larry elbowed their way to the front seat. Climbing into the back with Paul, Jim, and Jack, Lou stood and hung on the back of the driver's seat as his dad slid in and closed the door. In fascination, he stared at the silver button on the dashboard.

*Maybe this time it will work*, Lou thought. "When he pushes that button," he reminded Paul, "the wings are gonna pop out the sides of the car and we'll fly." Lou tightened his grip, bracing for the liftoff.

Butch and Larry, in the front seat, looked dubious. But Lou believed and he gripped even tighter as his father said, "All set? Here...we... go!" Then, extending his index finger, he poked the silver button and waited, his hands firmly on the steering wheel.

The car wasn't moving. His father looked out his window and then craned his neck to see out the passenger window. Lou watched as his dad's face first looked confused, then disappointed.

"What? It's not working again? When I came home from Milwaukee last night, it was just fine. I'm sorry, guys. I'll have to take 'er back to the shop to get it repaired."

With substantially less enthusiasm, six small passengers climbed out of the car. "Maybe another time I'll be able to take all of you on the ride of a lifetime," his father said.

Lou looked up at his dad and felt pride swell inside. His father could make a car fly. No other dad could do that. He knew that for sure. Right then and there he made a promise to himself. When he grew up, he was gonna be just like him. He, his brothers, and his dad were going to do amazing things together.

# 14

# The Early Beginnings of Sargento
# Spring 1955

DOLORES HAD GONE to bed ahead of him.

Shortly after midnight, Leonard joined her. He reached over, switched off the light, and regretted he could not do the same with his mind. It raced on, unproductively pouring out an endless list of things to consider, to do, to discuss, to explore, to test.

Three years had passed since he started Sargento, and the enormity of the challenge—physically and mentally—exhausted him. Each day he battled that bottomless to-do list as, each night, it preyed on his mind, preventing the rest he needed.

He rolled to his side, seeking a more comfortable position in bed, willing his body to relax and his mind to go blank. Sleep spurned his request.

Leonard pictured the second floor of the carriage house. Off to one corner, Leonard and Bill Linstedt had built a small, makeshift machinist shop. There, in that scatter of tools and dismantled machine parts—there taunting him—sat the vexing dunk tank.

They had designed that tank to wax multiple wedges of cheese—eighteen at a time. Too frequently the cheese tumbled from its rack,

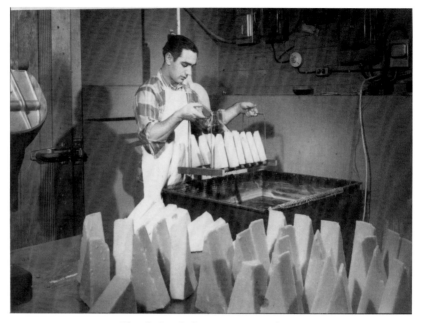

Chuck Strobel wax-coating cheese

plunging into the steaming pool of black paraffin. The dunking apparatus failed to completely coat the cheese in one dip, requiring extra dipping and cooling time. The heating unit with its uneven, inconsistent temperatures left an unattractive appearance when the wax cooled. They needed more efficiency and better-looking products.

Leonard swept that problem from his thoughts, only to allow a problem with their carton supplier to fill the void.

Rolling to his back, he stared into the blackness of the bedroom, listening to the soft breathing of Dolores next to him. His mind refused to surrender.

In many ways, Leonard believed that he and Bill Linstedt were cut from the same fabric, sharing a common passion for mechanical design. Bill's unusual insights led Leonard to believe that Bill might be a genius at seeing uncommon uses from common materials.

Scattered about his yard or in Bill's home workshop, it might be feasible to find the ringer from a washing machine, a gear drive from a bicycle, or maybe a collection of various cooking implements. Each had been dismantled to understand their construction. Each studied with fascination and curiosity. Each reassembled again, not always for their original function.

Bill Linstedt

Several of these items migrated from Bill's workshop on Bishop Avenue to the second floor of the carriage house, where they took up residence with an assortment of odd parts and pieces that Leonard had garnered.

To an outsider, Leonard considered, it may have looked like small piles of junk. Instead, he and Bill viewed them as pathways to continual learning—latent wellsprings, bubbling up some yet-to-be-imagined machinery.

In growing frustration, Leonard threw off the bedsheet. He was too warm. Then, as his body cooled in the night air, he pulled the sheet over himself again.

Recently, they'd focused on simple tools: grinders, slicers, and cutters—and that blasted dunk tank! Oftentimes, Leonard invested hours at Bill's small shop. Some days, Bill drove the five blocks to the carriage house, carting unrecognizable contraptions jutting from his car trunk.

Together, they worked as a catalyst, rapidly accelerating change and innovative ideas, uncovering previously unconsidered directions neither one of them may have entertained on their own.

As if he didn't have enough to worry his mind each night, Leonard also longed to develop another product to sell in stores: sliced cheese. In all the stores he had visited—and it seemed to him he'd visited every one of them within driving range—he could not recall any store selling prepackaged, sliced natural cheese.

If asked, a store clerk would slice cheese from a block of cheddar and wrap it in white butcher paper. Leonard imagined something different: presliced cheese, in plastic packages. Offering, like his assortment at the Plymouth Cheese Counter, more varieties than just cheddar or Swiss.

He had purchased a secondhand meat slicer and jury-rigged odd parts onto a device that fed long loaves of cheese through its spinning blade, producing a fresh stack of sliced cheese. But how could he keep the cheese slices fresh? Certainly not by dipping them in wax.

Fruits and vegetables preserved their freshness in vacuum-sealed cans. Similarly, Leonard imagined a vacuum-sealed plastic bag. A few scoffed at that notion. No one had perfected a package film capable of holding a vacuum, nor the equipment to mass-produce them. Two significant problems.

When he had the chance to rest—like this night—his mind rummaged for answers. Pulling the sheet around him, he rolled over again in search of sleep, only to hear the soft *tick, tick, tick* of the clock on the bed stand. Time bleeding out.

By chance, flipping through a magazine one day, he had noticed an H.P. Smith Paper Company story—an article he nearly overlooked—announcing the development of their new film structure and its ability to hold a vacuum. He couldn't believe what he was reading!

Within minutes, he had placed an urgent phone call to that Chicago-based company and learned that H.P. Smith's recent innovation had yet to attract any serious manufacturers. Within days, he met the head of that firm and, subsequently, reached an agreement. Leonard would be one of the first to use their new film.

With a possible answer to the first hurdle, he faced the issue of mass production. For the packages to be properly sealed and hold a vacuum, what type of machine would he and Bill need to design?

Daily, the two of them tinkered with equipment, getting little reward for their efforts. With so many variables, so many opportunities for things to go awry, he outlined a disciplined methodology on paper. During the day, while hoping to concentrate on other issues, Leonard's mind scoured over the process. Perhaps they were overlooking the obvious. He imagined the package-producing cycle, mentally watching each interval in slow motion.

Nightly, he climbed the stairs to the small work area above the Cheese Counter in search of an answer. He fiddled with the package-sealing mechanism, levels of heat, length of contact time with the sealing bar. The combination of variables seemingly endless. Forcing oxygen from the package prior to sealing challenged his understanding of physics and chemistry as well as his sense of timing. Later each night, he descended those same stairs with no better answer.

It was the very reason he fell into bed so late this night.

The film occasionally disappointed, falling victim to cracking, pin holes, and tears when stressed. These nettlesome and somewhat disheartening problems he could resolve. More concerning, the seal often failed. On rare instances when that closure held, he could neither fathom why it held nor could he consistently duplicate its success.

*Tick, tick, tick.* The clock nagged, as if mocking his inability to unravel the riddle. It was like, he imagined, the slow leak allowing air into his packages. The tiny *puff, puff, puff* of air sneaking back, marginalizing his efforts. Without a reliable seal, mold formed on the cheese within days.

Perplexing as that packaging challenge might be, he remained convinced an answer loomed just out of his reach. Not only did he believe there was a solution, he believed *he* would be the one to discover it. Night after night, he took the puzzle to bed with him. Morning after morning, he woke facing the same enigma.

Once more, in frustration, Leonard tossed in bed, this time more forcefully, as if commanding sleep to find him. Dolores, disturbed by this last jarring movement, threw her arm over him. He laid his arm over hers. Inwardly, he felt his tension unwind. He relaxed.

Then the soft *tick, tick, tick* dissolved into the night and he was gone. Sleep had mercifully taken him.

# 15

# Attempting the Impossible
# Fall 1955

BUBBLES, RESEMBLING A string of miniature pearls, raced to the surface of the water after Chuck submerged the sealed package of cheese. Had they been pearls, they might have partially mitigated Leonard's disappointment. Water bubbles, no matter how minute, only underscored their inability to manufacture an airtight package. If air bubbles could escape, the package just as readily allowed oxygen into the bag.

"You're wasting your time, Leonard." The words of a few well-meaning friends haunted him. "A plastic bag? Holding a vacuum? That ain't gonna happen. And if it were possible, some company with a lot of eggheads on staff will figure it out. Leave manufacturing innovations to the large companies with people and money to burn."

In those moments, Leonard would nod and smile. He welcomed ideas, not reasons why he shouldn't try. Anyone can give up. A man drowns only when he stops thrashing against the water. He wanted to hear ways it *might* be possible.

Dismissing all skeptics, Leonard redoubled his energies over the next few months. To near obsession, he and Bill adjusted, tweaked, and modified the equipment, hoping the next attempt would result in a consistent, reliable, airtight seal.

Several times a week, early in the morning, the local milkman, dressed in his white shirt, white pants, white cap, and contrasting black belt cinched at his waist, stopped by Sargento—not to deliver a quart of milk, but to pick up several cases of packaged cheese. On its delivery route, the refrigerated milk truck traveled over washboard roads, gravel, and the occasional pothole. The ride was jarring. Leonard's cases of cheese bounced and vibrated on the floor of that truck.

At the end of the day, the milkman returned to Sargento, unloading the exact number of cases provided that morning. The intent was not to sell cheese from the truck but rather to evaluate the effects of movement on the packages. Yet each subsequent day, packages submerged in the water tank revealed more "leakers" than airtight seals, sending a perplexed Bill and Leonard back to the equipment in search of yet another idea.

This morning, Leonard and Chuck loaded the milk truck for another "shaker test." Then, Leonard drove to Milwaukee to catch a flight to Pittsburgh.

This would be the second visit with Lou Mammone, their broker in that part of the country. Over the years, Lou had developed trusted relationships with all the key decision makers for the major grocers in the area: A&P, OK Grocery, Giant Eagle, and Kroger.

As quickly as Leonard landed in Pittsburgh, Lou Mammone ferried him to their first stop: one of the local A&P stores. The signature aroma of freshly ground coffee beans greeted him—as it always did whenever he entered an A&P. The two men went directly to the dairy case, made their purchase at the cash register, and left.

"I want you to get to know the Kroger buyer," Lou said as he pulled his car into the Kroger parking lot. "Nice guy. I showed him your stuff. He's interested but hasn't bought anything yet."

The wait in Kroger's lobby was brief and soon Leonard and Lou sat before the buyer's desk, exchanging pleasantries. Unlike other salesmen, Leonard never asked the buyer to purchase his products. Instead, from his briefcase, Leonard grabbed a few Sargento samples—bought at the A&P store that morning—and stacked them on the buyer's desk.

"This is what we're doing back in Wisconsin." Leonard leaned back in his chair, as comfortable as if he were swapping stories with an old friend. "Lou tells me you've seen these before. I'd just like to hear what you think of 'em."

Lou Mammone let Leonard do the talking. Despite Leonard's laid-back, relaxed approach—and amid some of the storytelling shared about kids, fishing, and business in general—the buyer became involved and implied he might consider stocking a few items as a test.

When Leonard called from the airport on his trip back from Pittsburgh, there was no mistaking the excitement in his voice. "I have great news, Chuck! I met with Kroger. Nice people. They said they'd like to work with us. I think they'll place an order soon."

"And I have news for you, too," Chuck echoed back. "You know the old post office building at 40 Stafford Street? Joe called yesterday and said, now that everything has been moved to the new post office, we can use the old building for a while. Just until we find something more permanent."

Leonard let out an unrestrained sigh of relief. Even though the added sales from the Pittsburgh market were paltry, they strained the company's ability to fill orders from the cramped space in the carriage house. Knowing it was time to look for a more suitable company location, he and Joe Sartori had explored locations that offered more permanent production arrangements. This was a step in the right direction.

Leonard held his hand over his left ear to block the noise of the passenger chatter at the airline gate. "That's a good-sized building, Chuck.

Can you let the post office know we accept their offer? I'll be back late tonight. We can work out the transition details in the morning."

After ten that evening, Leonard arrived back in Plymouth to find Dolores and the children asleep. Keyed up from the flight, he flipped on the lights in his funeral home office and thumbed through the stack of bills.

Covering his absence, Dolores had monitored the phone and responded to any funeral or ambulance requests. Leonard opened the funeral home log to the day's date. No activity. Not much of a surprise, although he wished for better.

In a separate ledger, the news offered more encouragement. Dolores had written a recent entry: two customer orders for Sargento products. Two good-sized orders, he noted, but week to week, demand remained sporadic. Inconsistent product demand defied his ability to provide steady employment for his employees. It was frustrating, but, he reasoned, it was likely to be the case until the company found its rhythm.

The house was quiet. He lit a cigarette and mindlessly smoked as he made notes and checked invoices. With the thought of grabbing a cup of coffee, he rose from his chair just as the phone rang. *Late-night calls never bring pleasant news*, he thought as he picked up the phone. The voice at the other end was unfamiliar.

"Leonard? My name is Gilbert Huss. Sorry for the late hour. I took a chance you'd still be awake. I saw your name and ad in a magazine and wanted to let you know I am interested in learning more about the funeral business you have for sale."

Finally admitting he was destined to be someone other than a funeral director, Leonard had listed the business in a trade magazine many months prior. Despite consistent placement of the ad, he'd not received more than a couple of inquiries. Still, he continued to advertise as his hopes waned with each passing month. The demand for funeral homes in small rural towns was limited.

"I'm a funeral director in Poynette, Wisconsin," Gilbert explained to Leonard, "and thinking of relocating my business. It's been a few months since I first saw your ad. Each month, I think about calling, but never did. Can you tell me if the business is still available and why you are selling?"

Leonard assured him the business was, at the moment, unsold, and through the conversation, he invited Gilbert to Plymouth to see his operation.

Leonard hung up the phone. Alone in the silence of the funeral home, he stared and mused. *There are times*, he thought, *when even the best efforts go unrewarded. Then, when least expected, they can suddenly blossom and bear fruit.*

The long hours, the sleepless nights, the frustrating challenges with the equipment—all those things—would still be there tomorrow and for years untold, he guessed. Yet as he took another draw on his cigarette and stared at the phone, he could almost perceive a shift, as if the ship he had been sailing for years had just found its long-awaited gust of wind.

The next day, Leonard shared a cup of coffee with Dolores as he replayed his conversation with Gilbert Huss. Then, after breakfast, he walked into the carriage house.

Already at the water tank, Chuck had arranged two bins: one labeled *Good* and one labeled *Leaker*. Next to him stood cases of packaged cheese from yesterday's milk run. Leonard shook out a Philip Morris and wandered over to view the customary water test.

Chuck submerged the first package. Nothing. Not one bubble escaped from the package.

Encouraging, but a good seal was not unusual. Occasionally, it happened. Chuck retrieved the package, dried it, and tossed it in the bin marked *Good*. With his other hand, he grabbed a second package and shoved it to the bottom of the tank.

Again . . . Nothing.

Chuck peered closely, expecting to see a bubble slowly forming on the edge of the closure. Patiently he waited and then shot a questioning look toward Leonard. Grabbing two more packages, he pressed them to the bottom of the tank. This time, he applied pressure on them with his open hands. Still nothing—no bubbles.

Hunched over the water, both men avoided any early speculation as Chuck plunged package after package into the water tank. There were leakers. Of course there would be. But amazingly, the percentage of poor seals was low—extremely low.

Leonard returned to Chuck's desk, pushing papers aside in all directions, in search of Bill Linstedt's notes. He needed to understand the adjustments made to the equipment. Bill's scribbled entries would detail modifications to the sealing plate, amount of time, pressure, and heat applied.

From under the spread of yesterday's mail poked a corner of Bill's black notebook. Leonard flipped to the last entry and ran his finger over Bill's scrawled notes. Then he stared, attempting to fully grasp the slight adjustments in this trial versus their previous tests. And why those alterations made all the difference.

With full understanding, Leonard tossed the notebook to the desktop and clasped both hands to the back of his neck in thought. *Thank God we wrote everything down!* How easy it would have been to tinker endlessly, hoping to arrive at an answer. How fortunate they both had the prior experience working for companies that demanded documentation.

In the thrill of pursuit, in the tediousness of recordkeeping, it would have been easy to abandon that discipline. With so many slight changes that could be tested, it would have been easy to jump into iteration after iteration, relying on memory, causing them to repeatedly explore the same failure paths.

Quelling his enthusiasm, he thought of the sleepless nights and then retrieved the notebook again, storing it safely in the desk drawer. This was not quite over. Multiple rounds of samples at the same settings would need to be run to validate this morning's results.

Leonard repacked all the "good" packages and stored them in the cooler. By the end of the week, he stacked even more cases of airtight packages in refrigeration as, run after run, most packages held their vacuum seal.

Weeks later, Sargento Cheese Company introduced buyers to two new items: Sliced Mozzarella and Sliced Provolone—and vacuum packaging! Sargento. Leonard's small cheese company in Plymouth, Wisconsin. Not a large company with great resources. Just a small company of nine employees with great determination.

# 16

## A Permanent Production Facility
## 1956

DEAD FOR NEARLY a decade—or perhaps the correct term might be *comatose*, thought Leonard—the sturdy brick exterior of the abandoned cannery belied its otherwise deteriorating condition.

The weather-worn door rotated heavily on its stiffened hinges, and an offensive scent assaulted Leonard and Chuck as they stepped inside. The fluorescent overhead lighting—those sections with some life—buzzed angrily, as if the act of rousing them from their dysfunctional slumber was borderline rude and disrespectful.

"Well, we own this now. The old Elkhart Lake Canning Company," Chuck said as they walked through the building. "The place needs a lot of work, but look at all the space. Just a little elbow grease and this place will shine."

Leonard grimaced. It was true. The building needed attention. Small piles of torn cardboard, an occasional empty tin can, cobwebs—lots of cobwebs—and a prevailing layer of dirt accented the otherwise vacant rooms.

There was little that could be done to gild the truth. The building had lived in neglect for years. As Sargento continued to grow, adding

The first permanent production site for Sargento

new customers, employing more people, the company begged for more room. Leonard considered himself lucky to be able to move into this building, despite the renovation needed.

Sargento had quickly reached a point where, without more production space, the company risked disappointing customers—or losing them—causing the company to stagnate or to collapse, stymied in its own inability to evolve. There just didn't seem to be any funds available to expand. Joe Sartori had already invested heavily in the company and was not likely to invest further. Leonard, laden in debt, held only a remote chance of finding additional funds from a bank.

Chuck, well aware of these barriers and their ramifications, had surprised Leonard with a check for $6,000—a substantial amount of money, enough to buy a vacant building if necessary. "It's all Marge

123

and I have been able to save over the years. We did it by skimping on things that other families would consider necessities. We've been frugal. Very frugal. Each paycheck, I've been holding back a little. It was intended to be a financial cushion for my family." Chuck paused a beat as if reflecting. "Firsthand, growing up, I saw how my mother struggled when my father left her without an income. I didn't want that to happen to Marge and the kids. If something should happen to me..." Chuck lowered his eyes and let his words fade.

"Chuck, it's a nice gesture...but I can't accept this. Hang on to that money. We'll find a way to work things out. Maybe we'll find another investor or a lender that won't mind giving us another small loan."

Chuck remained silent and then blew out a sigh as if underscoring their difficult choice and firm resolve. "We talked about it—Marge and I. This is what we want to do. We're putting our faith in Sargento. From the beginning, Marge provided the artwork needed for advertising and packaging. I sacrificed days on the road away from my family. We've invested ourselves in this business. We don't think we should stop now." He threw his hands up in a gesture indicating an end to the debate. "We believe in Sargento. As we grow, we know you'll pay us back. This is just a short-term loan."

The risks were high. The chances of success—butting heads against a large, better-funded cheese company—were marginal, but they were at a crossroads. Because of Chuck's faith—and Leonard's promissory note—Sargento had the needed influx of cash. As a result, they owned the vacant canning factory building and a large cheese dryer.

"Before we bought this," Leonard commented as he studied the lobby, "Joe and I had it inspected. You're right. There'll be some upgrades, of course."

The building tour provided them the opportunity to agree on the layout of the equipment, including the location of the large cheese dryer Leonard had recently purchased. The dryer, designed to extract moisture, allowed Sargento to manufacture grated Italian cheese: Parmesan and Romano. Somehow, they would need to wedge that monster of a machine into one of the rooms.

"Perhaps we could hire a few high school boys to sweep, clean, and paint," suggested Chuck as he poked at a pile of debris with the side of his shoe.

Chuck opened one of the interior doors and switched on the light. Tugging on a faucet handle, he stepped back as it sputtered pockets of air and liquid and then oozed orange water, flecked with rust flakes. With the base of his palm, he all but pounded the handle to stop the flow of water.

He ran his hand down the wall. Random sections of paint, defeated by the annual battles of cold winters and wet springs, flaked and blistered, falling into small colonies on the floor. "I think this place will work out just fine."

"I found out that old building over there"—Chuck turned to look as Leonard pointed out a cracked and dirt-caked window—"also belongs to this property. It was the old schoolhouse for Elkhart Lake. I've been inside. It looks like the cannery used it to store supplies. It's a mess, but we'll focus on this building first. Down the road, I'll want to use that place for our machine shop."

Leonard studied the interior, visualizing it fully operational. "Here's what I want you to do," he finally said. "We won't need high school boys. Our customers are not providing enough orders to keep everyone working a full week. On the occasional slow production days, have our employees come over here to get this place in shape. I'll pay their wages to do it."

Leonard watched Chuck jot notes in a pocket notebook. He was grateful for Chuck's generosity, and there was no person he trusted more. Chuck had a head for business, and while Leonard would have enjoyed leading the restoration and relocation, instinct told him that life was about to get more complicated.

In no time, those instincts proved right. Everything sprung into motion at once, as if someone had lifted the needle from the record, sending everyone scrambling for a vacant spot in a game of musical chairs. Never had Leonard simultaneously negotiated so many activities.

The previous December, Gilbert Huss announced his intent to buy the funeral home and move his family from Poynette, Wisconsin. That news had forced Leonard to accelerate his timetable for the construction of his new home, the house he always promised he would build for Dolores.

With the projected completion of their home scheduled for the fall of the year, Leonard scrambled to find temporary housing in neighboring communities, first in Elkhart Lake above the clubhouse at the Quit Qui Oc golf course and then later in neighboring Crystal Lake. As the Huss family moved their sofa into 728 Eastern Avenue, Leonard and his family moved their sofa out. Or perhaps it only seemed that way.

The new funeral business, now called the Gentine-Huss Funeral Home, hoped to transition Leonard's small customer base to its new owner. Regrettably, despite his best intentions to work months in tandem with Gilbert, Sargento demanded Leonard's full attention.

Relocating Sargento from the basement of the old Plymouth Post Office to the neighboring town of Elkhart Lake could not have been less straightforward—it required a complex choreography of people, trucks, and equipment over many days. After the employees improved the condition of the building, they transferred machinery between scheduled production runs and over weekends.

Often, Leonard was the first to grab a crescent wrench, disassembling cutters, slicers, packaging units, conveyor belts—everything.

Those days offered little sleep and long hours. With heavy-lidded eyes, weary bodies, and little energy remaining, nine men and women reassembled the slice line. The relocation of the chunk line followed in turn.

Unfortunately, during the days following the reinstallation, the equipment no longer functioned effectively in the new Sargento building at 305 Pine Street. It was as if the machines, like the employ-ees, needed rest and time to adjust.

After Sargento completed its relocation to Elkhart Lake and Leonard and his family relocated to temporary housing, Leonard invested more of his time alone in the car, driving from one store to the next. Each stop was a reprieve, providing the opportunity to talk with store man-agers, balancing his isolation on the road.

"Shoppers purchase Sargento products more frequently in stores where I spend the most time talking with store managers or dairy clerks." Leonard shared this observation with Joe Sartori over a lunch at the Mitchell. "That made no sense to me."

"That's probably just a coincidence," suggested Joe.

"No. You know what it was?" With the handle of his fork, he tapped the table to emphasize his travel route. "I talked to a store manager in Milwaukee. One in Racine. Another in Kenosha. All three good-sized stores. I asked them what they thought might be the answer."

"And?" Joe cocked his head, pursed his lips, and waited.

"Their responses weren't word for word the same, but they were similar." Leonard grinned at his new discovery. "It comes down to this. Where I had the strongest relationships—knew people's names, a little bit about their families, things like that—those were the stores that were generally selling the best. Turns out, the store managers—or sometimes the dairy managers—were doing me a favor. If the space allowed, they gave me an extra row on the shelf. If there was even more refrigerated space, they filled the bin with extra cases."

"So"—Joe extended the thought—"because those store managers gave you more visibility at the shelf…"

"Exactly!" With enthusiasm, Leonard leaned over the table in Joe's direction. "That exposure caused more shoppers to see the product and give us a try. What we gotta do—Chuck and I—we gotta spend more time with our customers. Build relationships."

Leonard grew somber. "But our interest in buyers and managers has to be sincere. People can easily spot a phony."

"Len, you don't have the ability to spend any more time on the road. You're traveling days on end already. You've got a company back here to run."

Leonard gave it a moment of thought. "I know just the person that can take care of things while I'm gone."

Bob Gilles

Bob Gilles, a man that Leonard hired while Sargento operated out of the carriage house, owned a farm on the edge of town. Strong work ethics stemmed, most frequently, from those raised with rural responsibilities, Leonard firmly believed. Cletus Wieser, another hardworking, model employee, also owned a farm. Leonard knew, remembering days when he stayed on his grandparents' farm, the self-discipline that lifestyle taught.

Farm living had an unspoken rule: Everyone pulled together for the common good. If one family member failed to live up to their responsibilities, it impacted the entire household. That same philosophy readily translated to the business world.

Bob exhibited that work ethic and then some. Believing him to be the ideal man to operate Sargento in his absence, Leonard named Bob Gilles as the company's production foreman.

On days when he remained in town, Leonard watched as Bob began his morning, tossing the loop of his white apron over his head and tying the strings behind. Immediately, Bob took charge. But it was Bob's hat that most intrigued Leonard.

If Leonard needed something specific accomplished that day, Bob scrawled a note on the face of his paper hat. "You're a walking to-do list," Leonard teased.

Often the hat offered limited space. By the end of the day, obsessed with details, Bob frequently scribbled notes on both sides of his hat, on his apron, his arms, and his hands. Employees knew the day's priorities by merely glancing at him.

What most endeared the new production foreman to Leonard was that Bob led by example, oftentimes placing his name next to tasks requiring the greatest amount of physical labor. Just as important, Bob also believed in balance and would be the first to initiate humor or an end-of-the-day celebration.

In addition to promoting Bob, Leonard hired Harriet Hawkins to serve as the company secretary for Leonard and Chuck, freeing Dolores of those duties. Except for Lee, all of Leonard's children attended school. Accordingly, on days when Dolores had obligations outside the home, Leonard refrained from traveling and brought Lee to work with him.

Harriet, among her other duties, entertained Lee during his visits.

"Good morning, Uncle Chuck," four-year-old Lee said politely one day as Leonard ushered him into the office.

"Good morning, Lee. And how are you this morning?"

Leonard placed a hand on his son's shoulder and peered into Chuck's office. "Lee's offered to help us this morning." Then, bending down and looking his son fully in the face, he added, "But first, Mrs. Hawkins has a surprise for you, Lee. Sit over on the couch. Mrs. Hawkins told me she'd be right back. I think she's making hot chocolate for you this morning."

"Here you are, Lee," said Harriet as she walked briskly into the room, cup in hand. "It's hot so let's put it on the table over here to let it cool." She looked at the clock on the wall. "It's after eight o'clock. You know what that means. We need to open the safe. And like before, I need your help."

Lee slid from the couch and rushed over to the large Wells Fargo safe as Leonard watched. Harriet squatted and began spinning the dial in a series of left and right turns, allowing the tumblers to fall into place. "OK, you ready? Push the handle down and pull the door open for me."

Once Lee swung open the heavy door, Harriet helped him remove the entire contents of the safe: an array of wooden toys, stuffed animals, and a collection of small cars and trucks.

Arms crossed and leaning in the door frame, Leonard shook his head. *That's all that's usually in that safe*, he thought—*Lee's toys. One day, we might actually store cash and receipts there.* For now, the cigar box on his desk served that purpose. If he lifted the cigar box lid and found cash, it was a good day. If the box was empty, that meant he needed to work a little harder.

It was a year of new beginnings: a new location and new growth. Leonard intended to add a new product to the line, too. He had been mentally tinkering with the idea, but it would require tackling the impossible—once again.

# 17

# Sargento Widens Its Reach
# 1958

Sammy Sargento, drawn by Marge Strobel

LEONARD NEVER IMAGINED the ramifications. The simple act of treating others with respect, taking an interest in the lives of others, offered respect in return.

It was a magnification of the relationship-building observation he'd mentioned to Joe a couple of years earlier. But this was much different, more complex.

In his frequent meetings with buyers and store managers, Leonard developed close friendships. He knew the names of their wives, their children, and sometimes the names of their pets. They shared interests in hobbies, sports, hunting, and fishing. They swapped business stories over drinks.

The ability to stay overnight in a city extended other opportunities. If schedules permitted, Leonard invited the store manager and his wife to dinner. No sales pitch with the meal—he was never about selling anyway—just a chance to know each other, to have a relaxing evening together.

"You should bring your wife along sometime," they would occasionally suggest. He would wholeheartedly agree, but the coordination of that with Dolores and the children was a challenge. He would be sure to bring her with him someday.

As Leonard and Chuck expanded these friendships in the grocery industry, sales increased. The small cheese company back home began to experience a consistent flow of orders. But just as Leonard could clearly understand their growing success when looking back, he saw with equal clarity the challenge that lay ahead.

"We're growing, Chuck," he had said in one of their Saturday morning meetings. "The company's getting bigger. Bob Gilles is hiring more people to fill the orders. You and I are stretched as far as we can be. We can see only so many buyers in a week."

Leonard took the cigarette from his mouth and looked at the smoke rippling upward. "We never could hire another man to help us talk to retailers. Never could afford to do that." Leonard paused. "I think it's time."

Chuck thought a moment. "How do you suppose we go about finding a good salesman?"

Leonard inhaled and the tip of his cigarette flared, the ash growing longer. He stared ahead in thought. "I have someone in mind." He stubbed out the half-smoked cigarette. "I'll ask him tomorrow."

Leonard slapped the car visor down to cut the glare from the May morning sunrise. Once more, he sat behind the wheel of his car, driving to catch a flight to Pittsburgh. Unlike his trips of the past, this time Leonard would not be flying alone. Next to him, in the passenger's seat, sat Harold Ziegler, the company's newest salesman.

As they drove, Harold confessed his self-doubts. "Thanks for giving me this chance and this job, Leonard, but I gotta tell ya, I'm not a salesman. I've tried it before and…Let's just say, I don't think it's my calling in life."

"Harold," Leonard explained, "look at Chuck and me. We're not salesmen. We go out and explain what we got. We just tell 'em what we're doing. That's all. Show 'em our products. Let 'em see the type of things we're making. That's all you need to do."

Leonard tapped the car signal and took the exit toward the airport. "You've only worked for a couple of weeks. Give it time. I have faith in you."

Harold's expression grew grim as he launched into his account of his short time at Sargento. "It hasn't been the best two weeks, calling on buyers and store managers. They would rather be dealing with salesmen from much larger companies, ones with larger wallets and more perks to offer.

"'What company are you with?' they would ask me. I'd tell them I'm with Sargento. We're a cheese company out of Wisconsin. I'd notice their forehead wrinkle, and then watch their face go blank and say, 'Nope. Never heard of ya.'"

Leonard shook his head at Harold's story. Often, buyers and store managers he met dismissed the need to carry Sargento products. They considered the products a fad, a flash in the pan, too small a niche to be of any interest to their regular shoppers.

"It'll take time for some people to appreciate the benefits of our products," Leonard assured him. "For anything new, there'll be those that go with it right away and others that'll want to wait. It's more important that we let 'em know what's available and let 'em make the decision when it's right for them."

"When we get to the broker," Leonard continued, "I want you to pay attention to the way the buyers we meet appreciate our products. Pittsburgh's a growing market for us. Lou Mammone's doing a great job."

Exposing Harold to a few success stories had been the primary rationale behind this trip. Just a few minutes in front of the A&P buyer, thought Leonard, should have a lasting impact on Harold.

Lou Mammone met the two men at the Pittsburgh gate and then, after lunch, drove them to meet the regional buyer at A&P—the buyer for the food chain's largest warehouse.

As he did hundreds of times in the past, Leonard laid samples of his 4-ounce wedges on the buyer's desk. Then he proudly revealed his company's latest innovation—vacuum-packed sliced cheese. He never asked for the order. Instead, he spoke about the things they were testing at the company, asking the buyer for his thoughts or ideas.

"What would help A&P stores bring in more sales?" Leonard asked at the end.

Picking up one of the wax-coated samples from his desk, the buyer turned it over and over in his hand. "Last week, we received a memo in the mail from our corporate office," began the buyer as he rolled the package between his fingers. "They want us to find ways to cut our costs at the store level. Our profits aren't where they want them to be."

The buyer paused, stacking the samples one atop the other and sliding them aside with the back of his hand. "There are a lot of hidden costs related to the cheese we sell in our stores. The clerk cuts a chunk from the wheel in the cooler. Then he weighs it, wraps it, seals it with a hot iron, and then puts a label on it and hands it to the shopper. The labor costs are hard to account for, but I have to believe they are costing us far more than we realize. I'll bet you could probably do it cheaper if there was only a way to do that for each one of our stores."

Sargento wax-coated cheeses reduced some store labor. Interest in Italian cheeses was growing, but those cheese sales still paled in comparison to frequently purchased varieties such as Swiss and cheddar.

This was a broader conversation—a more expansive idea. The buyer challenged Sargento to help them find a way to reduce their labor-laden process. Completely remove their clerks from the equation by offering precut, packaged cheese. Each package need not be restricted to the same weight. Sargento could offer various packages with slightly different weights—the buyer had called them random-weight packages—each package falling within a specific price range.

On their flight back to Wisconsin, Leonard was unable to contain his enthusiasm. "Did you hear the guy at A&P say it costs them a lot to provide cheese for their customers? He said I could probably do it cheaper. And he's right. I can! Harold, we gotta get into that random-weight business. We can't make it on four-ounce products. If we can get into Sargento eight- to twelve-ounce random-weight cheese chunks—and larger—we can ship cheese by the ton instead of by the pound."

The more Leonard thought about the potential, the greater grew his excitement. During the next Saturday management meeting, Leonard enthusiastically shared this opportunity with Joe Sartori.

Joe listened quietly. In a full measure of fervor, Leonard recommended that Sargento develop a random-weight program. Joe pondered the proposal but could not agree with the direction. The timing was bad. Moving in that direction stretched the company resources too quickly. Sargento was still finding its footing.

"Keep to your original premise," Joe urged. "There's plenty of opportunity to gradually expand on the type of items you have already developed."

Reluctantly, Leonard reined in his enthusiasm but continued to feel the pull of the opportunity. Admittedly, it was only one A&P buyer's concern for store-labor costs. But how long would it be before other customers awoke to the realization that labor costs could be removed from their bottom line by assigning the cutting and wrapping responsibility to a vendor? Leonard wanted to be that vendor. There was growth in doing that. There was profit in doing that. It would keep more of his employees working full time.

Joe clearly underscored the managerial direction for Sargento. Still, it would prove hard for Leonard to let that opportunity slide to another company. The idea gnawed at him.

Later, Leonard pulled Chuck and Harold aside. "Casually ask other buyers for their opinions on this," he said. "Listen to their thoughts. Make no promises—just listen."

# 18

# Leonard Impacts the Cheese Industry—Again
# 1958

Cletus Wieser operating the cheese dryer

RIVULETS OF SWEAT branched below Cletus Wieser's paper hat as he loaded precut sections of Parmesan onto a metal-mesh conveyor belt. The air hung heavy and hot.

Heat radiating from Leonard's big, bulky green machine reached 120 degrees. On a summer day, with the morning temperature rising since nine o'clock, Bob Gilles struggled to find anyone, other than Cletus, willing to operate that eight-by-forty-foot piece of equipment.

As if the heat from the machine was not enough, the smell of cheese drying permeated clothing and hair, and became the only scent Cletus could smell as he drifted off to sleep each night. Most people preferred working across the hallway, under cooler temperatures, slicing cheese or wax-coating chunks.

Yet Cletus boasted of his job at Sargento and proudly pointed to the 4-ounce grated cheese canisters in the local grocery stores. "I make those products!" he would brag. The stubborn aroma of Parmesan or Romano imbued him with a certain "air of authority," and most people listened to Cletus's pride in his work from a respectable distance.

With Harold Ziegler firmly ensconced in his sales territory, Leonard found some flexibility to pursue his other passions: tinkering with equipment and developing new products. Although just as enamored as Cletus with the cheese dryer and the products it produced, Leonard longed to market a product he felt held even greater potential— products different from those Cletus made for Sargento. Cheese items he'd been considering for the past two years: shredded cheese, not grated.

"Housewives use cheese graters to shred cheddar, Swiss . . . sometimes mozzarella," he said to Bill Linstedt. Bill listened but his attention was directed toward a disabled cheese slicer. The chain had snapped.

Leonard handed Bill a spare chain from a shelf and continued his thought. "And I can tell you, cleaning a kitchen cheese grater is not easy. Those scalloped edges rip dishcloths and dishtowels. Ever scrape your knuckles on a grater?"

"Yep," grunted Bill, his voice partially lost in the machinery next to his face. "It hurts!"

"So here's my question, Bill. How can we produce something in the factory to fix those problems? How can we manufacture a line of shredded cheese so housewives never have to take the grater out of the kitchen drawer? No company is making shredded cheese. But that doesn't mean it can't be done."

Bill snapped the new chain in place, gave the cutter a few test cycles, and then wiped his large hands on his apron. "Shredding cheese? That's what you want to do?"

Leonard nodded.

"Sure, I'll help you with that. I'll need some time to think about it."

A commitment from Bill was all Leonard sought for the moment.

Pioneering new product ideas, Leonard began to understand, took a familiar route. At first, the idea could look ludicrous, impossible to achieve. Fatigue and frustration battered them. Disappointments. One failure after another. But those defeats eventually led to new knowledge, new skills, and—if patient enough—success.

Leonard encouraged their newest machinist, Norman "Bud" Dick, to join them, too. With the three of them wrestling this challenge, their odds of success could only improve.

"Would the machine move a block of cheese back and forth across an oversized grater—simulating what a human would do?" Leonard asked as the three of them gathered weeks later. "Or would the machine scrape its rough edges across a stationary block of cheese?"

At the outset, Leonard believed those were the two primary development paths to consider. Either direction they chose would absorb hours of mechanical design and much of their resources. Accordingly, he needed consensus to pursue only one direction—the path that offered the greatest opportunity for success.

They were deadlocked, unable to agree on an approach.

Chuck Strobel, having recently returned from his week on the road, reported discouraging news at the weekly Saturday morning meeting. "According to one of the buyers I met, Kraft has been promising they'll soon be offering a line of vacuum-packed sliced cheese."

Joe Sartori cleared his throat and then flattened his hand on the table. "We should file for a patent on our inventions. When we don't, we make it too easy for the competition to copy us."

Leonard shook his head. "I would prefer not to patent our ideas. Let the competition take what we've done and improve it. That makes a good idea even better and helps the whole industry."

"I'm sure the industry is grateful," said Joe with a hint of sarcasm. "Think, for a moment, of all the hours this company invests. All the cost of the materials. It seems to me there should be some reward for doing all that. A patent would give Sargento something unique to sell. Build our business faster."

Leonard shrugged his shoulders. "You may be right, but we're doing fine. Sargento is in"—Leonard mentally counted—"six states. Not in every grocery store in all of those states, but in many of them. And A&P carries a few of our products wherever they have a store. Most of the time anyway."

"What surprises me," Chuck chimed in, "is how quickly they were able to copy us. Their salesmen must have spotted our packages in the store and mailed them to Kraft headquarters."

"If I had to guess," said Joe, crossing his arms before him, "they

Joe Sartori and Leonard Gentine at a trade booth

probably saw our products at the couple of trade shows where we had a booth. There were plenty of customers that stopped by. I have to believe our competition did the same. And there, on the table, each time, was our vacuum packaging. Front and center. They would've been blind to miss it."

Leonard was ready to move on. "Let's not worry about what the competition is doing or not doing. We've other irons in the fire."

The brightest glowing iron in that fire was his stalled, shredded cheese project. Although this was not the time to discuss its slow progress, he felt confident there would be news soon. He held to a simple belief: a problem cannot persist if enough thought is placed behind it. That had always proven to be true in the past. He had no reason to doubt it would be any different now.

The next morning, in that small window of time between dreaming and waking, Leonard again struggled to visualize a machine shredding cheese. They had approached this riddle by duplicating the action in the kitchen. What if they studied the problem from a different perspective?

Taking a cue from Bill Linstedt's approach to mechanics—finding uncommon uses for common materials—Leonard thought, what machine was already in use that could produce the shape of a shred of cheese?

Leonard first imagined a meat grinder. That would extrude long strings of cheese, but he couldn't imagine thrusting a block of cheese into a grinder's throat, hoping to achieve consistent shreds. That machine would produce more "cheese dust" than the shreds he wanted. Not a meat grinder. There was a machine in existence that would better produce the shape of shredded cheese. He sensed it, like a word that rested just on the tip of the tongue.

Then, in an instant, in a flash of clarity, he pictured it. Something that just might work. After breakfast, he'd stop at Bill's house to see if he had one of them in his collection of parts and machinery.

"Leonard! I hope this doesn't mean there's a problem again," Bill said as he responded to the knock on his door. "Something break? Need me to take a look at something in the plant?"

"Naw." Leonard shook his head. "I just wanted to get your thoughts on an idea. It's the shredded cheese project. Mind if I come in?"

"Sure, come on in. We can talk in the living room. Can I get you anything? Coffee?"

"I'm fine," Leonard said as he settled on the cloth couch. "Did you have any other thoughts on the type of equipment we would need? Anything come to you?"

"Nothing worth talking about at the moment, I'm afraid."

Leonard described the thought that sprang to him as he woke up that morning. "Would you happen to have one of those in your shop?"

"I'm sure I don't. I might know where I could find one. Did you want it today?"

"Or tomorrow," said Leonard. "I just had an idea I wanted to try. But I need to see how it operates to be sure."

That afternoon, Bill stopped by the Sargento office in Elkhart Lake. Tucked under one arm bulged a corrugated box. The sound of the carton as he plopped it on Leonard's desk gave testimony to its heft and durability.

He beamed. "Got what you wanted."

Leonard pulled open the cardboard flaps and peered inside. There rested an old pasta cutter. Placing it on the corner of the desk, Leonard inserted the crank handle and gave it a full rotation. The machine may have logged some mileage since it was new, but it worked just fine. In fascination, he watched as the smooth-cutting rollers revolved when the crank turned. Metal cutters pressed against other metal cutters with the sole intent of converting fresh dough into strands of pasta.

Eager to test it out, Leonard carried the machine out to the production line and attached the cutter to a table with a C-clamp. Lifting a 4-inch-square slice of mozzarella from the production line, he inserted it between the rollers as he cranked the handle. Out rolled fettuccini-shaped cheese—4-inch-long ribbons of mozzarella.

Leonard gave Bill a wry smile. It had worked, just as he thought. But the size of the ribbons concerned him—too wide. As he picked up a second slice of cheese, he moved the handle to a different roller setting and cranked again. As he rotated the handle, fine threads of mozzarella "spaghetti" rolled out. That was more in line with his expectations.

But a couple of nagging concerns remained: 4-inch shreds of cheese were too long, and bits of cheese, he noticed, clung to the rollers. How could they resolve those issues? Also, he would ask Bill or Bud to attach a motor, allowing a hands-free operator to feed slices of cheese into the machine, making it more efficient in the plant.

Months of testing and refinement led to a final test run. Leonard parked his car and walked toward the old Elkhart Lake School they now used as a shop. Even before he opened the door, he heard the growl of a motor. Except for the light from an old classroom, much of the interior was dim.

Seemingly endless equipment modifications to the pasta cutter had culminated in this moment. Bud Dick had installed custom-designed cutting rollers and a flywheel to the drive shaft to provide a smooth, continuous operation.

The trial run focused on durability. How long would the machine operate before cheese gummed up the cutters? How fast could the cheese slices be fed? As Leonard entered the old classroom, he found a circumscribed audience around the modified pasta machine. Each took turns feeding sliced cheese, watching the 1-inch cheese "noodles" fall into a plastic bin below.

Early on, they learned—just as they would have surmised—that the cooler the core temperature of the cheese, the easier it flowed through the machine. Too warm and the cheese clung to the blades.

Bill shouted in Leonard's direction, his voice rising above the motor. "Here's what it looks like, Leonard! We've been going at it for about two hours now."

Reaching into the plastic bin with both hands, Bill scooped up a small pile of shredded cheese. With his index finger, Leonard poked a few shreds around in Bill's hands to check consistency and examine the cut.

The test run proved better than expected. In turn, Bob Gilles promised to install the pasta cutter in the manufacturing facility next door, order packaging film, and plan a production schedule. He would package the shredded cheese from the test run for sales samples.

Their competition was now offering vacuum-sealed sliced cheese. But Leonard smiled, his worry temporarily subsiding. Those other companies had learned how to seal packages of sliced cheese, but Sargento would now be the first to offer family-sized packages of *shredded* cheese.

# 19

# Leonard's Focus Narrows
# May 1963

A STRIP OF bells clanged against the windowed door of the Plymouth Cheese Counter as Jerry Eigenberger opened it and stepped inside. Huddled at the far end of a long counter, Gramma Gentine and Leonard turned in unison, as if an invisible string attached them to the door, its opening jerking their heads in that direction.

Leonard threw him a smile. Jerry and his wife, Virgie, played couples bridge with him and Dolores, but this was the first time Jerry had been in the Cheese Counter. "Jerry! Did Virgie send you shopping for cheese?"

Jerry moved toward them as he scanned the room. "Virgie and I were talking the other day and she said this was the most interesting place she'd ever seen. That I needed to stop by sometime to see it for myself. So here I am." He looked about the room and then said, "She mentioned something about a walk-in cooler?"

"Well, let me give you a tour. My mother and I were just putting together an order for a cheese shipment. We can do that later." Anna looked up and nodded her consent.

Flagging Jerry in his direction, he said, "Let me show you the cheese room. That's the cooler Virgie was telling you about."

The two men pushed through a door, causing Jerry to involuntarily hunch his shoulders against the cold air. Metal shelving filled both sides of the cooler, each storing blocks and wheels of cheese. Below each cheese hung a small card with a name.

"So many different kinds! Pro-vo-lone." He carefully sounded out the name. "I wouldn't even know what to do with a cheese like that. And cheddar and... English cheddar? What's the difference?"

"Let me cut off a little piece for you to try." Leonard grabbed a small knife from the shelf and freed a small portion from three different cheddars.

"Oh, you don't need to destroy a block of cheese just so I can taste it."

"Jerry, this is what we do. Customers can taste any cheese they want. We can show 'em how to cook with 'em. Things like that. If they wanna buy some, however much they want, we'll wrap it up or dip it in wax to keep it fresh. We even have a small machine now that'll vacuum-seal it."

Jerry popped the three different cheddars in his mouth, one at a time, nodding as he chewed. "That's amazing. There is a difference."

Leaving the cooler, Leonard showed him the supply room and even walked him upstairs, pointing out the small areas Chuck once used as his office and he once used as his workshop. Stepping down the steep stairs back onto the sales floor of the Cheese Counter, Leonard asked what he thought of the place.

"Very impressive," Jerry said as he took a closer inspection of the shelves displaying an assortment of syrups, honey, locally made products, and other paraphernalia representing Wisconsin.

"Like it?" asked Leonard.

"Mm-hmm. I do."

"Well, if you like it, why don't you buy it? It's a great little business."

Jerry just grinned and thanked Leonard for the personal tour.

In a turn of events that surprised even Leonard, several days later, having given the matter some thought, Jerry returned. "That offer to sell this place still good?"

"It is. And it's been one of my most profitable businesses."

Jerry looked around the selling area of the Cheese Counter. "Well, I'm interested. A couple of weeks ago, the company I work for said they were going to transfer me...again! They keep moving me around the country. A good sales manager's gotta keep moving, they tell me. Learn different parts of the business. Learn different customers."

"I certainly understand what it's like to be on the road all the time," said Leonard.

Jerry wagged his head. "I just finally got back to my hometown, and the more I thought about it, I've got no interest in leaving. This looks like a better deal to me. I'll pull out some money from my savings and then get a loan from the bank in a couple weeks. That work for you?"

"That'd be just fine, Jerry." Leonard shook his hand to seal the deal. It would be the last of Leonard's businesses sold—those ventures launched in his earlier years.

Now, only Sargento remained. Unfortunately, with Joe's part ownership, he could never consider the company a true family business.

His children were growing. Butch had reached his twenties. Larry and Lou attended high school, with Ann soon to be a freshman. The youngest, Lee, recently turned eleven. Ironically, Leonard wondered if he should consider starting another small business. Perhaps funded with Sargento profits.

In truth, the financial results for Sargento had improved marginally over the past five years with revenues modestly covering wages, supplies, repairs, and equipment modifications. Ron Begalke, their outside accountant, remained indispensable in his role, establishing payment schedules and overseeing product costs and pricing.

Although the financial picture at Sargento improved, any accountant would be hard-pressed to classify the company as financially sound, insulated from a downturn in sales or the economy. Leonard realized this but tended to understate the potential threat. It took money to run a business, and there were certain things that he believed to be necessary for Sargento.

As Leonard began to see each employee as part of his extended family, he counseled, coached, and cajoled over cups of coffee. Or he took an empathetic role, comforting or consoling an employee struggling through one of life's many challenges. Occasionally this extended to the use of company funds to aid an employee financially.

He believed consumers should get a fair shake. "If the bag of Sargento cheese says four ounces, there had better be at least that much in the package. We're in the business to give people our best. If we have to give away a little cheese, that's fine with me," he affirmed.

At other times, Leonard donated to charitable causes, or helped fund civic projects. *What's good for the community is good for Sargento*, he believed. He considered such actions not only a personal obligation, doing the right thing with available resources, but also a corporate responsibility.

Constantly, he spent funds to design or improve the equipment. Pasta cutters gave way to more sophisticated shredding equipment. Package-filling machinery replaced the need for employees to hand-fill each package. Rare was the week that he and Bud Dick weren't working on some new piece of machinery.

New products, new ideas defined Sargento. Their development cost money.

Layer upon layer—new products, new equipment, new employees— Sargento found a need for more cooler space and more production space. The manufacturing location in Elkhart Lake, once considered spacious, was now cramped and inadequate. Sargento would soon need to fund a building expansion or a second location.

Much of these expenditures immediately impacted the profit line or loomed on the near horizon, keeping Ron ever vigilant. Could there also be enough dollars available to start a new business? Leonard toyed with the thought.

He'd given thought to something else as well.

The world was changing, and the cheese industry was evolving along with it. Improved refrigeration and transportation had far-reaching impacts. More regional cheese companies clambered onto the bandwagon, each extending their grip with a regional presence.

Leonard Gentine, in that changing world, refused to step down as a change maker in his own industry. Now, in the early 1960s, he planned to carve out a business path that would set Sargento on a course—one completely unexpected by his competitors.

# 20

# Central Wrap
# 1964

SIXTEEN-YEAR-OLD LOU GENTINE slapped the 40-pound block of cheddar on the roller conveyor, his arms aching from the full truckload of cheese he'd partially unloaded that morning. And the two semis he'd unloaded the day before. Each night he tumbled into bed weary.

Like his brother Larry, Lou spent his summers working for his father. It was a job and he needed the money—some to spend, some to set aside for college.

In 1962, Leonard formed Central Wrap with Bud Dick, the local machinist who fabricated much of the equipment for the new company. Central Wrap was one more company added to the long list of businesses launched over the years. Leonard—the name he asked his children to call him while at work—and their uncle Chuck managed Sargento while Butch supervised the operations at Central Wrap. After a few years, Leonard elevated his son's title to president.

"Got that truck unloaded yet?" Lou snapped his head up to see Jerry Robb, the production manager, entering the loading dock area.

Leonard and Butch Gentine

"Almost," Lou replied as he blotted the sweat from his forehead with the bottom of his apron. "Jerry Kraus was helping for a while, but one of the label machines jammed. He went to fix it." Lou peered into the partially empty truck. "This should be empty soon."

"We need that trailer," Robb said in a no-nonsense tone. "As soon as you can get it empty, I want you to start hauling the cases of finished product back into it. This load's gotta get back to the A&P warehouse before they close today." Not waiting for a response, Jerry turned and walked through the door in the wall partition, toward the end of the production line.

Lou looked at his watch. He had no interest in staying any later than he needed to. He had plans for the evening. After all, what's the use of earning money if you couldn't spend a little with high school friends?

Sliding his box cutter around the top edges of the case of cheddar, Lou removed the top and ripped the remaining cardboard free. A shove sent the cheese forward, spinning over aluminum conveyor wheels. Down the line, another employee waited to push that massive block of cheddar through three cheese harps—sets of parallel wires—cutting it into slabs, then into strips, and then into rectangular blocks.

Jerry Kraus banged open the aluminum partition door as he rushed into the loading dock area. Lou smiled. He could imagine the recent conversation between Jerry Kraus and Jerry Robb.

"Robb says I'm to help back here now." Kraus sprinted by Lou and into the truck. Then, raising his voice to be heard, "The labeler's running again. An easy fix this time. Robb says Butch's got another A&P order coming our way tomorrow. Time is money!"

"So I keep hearing," said Lou, growing weary of the shopworn phrase, canonized through repetition.

The conveyor rattled as Jerry slammed a cardboard case next to Lou, rocking the support stand slightly with the blow.

"You know, your brother's a legend," Jerry said over his shoulder to Lou as he ripped the cardboard free from the cheese. "I bet I heard a hundred stories about him since I've been working here."

Jerry hastened back into the cavity of the trailer and raced out with another case in his arms. "A guy I know was telling me a story that he had heard from a friend. About when Butch was in school at the University of Wisconsin in Oshkosh ordering pizzas from Gino's, a—"

"Yes," interrupted Lou, "it was a pizza parlor that bought their cheese from Sargento and Butch kept telling the owner to deduct the pizzas from the Sargento invoice. Sargento ended up owing the pizza place, not the other way around." Lou shook his head, waving off the story. "It's an old story, Jerry. I think everyone's heard it by now."

"It's still funny," Jerry countered. "And then I heard"—Jerry Kraus looked to see if Jerry Robb might be heading their way before continuing—"that Butch hired Robb at a stag party. Just started talking to him at the party and then said, 'Jerry, I'm gonna be running a new cheese company. Why don't you join my company?' Offered him a job right at the party."

"I suppose that could have happened," Lou replied. "College didn't interest Butch, and I know that my father was excited when Butch came back and joined the company. Who knows? Maybe I'll do that, too, someday. Butch is going to do whatever it takes to be just as successful as my father by hiring good people. Robb's a smart cheese buyer. Does it really matter when or where Butch asked him?"

Jerry Kraus shrugged as he pushed a block of cheese down the conveyor.

"C'mon. Let's get this thing unloaded or Robb's gonna be all over us." Lou leaned to peer inside the truck. "Tell you what, you unload the last few cases and I'll head to the end of the line and begin bringing the pallets of finished product back here. We have only a couple of hours to deliver the cheese back to the A&P warehouse. And I want to get out of here tonight. I have things to do."

With that, Lou pushed through the swinging door, grabbed a pallet jack, and dragged it toward the jumble of pallets scattered to the corners of the building.

Since A&P paid Central Wrap for each package it produced—a deal Leonard arranged with Bob Griese, president of the A&P Dairy Division—time did equal money. Speed was king. The greater the output, the more money they would earn by the end of the day. Hence, each employee felt the pressure to go faster and, if possible, faster yet.

In 1962, as with most of his ventures, Leonard had started producing Central Wrap products out of the carriage house. Gilbert Huss, the funeral director in Leonard's old home, had no interest in the old building, and Jerry Eigenberger—the new owner of the Plymouth Cheese Counter, still operating out of that carriage house—provided Leonard the space. But the cooperative arrangement was short-lived. With eighty thousand pounds of cheese cut and wrapped weekly, Leonard immediately recognized the space limitation, thwarting his ability to accommodate the sizable shipments in and out of that building.

Easing that pressure point, Leonard had met again with Bob Griese. He negotiated the use of the space behind the Plymouth A&P—the back end of the building where A&P once candled eggs—and an agreement with Bob, making Central Wrap the sole company converting all of A&P's bulk cheese into random-weight, store-brand packages.

As he pulled the pallet jack to the opposite end of the building, Lou watched employee Lorna Preder pack a carton at the end of the line and then stack it on a skid. In a wide sweeping arc, Lou clanked the tapered fork of the jack into the open end of a pallet near Lorna. Pumping the handle, the pallet rose from the floor.

Lou banged through the door of the loading dock and angled the pallet to the side. Since Jerry Kraus hadn't emptied the trailer yet, Lou lowered the skid to the floor and dragged the jack back to the end of the line in search of the next pallet.

Jerry Robb looked in Lou's direction. "Lou. Got that truck empty?"

"Kraus is working on it," Lou shouted back over the machinery.

"Go back and give him a hand. We need it emptied and then filled with finished cases."

Butch, stepping from his office, pulled his head back and gazed across the room at his brother. "You had your break yet?" he asked Lou.

"No, but that's OK. I want to get this truck loaded so I can get outta here. After work, I'm going to—"

"Lou." Butch jerked his head toward the break station at the top of the stairs. "Come join me. I'll buy you a soda." Then turning to his production manager, he said, "Jerry, my brother needs a break. Take one of the guys to cover for him."

Lou preferred to just get the work done so he could punch out and leave. A can of Pepsi was low on his priority list. Reluctantly, he followed his brother up the stairs, leaving Jerry Robb silent but in passive protest.

At the top of the stairs, Butch turned to view the production floor. "Just take a look, Lou. This is what it's all about. Building a company for people. And it's important to get to know each of them personally."

Lou saw the pride on his older brother's face and then watched the broad smile lines melt as if something caught his attention. Turning in the direction his brother was staring, Lou recognized Ron Begalke. The company's outside accountant had just entered the building.

"Go grab a seat." Butch motioned to Lou. "I'll join you in a sec." Then, cupping his hands around his mouth, Butch shouted, "Hey, Ron! Got a minute? I need to talk to you."

Ron stretched a tight smile and gestured that he would be up in a minute.

"Come in. Join us." Butch waved with a wide sweep of his arm when Ron entered the break area. "I was hoping I would see you when I stopped over at Sargento later. I need to talk to you. So...as long as you're here..." Butch partially rose from his chair, reaching for one of the mugs on the counter. "Can I get you a cup of coffee?"

"No, thanks." Ron dragged a chair and took a seat, back straight, next to Butch, who threw him a broad, warming smile.

"Say, I was just telling Robb," began Butch, "that I plan to meet with a retailer in Chicago tomorrow. I've been calling on him. I think I can convince him to let Central Wrap produce their store products. But here's what I wanted to see you about. I need a hot deal to offer them. You know what I mean?"

Ron looked at Butch. "I think our price list is already very competitive. Are you now thinking that's not enough?"

Butch narrowed his eyes and tightened his face. Shaking his head, he said, "Not for Chicago. We need to sharpen our pencil if we plan to get business down there. I'd like to offer them a deep discount. Maybe even throw in a free case of product—one for every one of their stores. One case per store. A sorta introductory incentive."

Ron rocked back slightly as if Butch's words carried a physical punch. "Butch, we've been down this path before. The pricing we agreed upon already cuts a thin margin. Go much deeper and we won't be making any money at all. In fact, without doing the math, I'm pretty sure an offer like that would actually lose us money."

"Well, I'm sure we can find a way to make this happen. This is Chicago, Ron! The Windy City! This is our chance to grow. To push more cheese through this plant. To add more people to the payroll."

"That's just it," Ron countered. "All those things—adding more people, maybe running an additional shift, lights on more hours of the day, added stress on the equipment—they all add to overhead, the cost of goods. My recommendation would be to go in with the pricing we agreed upon. It's a fair price."

Lou watched as his brother sat straighter in his chair.

"Maybe we lose a little money at first," suggested Butch. "But we'll make it up down the road." He paused. Then a more deliberative expression softened his face. "We need the business if we're to grow."

Absorbed in the conversation, Lou internally processed both sides of the argument and then sat in the silence that followed.

Perhaps in thought, Ron glanced at Lou.

Throwing up his hands, Lou quipped, "Maybe we can give them a deal on A&P cheese. It seems like I'm forever hauling it back and forth."

It broke the tension.

"I know how important this is to you, Butch. But we need to make money. To pay those people out there." Ron nodded in the direction of the production floor. "Let's just see what they have to say with the pricing we have. If we need to...perhaps...we can discuss if it makes sense to pursue this customer or if we look elsewhere for business."

Butch lowered his gaze and then slowly nodded as if in agreement. That was how Ron might have interpreted the nonverbal response, thought Lou. But he knew his brother much better. To Lou, it meant his brother was pondering, weighing his options. Perhaps considering how he could make the offer that he wanted. Maybe apologize later.

Believing the matter settled, Ron returned to the production floor to speak with Jerry Robb. Lou drained his Pepsi, wished his brother success at his meeting in Chicago, and resumed hauling pallets.

Butch walked about the plant, talking with each employee, his deep laugh rising over the mechanical din. And then, as if the walls and the equipment of Central Wrap had suddenly absorbed him, Butch was gone.

Lou knew his brother's determination. Whatever it took, Butch wanted to demonstrate to Leonard, the community, the retail customers, and to himself that he had what it took to be a savvy businessman, equal to his father.

Another day, perhaps, Lou would learn about that Chicago meeting. At the moment, he had a truck to load. He glanced at his watch and picked up his pace. Time was running thin.

# 21

# A Shift in Sargento Ownership
# 1964

LEONARD WRESTLED WITH a proposal. If he suggested the idea to Joe Sartori, it might imperil their close friendship. On the other hand, if he chose not to propose the idea, it could delay the vision he held for his family's future.

For months, he'd considered the potential of one trade-off versus the other, ruminating far too long on the issue.

*It's time to get this resolved*, he thought.

Leonard pulled into the restaurant's narrow parking lot, made all the smaller by the mounds of January snow plowed and piled along its edges. Earlier that morning, he had called Joe, asking if he had time to meet at Q's Quarters right after work, just for a quick martini or Manhattan.

For a moment, with the motor pumping heat into the car, he remained, watching patrons park and enter the restaurant. To his right sat Joe's car, its windshield still clear, light flakes drifting down, melting as they landed on the glass. A sure indication that Joe had arrived not long before him.

For twelve years, he had partnered with Joe to build Sargento. Together, they felt the pains of launching a new business: the sudden, unexpected missteps; the frequent equipment failures; the inconsistent customer orders. Save for the few initial years of negative revenues, Sargento contributed small annual profits. With Joe's guidance, their little company was healthy and growing.

Just last year, once they paid all the taxes and bills, Sargento surprised them with a profit close to twenty thousand dollars. Of course, other businesses in the county overshadowed that success. Still, they had been methodically expanding products, approaching new customers, and Leonard had no intention of subverting that success path for Sargento by cutting company spending.

He switched off the engine and carefully walked over the hard-packed snow in the parking lot, treacherous footing for his smooth-soled dress shoes. As he tugged open the door and entered the dimly lit restaurant, Leonard waved a greeting at its owner. Bernice Quella returned the welcome.

"Evening, Bernice!" Leonard draped his coat and hat on the nearby hook. "Joe Sartori is meeting—"

"He's over at the table by the bar." Bernice threw her head in Joe's direction as Leonard gestured a silent thanks and walked in that direction.

"Thanks for coming," said Leonard as he slid into a chair opposite his business partner. "I see you've ordered your Manhattan already." As the waitress approached their table, Leonard pointed at Joe's glass, indicating he'd have the same.

"It looks like we're heading into another good year for Sargento. Customer orders were strong again this week."

"I haven't looked at the latest shipment report," said Joe, "but with the past holidays, I would guess those seasonal products you offered— the cheese nut rolls and spreads...and the small square slices of cheese"—Joe gapped index finger to thumb as he sized the cheese— "that snack cheese in the plastic tray..."

"Cracker Snacks?"

"Yes. Cracker Snacks." Joe took a quick swallow from his glass and then leaned back in his chair. "I would bet those items did pretty good over Christmas and New Year's. I have to tell you, I'm a bit surprised. Have stores been ordering them regularly before the holidays?"

Just the opening Leonard hoped for. He nodded. "Doing good. Doing very good. Both varieties of Cracker Snacks."

"Hmmm." Joe shook his head as if in disbelief. "They are a bear of a product to make. Not like our shredded cheese or our sliced cheese. All those little square pieces of cheese. Placing them in those gas-flushed tray packages as they zip down the line. Your people have more patience than I have to make those things."

The waitress delivered Leonard's Manhattan, and he took the time to absently study the maraschino cherry speared at the top of the glass, allowing a moment to pass between them.

Leonard drew his lips tight, then looked at Joe and began to proceed with the purpose of their meeting.

"You and I know I've been pushing the company and products in ways that we…sometimes…see differently," Leonard began. "Products like those Cracker Snacks."

Leonard looked across the table, attempting to read his friend's thoughts, but Joe remained inscrutable.

"The company's doing fine," Leonard continued. "I've been noticing that some people are beginning to recognize the company name. But all this hasn't happened without our occasional disagreement on some things. We've always found a way to resolve those differences, but I'd hate to see business decisions ever come between us."

Leonard paused, giving emphasis to what he was about to say, and watched as Joe's eyebrows furrowed. "I place a high value on our friendship, Joe."

Joe's face lightened as he smiled. "And I value your friendship, too, Len."

Both men sat in momentary silence as Leonard mentally switched gears.

"I saw your son, Paul, the other day." Leonard leaned back, relaxed. "Your kids are growing up fast. You've got to be proud of them. The way they've grown into adults. It won't be long when you'll pass along S&R Cheese to them."

"With Paul already interested in the business, I'm afraid that day is coming sooner than I would imagine," agreed Joe.

"Just as your father passed the business on to you, you plan to pass it along to your children..." Leonard looked downward in thought. "I'd like to do the same with my children, Joe."

"With Central Wrap?"

*Well, no, not Central Wrap*, thought Leonard. For a number of reasons, that company was not living up to expectations.

"Central Wrap is holding its own," said Leonard, but even he heard the disappointment in his own voice. "A&P has been very good to us and Butch is constantly drumming up new business. Long term...I'm not sure I see that much opportunity."

Joe offered a short nod as if acknowledging earlier concerns he had offered for exploring that business direction.

"So I was wondering..." Leonard threw his hand up to soften the question. "And you don't need to answer today, but I'm asking you to give it some thought. Would you consider allowing me to buy out your shares of Sargento?"

From the look on Joe's face, the question had come unexpectedly. Leonard watched his partner take a moment, tapping his fingers on the tabletop as if deliberating over his response.

"If that's what you really want to do...sure...I'd be willing to sell my interest in the company." Joe seemed to be studying Leonard's face. "Can you afford to do that?"

"I'll need some time to pull the money together, but I wanted to learn if you were open to the idea."

"Take the time you need. When you're ready...if you still want to do this...let me know. I'll have an attorney draw up the papers."

Leonard nodded in thought, his unfettered mind racing ahead on the next steps, the things he would need to do in the days ahead.

He immediately felt a confluence of emotions—exhilaration and uncertainty. Together, he and Joe had found a small home in the marketplace for Sargento products: a chain of grocery stores here and another chain of stores there. Over time, they'd expanded the company from a local cheese company to a regional cheese company—distributing products to stores in a few states.

Based on Joe's calculations, the value of Sargento shares held by S&R and Joe would be worth approximately $153,500—a daunting sum. It was more money than Leonard could have ever saved.

Believing there might be a way to purchase the shares with assets currently owned by Sargento and Central Wrap, Leonard later asked Ron Begalke to review the financial opportunities of both businesses. What could they sell? What expenses could they delay?

Unfortunately, Ron's review of the two companies only validated Leonard's suspicions: the companies could not support the cash needed. Leonard would need to source the money elsewhere. Within a week's time, he and Ron drew up a list of lenders they believed offered a reasonable degree of success.

To secure a loan, Leonard relied on his greatest strengths: his down-to-earth personality and his sincere interest in others. He invited friends in the banking industry to lunches and dinners. Those he knew on a more personal level were invited, along with their wives, to tour Sargento and then later attend a social event.

Others, he courted in the more traditional manner, scheduling business appointments and supplying them with charts, graphs, financial statements, sales trends, and sales projections. He emphasized the company's reputation for innovation: the first to offer family-sized packages of cheese, the first to offer vacuum packaging, the first to offer natural sliced cheese in a package, the first to offer packaged shredded cheese. Sargento, he reminded them, led the industry with new ideas.

Each potential lender expressed interest and empathized with Leonard's situation but believed the venture posed risks they—or their management—were unwilling to shoulder. Reluctantly each declined.

It was an exhausting and frustrating exercise. "Most lenders only want to lend money to those who don't need it," Leonard complained to Dolores, "and deny it to those who do."

It was not until Leonard visited Clarence Weber, a bank officer at Security First National Bank—a financial institution with similar entrepreneurial foresight—that Sargento finally found its funding. Still, to acquire the loan, he put everything on the line. Everything. He swallowed hard, knowing that, should Sargento fail, he'd lose more than a business. He'd lose his home.

With the funding in place, they met at the attorney's office. When Leonard and Ron entered, the secretary looked up quickly from her typing and then resumed her clacking at the typewriter. At her side hunched the attorney, assumingly making last-minute adjustments to their agreement.

"Leonard! Ron!" the attorney enthused as he pumped their hands. "Let me get you back with Joe while we finish this up."

In the paneled conference room, Leonard found Joe, head bent, studying a carbon copy of the agreement. Joe cast a glance in Leonard's direction, smiled, and angled his arm upward for a handshake. Leonard took a seat next to him and pulled a copy of the agreement toward him to study. As they read, Ron straightened his tie, unsnapped the briefcase clasps, and waited for the attorney.

Barely a minute had passed before, with a click of the door handle, the lawyer unhurriedly ambled into the room with his pad of paper, pen, and revised copies of the agreement, fresh from the typewriter's platen.

Taking the chair opposite the three men, the legal counsel shoved carbons of the revised agreement across the table to Leonard and Joe. With little more than a few opening comments, he summarized the language and terms of the agreement for each man's benefit.

Subsequently, with the legal language broadly restated, the attorney called for questions. Hearing none, he languidly pushed spare pens to both Joe and Leonard. Joe signed, once on his behalf and a second time on behalf of S&R. In turn, Joe slid the paperwork to his right, allowing Leonard to countersign and Ron to scribe his signature as a witness.

With all copies signed, countersigned, and witnessed, Ron flipped open the lid on his briefcase and withdrew the two company checks: payment made in full for the 250 shares owned by Joe and his company.

It was now a matter of public record. Leonard took sole ownership of Sargento Cheese Company. A jubilant and energized Joe Sartori and a cautionary Leonard Gentine posed for a photo to document the transaction.

Ron Begalke, Joe Sartori, and
Leonard Gentine

Joe promised to remain as an advisor. That said, all decisions for the company now rested squarely on Leonard's shoulders and his management team.

At nineteen years of age, without money to pay for damages when he crumpled the rear of Hobart Brigden's hearse, Leonard had traded his labor as payment. Years later, his mother and father lent him the money to launch his funeral business in Plymouth.

To begin the gift box business in 1949, Leonore Meltz—Dolores's long-time best friend and godmother to Leonard and Dolores's son Lou—provided $1,500, a sizable loan at the time.

Chuck and JC helped to fund Genstrupp, and Joe—with the support of S&R—supplied much of the capital to launch Sargento. Now, a banker offering the unimaginable sum of over $150,000 replaced the past support of friends and family.

Life would be different. It was not the ranks of family and friends that would nod in sympathy if the unexpected happened. It was a third party holding the rope. And lenders, Leonard knew, tended to be less forgiving.

# 22

# For the Love of Plymouth
# 1965

LEONARD PULLED AT the sleeve of his dress shirt, exposing his watch. Jack Anton was late.

It didn't surprise him. Jack, a local businessman with a tireless commitment to a long-term vision for Plymouth, spent the long hours of the day juggling one appointment after the other. *Quite possibly, a protracted phone call caught him at the last moment,* thought Leonard.

To accompany his second cigarette, Leonard ordered another cup of coffee from the Mitchell Hotel waitress. Most of his meetings or conversations with other businessmen happened in restaurants during lunch or after work. In many ways, he preferred that. Business during meals allowed more to be accomplished each day.

*Ah, there he is,* thought Leonard. From the window, he watched Jack vault the hotel's outside steps two at a time—spry for a man his age.

"How ya doing, Leonard?" asked Jack as he simultaneously sat, shot a warm smile, and unconsciously grabbed the menu. The waitress scurried over and took their order.

"I never had the chance to talk with you about your January trip overseas," said Jack, wasting no time advancing his agenda. "The paper

The Mitchell Hotel

said you and the others believe there may be some opportunities for exporting cheese. That so?"

Over a year earlier, Leonard unexpectedly invited Wisconsin cheese makers to his house to propose forming an organization dedicated to educating retailers on how to better merchandise and sell cheese in their stores. Within a year's time, members of that newly formed industry association also explored opportunities and hurdles in exporting Wisconsin cheese.

"It was an exhausting trip," said Leonard. "All ten of us were dead tired when we came back from that six-country visit. And a bit disappointed. At least I was. Only Beirut, Hong Kong, and Rotterdam looked like possibilities—all of them free ports. Not restricted by all that government red tape. But a lot of other countries with cheese businesses got there ahead of us and locked up some of the markets with contracts."

"So do you think we might see a few international sales with Central Wrap or other Plymouth cheese companies?" Jack shot Leonard a hopeful look.

Leonard should have anticipated the question. After all, Jack made it his personal mission to draw additional business into Plymouth.

"Well, if there's opportunity," sighed Leonard, "it won't be with Sargento or Central Wrap. Maybe some of the other cheese companies in the state might get their foot in the door."

Jack fidgeted with his silverware, evenly spacing them, moving each minutely one direction or the other as he listened and thought.

"The newspaper article in the *Plymouth Review* implied a stronger sense of opportunity." Jack brushed back his snow-white hair and with a weary sigh added, "Well, I guess that dampens hope for Plymouth to be involved overseas."

"For now, I suppose."

With forefinger and thumb, Leonard pinched the cigarette lodged in the corner of his mouth, moving it deftly to the ashtray before the precariously hanging, long gray ash disengaged. "I don't begrudge the effort, though. Nor the trip."

Leonard unfolded his napkin and laid it in his lap. "It's all a learning process. And it's what we need to do if we're to be any good at exporting. We need to ask questions, then stop talking. Asking a question, most times, gets you get an answer. But what I learned is that if you listen . . . really listen . . . that's when you start learning something.

"It's not our responsibility to know everything, to be the smartest men in the room. Ideas come from everywhere. From anyone. When I sit in front of a cheese buyer, I always ask questions: What are your consumers saying? Why do they purchase certain items? How often do they buy cheese? Which items sell the best? How can I help you sell more products?"

As Leonard talked, he watched Jack look around the room, expressing little interest in the conversation. With a gesture that clearly signaled an apology for the long-winded discourse, Leonard let the topic die.

Jack glanced at his watch. "Listen, I don't want to take up too much of your time. One of the reasons I wanted to have this lunch…and I need to bring this up again with the—"

"Your sandwiches, gentlemen," intoned the waitress. Jack paused until she placed each plate on the table.

When the waitress left, Jack began again. "It's April. The annual Cheese Derby Days are right around the corner. I'm the festival co-chairman again this year. I've lined up sixteen different drum and bugle corps for the parade. But we need funding. It's been disappointing that the other large cheese companies in town made only small donations this year."

Jack theatrically inserted a small pause, an atypical gesture for his traditionally effusive character, thought Leonard. That could only mean that Jack's sudden reticence was signaling a plea for a donation.

"I know you have contributed in the past," Jack continued. "Would you be willing to increase your donation a little more this year to help us cover that financial gap?"

Leonard took one last draw from his Philip Morris before crushing it in the ashtray. "Of course. How much are you short?"

Jack mentioned a shortfall greater than Leonard had expected.

"I'll throw some money in the pot," offered Leonard, and tossed out a figure far greater than he had donated in the past, but Jack's face telegraphed that it was less than he had hoped for.

As Leonard took a bite of his sandwich, Jack stole another look at his watch and leaned back in his chair as if to queue up his next topic.

"There is one other thing I wanted to ask." Jack toyed with the handle of his coffee cup as if in thought. "I know we talked about this many times, but I want to bring this up again. You know how the city is interested in drawing industry to Plymouth. We were a community steeped in cheese tradition. Still are. But there are those—and I'm one of them—that believe we need to better balance our industry with some noncheese businesses."

Jack looked out the large bay window next to their table as if seeing something beyond normal vision. "We have a large plot for an industrial park. You know. You've seen it. We've been having difficulties convincing businesses to locate there. We need a leader. Someone who can take the risk and build there. To let others see that it's a viable place for a business. You know how that goes, right? Have you given any thought to moving Sargento from Elkhart Lake onto that large plot of land?"

Leonard finished the last bites of his sandwich and dabbed the corners of his mouth with his napkin. *Here it is,* thought Leonard. *This is what Jack really wanted. More than money for a festival, he wants his industrial park project to be more than a failed effort.*

"I thought that business expansion project was dead, Jack. Didn't I read that the committee you headed up is now defunct?"

"Well…" Jack replied, avoiding eye contact. "I think Plymouth needs to do this. So, no. No, it's not dead. Maybe the council has given up hope. Not me. And I think you would be a great help to the cause. If not moving Sargento to Plymouth, maybe relocating Central Wrap?"

Leonard pushed his plate to the side of the table, making it easier for the waitress to retrieve it. He had just put everything on the line to buy out Joe Sartori. There was absolutely no way he could afford to fund a building in the industrial park.

"It's true we could use a little more space at Central Wrap," said Leonard. "That being the case, I just don't think we are in a financial position for something like that. Not yet anyway."

Jack lowered his voice and leaned forward, adopting a conspiratorial tone. "Of course, there are many ways to make this happen. I could talk to the city council members to see if they might be interested in loaning the money—or providing partial funding. Can you promise to give it some thought? It means a lot to Plymouth. I'm just asking that you think about it, that's all."

Little did Jack know his sincere interest in relocating Central Wrap, thought Leonard. With thirty-eight employees now crammed into the cinder-block building behind the A&P store, that business faced serious space issues. Truthfully, he had no money to fund a new building. As for seeking a loan…well, he had been fortunate enough to find a lender to purchase Joe's shares. Unless Jack could work magic, Leonard would have to do with the space he had.

Surprisingly, Jack did know a little wizardry.

By late summer, after months of negotiation with Jack and Plymouth, Leonard drafted a letter of intent to relocate Central Wrap from the back of the A&P store to the new industrial park. At the city council meeting on August 31, as Leonard sat in the audience, Jack Anton gleefully waved Leonard's intent to purchase in the air as proof that his industrial expansion project was very much alive.

Leonard had agreed to purchase the land for the sum of $500 per acre. Per their agreement, Jack explained, Central Wrap would design and build a 17,000-square-foot building, sell it to Plymouth, and then lease it back.

Jack's magic. Leonard smiled to himself in the audience that night.

With the announced relocation of Central Wrap, Leonard drove to Tupper Cheese. He still believed, given the circumstances, selling his interest in Genstrupp had been the correct course of action. Nevertheless, his departure from Genstrupp, its timing falling at the early development of the company, continued to weigh heavily on him.

He could not let it go. Overtly or subtly, he felt compelled to pursue opportunities to bolster JC's business success. Twice, Leonard offered to blend the two companies as one. Twice, JC had declined.

As he entered Tupper Cheese, Leonard flagged JC's attention. At the back of the building, in the small lab, JC tossed a smile his way. "Have a seat, Leonard. I'll be right there."

Dragging a chair from the table in the front bay window area, Leonard waited.

JC wiped his hands on his stained apron, walked to the front of the building, and took a chair next to Leonard.

"I don't mean to bother you," said Leonard. "When we move Central Wrap to the industrial park... I'm sure you saw the article in the paper, right?"

JC nodded.

"Well, anyway, when we move Central Wrap, we will have a lot more space. Quite a bit more space," Leonard repeated for emphasis. "There's room for two companies in the same building. Side by side. We could run a line for cooked cheese and have the room to put sliced cheese and shredded cheese lines in another section. I'd like you to consider joining me."

JC formed a thin smile as he looked around at the Tupper Cheese operation and the men and women running product that day.

"It's kind of you to make that offer again." JC hesitated. "I think I would feel out of place in a large company. This just seems like where I belong. Besides, like you, I want a small business that I can pass down to my children. Moving to your new building... a nice enough gesture on your part..." JC shook his head. "I'm gonna stay right where I am."

JC pushed back from the table as if to get up but remained seated.

"It's good of you to think of me. I do sincerely appreciate the offer." JC looked back toward the production area. "We're doing fine."

"I understand," said Leonard. He paused, searching for the right words. "We're family," he began. "What would you say to this? If any of your products are going to the same customer...or even to the same part of the country...we could put your items on our truck. We're shipping anyway. Might as well have the free ride. What about that?"

JC thought before responding. "I guess that could work. That's a nice offer."

"I'll not keep you any longer," Leonard said as he stood and headed toward the door. "I only wanted to see if you were interested in sharing my building." Leonard gazed at the cooker pouring steamy, melted cheese into the jar-filling station. "But I completely understand."

Then, as Leonard grabbed the door handle, he stopped as another thought occurred to him. "You know," he said, turning back to JC. "Central Wrap will be leaving the building behind the A&P. It would be a larger place for Tupper Cheese. That is, if you would have an interest. We could even help you move the equipment there."

"I'll have to think about that," said JC as he shared a nostalgic grin and returned to his lab at the back of the building.

That fall, when Central Wrap broke ground, Jack Anton approached other businesses with the hope of relocating them as part of his industrial expansion project. Once Central Wrap relocated to its new headquarters, Tupper Cheese occasionally shipped products to its customers via Sargento or Central Wrap semis.

Those semis picked up Tupper Cheese products, not from the space behind Sloan's Paint Store at 405 East Mill Street, but at Tupper Cheese's new location—behind the A&P store.

# 23

# Doing the Right Thing: Sowing Family Values

## 1967

*HOW IRONIC*, THOUGHT Leonard.

It had always been the lack of money that drove him to work harder, to stanch his concerns over a meager income by venturing in different business directions. Never did he and Dolores live in a state of penury, but for nearly thirty years, his dedication to building a business foisted his family into a standard of living that others not often realized nor would envy if they did.

Now, at the age of fifty-three, he would be defending the meager profits of his two cheese companies, citing their earnings as "appropriate." He didn't oppose profits. After all, earned income allowed Sargento to develop new products. It paid his employees' wages and granted him the freedom to donate funds for the betterment of the community. What he opposed was maximizing profits to the detriment of his companies' or employees' well-being.

It seemed to him that a long-term vision should never fall prey to what was managerially expedient. Doing what was right today, no matter the financial implications, offered the greatest promise for an ethically successful business—a business capable of transcending generations.

He flipped the page of his day calendar. The next morning, Ron Begalke would meet with him to discuss corporate profitability. As they closed the corporate books in June to end the fiscal year of 1967, profits were slim. Paper-thin margins, he remembered Ron had called them.

With Central Wrap now in its new building in the Plymouth industrial park, as Sargento slowly whittled away at the stiff loan required to buy Joe Sartori's interest in the company, Ron had been advocating that the company make decisions to maximize its profits by being more parsimonious in its spending—the very topic of the next day's agenda. Leonard was fully prepared to argue his defense.

A knock on Leonard's door interrupted his thoughts, and the somber face of Bob Gilles arced around the door frame.

"Leonard, the slice line is down. We got a truck on its way to pick up product. We're running out of time, and Chuck and I can't reach Bud Dick. I think he may be fixing a machine over at Central Wrap but I'm not sure."

*Here we go again*, Leonard thought. "I'll be right there."

With that, the production foreman vanished. "Hey, Bob," Leonard called after him. "You got the toolbox or should I grab it?"

"Got it already," came the response fading down the hallway.

Leonard pushed away from his desk. This was just another example of costs for tomorrow's discussion with Ron. The equipment could only run for so long without failing.

On the production floor, Leonard saw Bob standing next to an employee hunched over the meat-cutting machine, instructing him to manually pare the loaf of mozzarella into uniform slices. Others hustled about as if acting out a well-trained drill, pushing cases of product toward the end of the line as fast as they could.

How could you not admire these people, wondered Leonard. It seemed to him at any other company with any other employees, when a production line stopped functioning, people would go idle, waiting for someone to fix the problem. Here, everyone thought as one, looking for ways to keep the line running.

"The flywheel froze," said Chuck. "So I had the drive shaft disengaged from the meat slicer. I don't see any other option. We're producing the remaining cases manually. With the truck here around four thirty, we need to do whatever it takes to get this customer order out the door."

Taking note of the time and their approaching deadline, Leonard called out to Bob, "Have someone run back and get me that spare meat cutter. It's not in the best of shape, but we can jury-rig it so we can get another person slicing. Get someone on each cutter. Then have someone move the slices to the conveyor belt by hand."

Bob turned from the employee at the meat cutter and pointed to three other men, waving two of them over and sending the third in search of the dysfunctional cutter in the back.

"We need to set up a rotation," said Bob. "Keep the cheese coming down the line, but I don't want anyone injured. No one slices for more than twenty minutes before they get a break. Have 'em switch places with the one feeding the belt. Just keep rotating every twenty minutes."

Once the second meat cutter was pressed into service, Leonard, cigarette lodged in the corner of his mouth, yanked his tie open, grabbed a wrench, and on his back, snaked under the primary machine. Pounding on the end of the crescent wrench, he loosened the bolts securing the housing. Blackened oil and grease stained his fingers. Caked grease accumulated with the turn of the bolt and then dropped. He felt the impact as it landed on his pocket. *Dolores will not be happy when she sees this shirt*, he thought.

He shook his head as he unsuccessfully attempted to find a quick fix that would prod the equipment back into action. They would need to muscle both machines along until Bud, the one who designed the equipment, could get in and rebuild it. It had been pushed beyond its limit.

"Looks like the ball bearings also overheated," came Leonard's muffled voice below the cutter unit. "Seized up."

Bob released an exasperated sigh. "That's the fourth time in three weeks. How are we supposed to meet orders when the equipment keeps falling apart?"

Leonard dragged himself out from under the equipment and slapped the collection of cheese bits from his shirt and pants. Then, grabbing a nearby rag, he wiped the glob of grease from his white shirt, leaving a Rorschach inkblot as a reminder.

Down the line, the cardboard cartons were dwindling. With added manpower now repositioned as backup slicers, no one remained to supply the line. Leonard ducked into the storage area to replenish the inventory. Then, as each took their position to push out the needed cases, Leonard slid back under the disabled equipment. One way or another, they would complete this customer order.

In 1963, Joe Sartori had elevated Leonard's role in the company to president of Sargento Cheese. Today, he was also the sole owner of the company. Yet despite his executive position, Leonard refused to take on the airs and entitlements commonly associated with title. Never would he ask anyone to do what he wouldn't freely do himself.

On days when Bud Dick was unavailable—and this was one—Leonard attempted to repair faulty equipment without complaint. In fact, Leonard assumed most roles—when the situation demanded—blurring the lines between management and employee. Some days found him loading a semi or sitting on a wooden stool along the production line until backup support replaced him.

Not only did he consider this to be good business sense—meeting the needs of the customer, making the customer's needs their highest priority—it also served as a nonverbal communication that they were all in this together. For indeed they were. There could be no accounting for success unless each individual succeeded in being accountable.

By four twenty, the truck arrived at the loading dock. The driver found the employees in a curious state of celebration as he entered the building. Long before his arrival, the last case had been packed and stacked. Earlier, sensing their mastery over the uncooperative machinery, Leonard left to purchase pizza and beer, leaving his employees to finish producing the last hundred cases. With food and beverage in hand when he returned, he recognized each one for their undaunted effort to fill that customer's order.

The next morning, Bob Gilles was the first to arrive at the Elkhart Lake building and was surprised to see a body below the production line, legs precariously jutting out. He recognized the dress shoes.

"Leonard, are you still working on that cutter?"

"Yeah. I'm trying to repack the ball bearings. Each time I reconnect the flywheel, it stutters and refreezes. Frustrating.

"What time is it?" Leonard asked, more to himself than to Bob. Pulling his weary body from the floor and tugging his sleeve, he gathered the tools around the production line. "I gotta get home. I don't want to miss breakfast with the family."

It was then that Bob noticed the Rorschach grease stain on Leonard's shirt. "You damage another dress shirt? Dolores is gonna to kill you. Those stains aren't easy to get out."

Leonard looked down at his clothing. "Naw. These are the same clothes. After dinner last night, I came back. Spent most of the night here."

Following breakfast, Leonard returned in fresh clothes to find Bud Dick in charge of the disabled meat cutter and Ron Begalke waiting to discuss strategies for increasing profitability in the year ahead.

"Coffee?" Leonard offered as he ushered Ron into his office.

"That would be great. Thanks." Ron clicked open his briefcase, pulled out a stack of papers, and began separating copies for Leonard.

Setting two cups on the small table, Leonard took a chair. "In a few minutes, we should have pastry to go with that coffee. Harriet usually stops at the bakery before coming in."

Ron pushed the set of financial reports in Leonard's direction. "As we closed the year, you'll see that sales were up over last year...Over a million versus last year. A good year."

In silence, Leonard stared at the financial statement, sipping his coffee.

"A good year," repeated Ron, "if we only looked at company sales. Here's my concern." Ron poked his pencil at the report. "The profit line. Our earnings dropped to a little more than half of a year ago. That's worrisome. That left us with just a little better than breaking even. We're barely in the black."

Ron shuffled the financial page aside. "Now look at our expenses for the year. This is the problem. Many are typical expenses one might expect in a growing business. We added to our sales force—"

"Four men," Leonard interjected as he held up his fingers. "We expanded. We now have Jerry Schaefer, Ed Rammer, and Arly Hussin. Then I hired another guy—Jack Fernsler—out on the West Coast. That's a good cheese market out there. We need to grow that part of the country."

"Sorry to interrupt," Harriet Hawkins said, standing in the doorway. "I brought in some apple strudel. I can bring in a piece for both of you if you like."

Ron eyed the slice on the plate set before him as if deciding how best to tackle it.

Leonard pushed a fork in his direction. "The Sheboygan Bakery calls this one a topfenstrudel. But I don't think it's really that. It has apples and nuts in the quark cheese filling. A true German wouldn't consider it authentic. It's unusual but I like it."

"Hmm. You're right. It's good," said Ron, sampling from his plate. Then returning the conversation to business, he continued, "And you're right about the new salesmen expenses. They're normal expenses for a growing company but they did impact profitability. OK, here are a few other expenses that concern me." Ron underlined the items on his report and slid it to Leonard.

"This one"—Ron tapped at the figure with his finger—"is for the purchase of a car. A car for an employee. We pay car expenses for our salesmen. But this person—Gordy Abler—works in the plant. Why did we buy him a car?"

Leonard exhaled, stood, and riffled through a desk drawer for paper napkins.

"Here," he said, offering one before returning to his seat. "Those things can be messy." Then settling back in his chair, he said, "Ron, the man needed a car. If he doesn't have a car, he can't make it into work. Everyone has setbacks in life. But Gordy had a series of very unfortunate things happen."

"But buying him a car? Can't he buy one from the car dealer in town?"

"No. He'd tried that. He's a good man, Ron. They need a car but can't quite afford one at the moment. We can help. But don't misinterpret that. Sargento is not giving him a car. We purchased it, and we're taking a little bit from his check each payday until the car is paid off."

"It's an expense we don't need," Ron protested.

Leonard's face darkened and signaled the discussion was over on this issue.

"OK, OK." Ron pushed onward. "What about these expenses? For a company just barely breaking even, these are expenses we can forgo for now."

Ron tapped at one expense line after another. Money Sargento had given as part of a civic fund-raiser, funds for a new audio system in the grade school, and regular donations to a local food pantry. Sargento had donated funds, Ron pointed out, to refurbish an old building into a youth center and to supply some funds for a local festival, to partially cover the cost for the Fourth of July fireworks display.

Leonard offered his rationale for spending in each case. From the viewpoint of an accountant, the spending seemed unnecessary, at times reckless. From Leonard's viewpoint, these were obligations. Doing what was right despite the short-term implications.

"Many companies offer their employees a holiday gift at the end of the year," Ron said as he circled the amount Sargento had paid for the prior year's Christmas presents. "But here in June...and here in November...items you bought for each employee during the year."

"Uh-huh. I know." Leonard forked a piece of pastry to his mouth and chased it with a swig of coffee.

"Leonard, these are fine gestures." Ron paused. "Until we find stronger financial footing, let's cut back—or maybe go a year without doing anything—knowing that we'll resume the corporate generosity in the years ahead."

Dabbing the corners of his mouth with the napkin, Leonard looked down in thought.

"You know, a business can't continue on with one person. It takes people. People who don't just show up for a paycheck. They're here because they care. They care about their families. They care about what we're trying to do with this business and their job. And they care about each other. But it's not a one-way street. We have to let them know we care about them."

Leonard stared at Ron's pastry. "I see you haven't made much progress on your strudel. If you don't like it, don't force yourself to eat."

"It's OK. Different, but"—Ron shrugged his shoulders—"it's good."

"It's interesting." Leonard poked at the pastry with the tines of his fork. "So many different textures. A pastry crust. Bits of apple. Nuts. Quark. Have you had quark before?"

Ron shook his head.

"It's a type of cheese I discovered on my international trip with the Wisconsin cheesemakers. It's a soft cheese. Kinda like sour cream but…tastes different. Hard to describe. I've grown to like it. The cheese is solid enough to hold the whole thing together.

"Some baker tested it. He took a risk. He took the basic idea for a traditional strudel and tossed in something different. And discovered something better. That's called progress. Innovation."

Ron countered back. "But why risk trying something different when you know everyone's used to a simple strudel? Why not spend the time making what has worked in the past? If people don't buy the—what did you call it?—quark…if people don't buy the new pastry, you end up throwing it away. Losing everything."

Leonard paused for a moment. "You should've seen them yesterday. We had the equipment break down again. Before I could even reach the production floor, everyone was doing what they needed to do to make the customer happy. It was as if they didn't even need me. Isn't that what we want? People who can make the right decisions on their own?"

Ron shrugged in agreement and then countered, "We just need to get better control of our expenses. That's all I'm saying. It's good to be philanthropic, but we do the employees no service if the company goes bankrupt in the process. No company. No jobs."

Leonard toyed with a rogue apple bit that had fallen from the cheese, poking at it with his fork, attempting to force it back into place. "You're right about that. And I think that we can find common ground where we are doing a better job spreading out the costs and being responsible to each other.

"Last year, we had the money. We made a little profit. Would it be nice to have made a little bit more? Sure. But it's not how much money we make. Not how much we can pile up. It's how we use that money. I'm investing in people.

"As far as the profits and expenses, you're the accountant. Help us find a way to negotiate better payment terms with our vendors. Or better terms with our customers."

Leonard reached out and set his empty plate on the corner of the desk. "With our four new salesmen…you wait, sales will increase. They'll be bringing in more orders than before. And then we won't be having these conversations.

"Next year we'll do better controlling our expenses. Profits will be where you want them, Ron."

# 24

# Betting the Future on Metal Pegs
## 1969

AS SARGENTO COMPLETED the first quarter of the next year, profits *didn't* improve. If anything, the financial picture grew bleaker than the year before.

As profits thinned, Leonard continued to invest not only in the package design but also in the containers used to ship the product. He enjoyed seeing Sargento products in grocery stores, but the problem was that he rarely could see them. Usually, the grocer laid the packages on their back on the shelf, leaving only the bottom end of the package visible on the shelf.

"You can't even tell what it is when you walk by the aisle," Leonard complained. "If they can't see the product, they're not going to buy it."

With his carton supplier, he designed cardboard sleeves that held a row of product and fit snuggly in a shipping carton. The extra cardboard increased their costs, and placing the packages of cheese in each sleeve slowed production speed, but if the increased visibility in the stores stimulated sales, it could justify the added expenses, Leonard reasoned.

As the product shipped with cardboard sleeves, Leonard visited stores to study the new visibility of Sargento products. Yet except for a few stores, the product continued to be stocked on its back.

"Have you been getting our products with the cardboard sleeves?" he would ask the dairy managers.

"Sure," they would assure him. "But I don't have the time to mess around with those things. I just pull them out of the sleeve and stack them on the shelf."

Too frequently, the cardboard and the investment were thrown in the trash. Product costs increased with little benefit. There was little he could do but stew over the outcome. He considered offering some form of incentive for those who used the sleeve, but he made little headway.

Unexpectedly, Chuck returned excitedly from a week on the road. "You've got to see what Oscar Mayer has done in the meat section. It's showing up in more and more stores."

The next day, Leonard and Chuck entered a grocery store in Milwaukee—the electric-eye door jerking open ahead of them—to the familiar sound of metal clanking against metal as shoppers dislodged carts at the front entrance. With aisles clogged with a slow-flowing river of shoppers, both men zigzagged their way toward the back of the store.

"There it is," said Chuck as he walked up to the rows of Oscar Mayer meats, bent a metal peg downward at a slight angle, and peered into the back of the refrigerated meat section. "The metal pegs are hooked onto some kind of metal bar. I'm told the meat salesmen are taking out the shelves in all the Oscar Mayer sections and replacing them with these pegs."

Products hanging on hooks. It always amazed Leonard what could be learned by studying other products in the store. For a small company like Sargento, unable to hire the best minds in the industry, being observant often allowed the company to tap into that unattainable talent.

Leonard drove his large hands into the hanging packages, tugging at several metal pegs to test their strength, pushing product this way and that to gain a better view of the peg bar support.

"I see how it's done," said Leonard. "They inserted a long metal bar with brackets in the back. Those brackets slide in the slots that the shelf brackets used. Then they hooked the pegs into that bar. It's the peg bar that holds all the weight of the packages."

Stepping back to view the entire section, he thought aloud. "I wonder if this is something the store bought or if Oscar Mayer is supplying them." Then, spotting a meat manager at the far end of the meat case, he added, "I'll ask."

Instinctively, as he approached the store employee, his eyes drifted to the name badge—"Brad" scrawled in Magic Marker—pinned to the strap of the butcher's white apron. "Brad? Hi. I'm Leonard Gentine from Sargento Cheese. Those pegs in the meat case down there"— Leonard gestured—"those are new, aren't they?"

Brad leaned over his work, looking in the direction Leonard had pointed. "Yeah, some Oscar Mayer guy was in last week and did that."

Leonard offered a smile. "Do you know if the store bought those pegs or if Oscar Mayer brought them in?"

"I haven't a clue," said the meat manager as he stacked the last of the ground beef in the meat case. "Maybe headquarters paid for them. The guy just came in, said he had approval to put them in the store. Then spent half a day making a mess. Ripped the section all apart. He had meat packages stuffed in grocery carts. I had customers complaining 'cause they couldn't find what they wanted."

The meat manager threw both hands in the air in front of him as if dismissing any responsibility. "They're up. They look nice, but if my department gets dinged for the cost, they'll be down just as fast."

With that, he grabbed his empty aluminum tray, turned on his heel, and returned to the meat-cutting area behind the swinging door.

"You gotta believe Oscar Mayer was having the same problem we were," said Leonard when he walked back to Chuck. "Their packages don't stand upright either. So stores always stocked them on their backs, too. Chuck, we gotta find a way to get pegs like these in dairy sections."

As they walked out of the store, Leonard found it hard to suppress his enthusiasm. "This could be the answer to the problems we've been having, getting our products seen. When we get back to the office, I'll call Oscar Mayer. I know a guy there. While I'm doing that, call Bud Dick. Bring him to this store. Let him see this. 'Course, I'd rather buy them from Oscar Mayer. They'd be cheaper that way. But if we have to, I think we can create our own version of those pegs and bar supports."

Back in Plymouth, Leonard researched the merchandising idea. The following day, he walked into Chuck's office. "Looks like Oscar Mayer owns a patent on the design of those peg bars. I told Butch to drive over to Madison to meet the folks at the meat company. See if we can use their system. If anyone can convince 'em, it'll be Butch."

"We're not competitors," said Chuck. "I can't imagine they'd have a problem letting us use the pegs in the cheese department, especially if we're paying for them. By the way, Bud and I went back to that store. He says he can make something like that. Maybe better."

When Butch returned from Oscar Mayer's headquarters in Madison, he brought promising news. "They're thinking about it," he said. "And I did find out who makes 'em for them." Butch handed Leonard the slip of paper with the supplier's name.

As the four of them scrambled to replicate the peg bar system, Leonard assigned Bud Dick an additional responsibility: design a means for adding one small package feature—a peg hole. It would be of little benefit to have metal pegs installed in dairy departments and have packages without peg holes. Of the two projects assigned to Bud—the peg bar and the package hole—developing a way to punch a small hole proved to be the greater challenge.

By midyear, with an agreement reached with Oscar Mayer, the peg bar manufacturer shipped pallets of heavy metal racks to the Central Wrap and Sargento warehouses. Months before those units arrived, anticipating the use of peg bars in a few grocery chains, Sargento shipped packages with a hole punch. Their competitors, unaware of any potential peg bar installations, did not.

"Got great news for you," Butch said as he strode into Leonard's office. "I took a load of peg bars down to Jewel in Chicago. Sold the idea to Stan Kouba, the buyer at that account, and we put pegs in six Jewel stores as a test. If sales increase, I have his word that Jewel'll put them in every one of their stores."

Convincing stores to revamp their cheese section met with more resistance than Leonard had anticipated. They needed evidence that the idea had merit. "You suppose Stan would let us share the results of the test with other grocers?"

"He's a straight shooter. I'm sure he'd do that for us. I'll talk with him." Butch paused then added, "Since competition has no peg holes in their packages, they'll be stocked on the shelf. Not on the pegs. If our sales increase and the competition stays about the same, that'll show the value of putting in a peg bar."

The test results—an inarguable correlation between a sharp rise in sales and items merchandised on pegs—could not have been more conclusive. Jewel showed no hesitation and immediately installed peg bar units in all their stores. The relationship Butch nurtured with Stan and Jewel only reinforced Leonard's belief that business was less about selling and more about being genuine, building friendships.

As Sargento shared the sales results of the Jewel test and other grocery chains agreed to have the metal pegs installed in their stores, Sargento shipped the peg bar equipment on their truck in tandem with the retailer's cheese order.

Shredded Cheese for Tacos

Sargento bore the cost of the equipment, offering the peg bars for free if the store ordered their newest product, Shredded Cheese for Tacos, and placed a minimum-case, multi-SKU order with Sargento. Leonard covered the installation costs as well, using his sales team to install the equipment. Remembering the comment of the meat manager that shoppers had been inconvenienced when the meat section had been reset, an agreement was made with each store to install the peg bars after hours, when the store was closed.

The expense of Leonard's peg bar program was greater than any expense Ron Begalke had seen to date. He took shallow breaths as waves of invoices pounded the profit line. "You have salesmen going from store to store installing peg bars," said Ron. "They sleep in hotels during the day and work every night until store opening. Most times you have two or three salespeople working per store."

"That's so we can get more stores done per day," responded Leonard.

"Most times, in one night, they can convert three stores as a team, where, alone, each person would only be able to do one. Redoing a section is time-consuming."

"But do you have to give the equipment away?" protested Ron. "Maybe we could charge just a little?"

Leonard shook his head. "These peg bars are the best thing going. When the pegs go in, there is an immediate increase in sales. Immediate. They make a huge difference for Sargento and for the store. We're gonna put a peg bar in every store in the country."

"I can't argue the impact on our sales, Leonard. I just think the costs are too high for Sargento to bear. We're a small company. Putting a peg bar in every store would be…" Ron closed his eyes, inhaled deeply, and then, reestablishing eye contact, continued. "Leonard, we simply can't afford to do that. The plan could be financially devastating even if we just put them in the stores where we sell product."

Chuck added his thoughts. "I agree with Ron. Let Kraft pay for some of them."

"No," Leonard shot back. "We're going to take full responsibility for getting 'em into stores. Besides, Kraft won't put in the pegs. Why would they? They're the leaders. They're selling cheese and making money. But there's a benefit here for the retailer. We owe it to them to do what we can to help them sell product. And they're seeing it, too. We've got customers crying out asking for these things to be put in their stores."

"Well, I don't hear the crying out as much as the grumbling," Chuck added. "Some of the salesmen are getting tired installing peg bars. They joined Sargento to sell. They're beginning to feel like store installers."

"I'll talk with 'em, Chuck. We can add more salesmen. Set up teams for resetting dairy cases and rotate them so that they're not always installing peg bars. We just gotta do this."

That year, with added salesmen and the installation of peg bars in as many stores as they could install, sales rose 20 percent over the year before. Leonard had been correct. The peg bars brought a dramatic impact on sales for retailers and for Sargento. Encouraged, Leonard planned to increase the number of installations for the following year.

Those peg bars put Sargento, a regional company, on the competitive radar. As Leonard sensed the first sizable growth spurt for Sargento, Ron increasingly voiced his anxiety. Some of their suppliers agreed to longer terms, but it was still a juggling act, meeting payroll and satisfying vendors.

By December, the company was halfway through its fiscal year. Things looked grim to Ron. But Leonard needed to shift his attention to more personal issues.

The year was ending on a bittersweet note. His son Lou planned his December wedding to Michele Miller—a woman he had known since fifth grade and dated the last three years. It was a joyous family event, dulled only by Anna's failing health.

"You know how fond my mother is of her grandchildren," Leonard confided with Dolores one night. "She'll want to be at Lou's wedding. I just don't see how that would be possible. Each week she gets weaker. I'm sure Lou and Michele will stop by the nursing home after the ceremony."

Christmas Eve, Gramma Gentine's seventy-fourth birthday, the whole family gathered for a quiet pre-wedding celebration at the nursing home.

Two days following Christmas, the priest at the wedding rehearsal played out his traditional script, directing the wedding party. Not until the rehearsal dinner at Q's Quarters did the convivial tone shift.

"Leonard," said the restaurant owner in hushed tones leaning near his ear, "you have a call from Dr. Evers. You can take it in my office."

Leonard walked back into the restaurant, whispered to Dolores, and watched as her face drained of color. Then he walked over to talk with Lou.

Gramma Gentine had passed away.

There were no words to comfort the stunned. His mother—the one who had supported him every inch of the way—was gone. He felt a lump grow in his throat and shoved his feelings downward. He'd have time enough to revisit them.

Tomorrow, the family must do what his mother would want most: see her grandson marry and begin his life.

# 25

# Two Become One
## 1972–1974

LOOKING BACK, LEONARD almost regretted his carefully considered decision. Unexpectedly, it triggered a series of events that led to the unwelcome outcome he now faced with Butch.

Ron Begalke had seen the lean years ahead. With regularity, Ron mentioned the potential dangers. Yet Sargento and Central Wrap pushed on, each pursuing their separate visions, their separate sales targets.

Since launching its crusade—placing a peg bar set in every store—Sargento shipments increased each year. The company sold more products, in more stores, in more states than ever before. Disappointingly, profits from those rising sales barely outpaced the burdensome expenses of that expansion.

Central Wrap, over its nine-year history, reported increasing volumes as well but fared no better with its profits. Butch's spending—more often stemming from his heart and enthusiasm—continued unabated. In his desire to build Central Wrap to mirror the size and importance of Sargento, liberal decisions tended to overpower more conservative alternatives.

Although Leonard knew Butch had managed Central Wrap with best intentions, he often challenged his son on his expenses. "Yes, we are spending a little heavy with some customers. But it's investment spending," Butch affirmed.

Too often for Leonard, and for Ron, the dividends from those investments failed to materialize. Instead, some customers vehemently insisted the lower pricing remain—until the products found their footing. Another competitor always waited at the customer's door if Butch balked. It remained difficult for Central Wrap to walk away from the volume of business the customer offered.

By 1972, Leonard could no longer postpone a decision, could no longer remain hopeful for a dramatic reversal of misfortunes. Listening to Ron's frequent counsel, relying on Joe Sartori as a sounding board, Leonard believed it was time to decide which was the better horse to back and which should be pulled from the race. The dynamics of the two emerging businesses spread his limited resources too thin to remain with both.

Long, sleepless nights offered him little solace. Suspecting the risk, yet believing he could contain it, Leonard made an appointment with an attorney.

"I'm gonna merge the two businesses," Leonard later shared with Butch. "I'm having the paperwork drawn up. Central Wrap will become Sargento."

Butch failed to immediately respond but, instead, listened with a stillness that left Leonard unsettled. He had been prepared for a verbal response.

"The production lines we use to produce store-branded products at Central Wrap," Leonard expanded, "we'll gradually convert those lines to produce more Sargento-branded products. As we continue to expand our business, we'll need the extra capacity. Let the other cheese companies have the store-brand business," he added with a wave of his hand.

"What happens to me?" Butch gave Leonard a guarded look.

"I'll continue to serve as president of Sargento. Chuck and I will oversee both production sites." Leonard paused and studied his son's face. He could only guess at Butch's thoughts, but needed to emphasize the importance of his son's new responsibilities.

"I see our sales team as our greatest strength, Butch, and I plan to place you at the head of that. If we don't sell products, we aren't making any money. I can think of no one better at developing relationships. No one better at selling Sargento. I need you to train our salesmen to do what comes naturally for you. You'll have a totally new position at Sargento—sales manager. You'd be perfect for that."

Butch pursed his lips in thought and then slowly nodded in agreement to the new title and responsibilities, but Leonard read the disappointment. Going from a company president to sales manager was a blow to Butch's self-esteem.

Not long after, Leonard would recall as he reflected on the weeks that followed, Butch occasionally mentioned the topic of succession planning. It was a fleeting, sporadically offered comment at first. Leonard could see little value in dedicating much time to that. Not now anyway. In 1972, Leonard was only fifty-eight years old. Too young to even consider retirement—if he were to consider it at all.

"You never know what can happen," Butch had argued. "We don't like to think about it, but if something tragic should happen..."

By 1973, interest in succession planning waned as Butch found new, fertile territory—product promotion—as part of his sales responsibilities. Envisioning more than simple signs in the store, Butch retained an advertising agency—Biddle in Springfield, Illinois. Together, they commissioned the animation artists at Walt Disney Studios—the best in the industry—to develop and launch the first television advertising for Sargento.

"Television advertising is expensive," Leonard cautioned Butch.

The first television commercial for Sargento

But Butch fervently believed that the commercial would dramatically increase their sales. "In the long run," he assured Leonard, "the advertising will pay for itself."

Their cartoon commercial didn't air in many markets—just a few states—and it ran infrequently. The available corporate funds wouldn't allow much air time. Still, Leonard couldn't help but feel pride that his little company was mentioned on television. True to Butch's word, it began to build a small bump in awareness for Sargento. Demonstrating that the commercial increased sales, on the other hand, proved hard to quantify.

Almost with the turn of the calendar in January 1974, as the television advertising aired with its scant budget, Butch once again took up the banner he'd waved earlier: the need for a succession plan.

"Let's bring in a consultant." For the first time, Butch suggested soliciting the advice of an outside expert. "We'll get a disinterested third party that can come in, look at the company, and make an objective recommendation."

Given Butch's persistence and reluctantly admitting there would be a benefit for a plan "just in case," Leonard eventually agreed. Accordingly, he and Butch researched, located, and finally hired a firm to study the Sargento organization.

For weeks, that firm met with the managerial staff and many of the employees. Attempting to grasp an understanding of the company, its workings and its synergies, the consultant team asked pointed questions during one-on-one interviews. In time, an executive summary, replete with supporting evidence—typed and delivered to Leonard—provided an unbiased recommendation.

In his office, Leonard smoked his cigarette, absorbed in thought as he read and reread the consultant's report. Over the years, he'd faced numerous tough decisions. He'd battled financial issues. He'd experienced disappointment when the competition, a supplier, or even a retailer failed to live up to expectations.

The consultant's recommendation pulled no punches. It was direct, pointed, and supported by rationale. Its suggested course came as no surprise. Nor was it far afield from the conclusion Leonard had reached after his long rumination and conversations with friends.

Carrying the uneasy weight of the decision, Leonard stood from his desk, walked into Butch's office, and closed the door. Sitting opposite his son, Leonard began the conversation. "I've read the consultant's report." Glancing toward the closed office door, looking for the words, Leonard paused.

"Let me guess," said Butch. "They didn't recommend me as your replacement in the company."

Leonard took a long draw from his cigarette and merely shook his head.

"Well, that's just one person's opinion," said Butch. "I was president of Central Wrap. Doesn't it make sense that I would soon take over Sargento?"

Leonard studied his son. The task was difficult. "Butch, I think we need to at least consider the recommendation of the study. They think in the long run, the company would prosper with you in another role. Best for the company...for all the employees. Most of the study hinges on what is seen as a financial specter that has plagued the company's history. Our need, they believe, is to have someone with a strong financial background."

Butch raised an objection and Leonard overtalked him—each raising his volume as they exchanged point and counterpoint. The confrontation was difficult. "There're plenty of key roles in the company," suggested Leonard. "You're an excellent salesman. Think of the great things you've done...the TV commercial...the things you could do...by continuing to lead the charge on that!"

As each volleyed their thoughts back and forth, their voices escalated, not in anger, but in an effort for each to promote their viewpoint. In the end, Leonard walked out of Butch's office, returned to his office, closed his door, and finished his cigarette in solitude, repeatedly playing back the conversation with his son. Wondering what he could have said differently. The conversation dissolved without agreement.

Those series of events had led the two of them to this point in time. Now, Leonard wondered what Butch would do.

The dark day in 1974 unavoidably arrived as Leonard watched his oldest son toss a production-line cardboard box on his desk, fill it with his papers and files. Butch walked down the hall and then out the door. He could and he would start another company. That had been his message on multiple levels, direct and inferred.

Leonard felt the weight of melancholy cloak him as he watched his son drive away. Yet he remained hopeful that what was done could be, later, undone.

In short order, Butch leveraged his relationships, built over the years within the cheese industry. He made known to all that Butch Gentine's new company—World Wide Sales Inc.—bought and sold bulk cheese as a brokerage firm. As a cheese broker, his company would source all types of cheese, some imported but primarily domestic.

Frequently, Leonard stopped by Butch's World Wide Sales office buoyed with the hope he could convince his son to return to Sargento. Butch refused each overture. There was no animosity. His admiration for his father and for Sargento remained genuine and deep.

"Now that this opportunity has presented itself," Butch told his father, "I'm looking forward to building and growing my own company. It's something I know I can do. A business I can pass along to my children one day."

Later, in 1974, the board of directors, signaling agreement to the consultant's succession plan, moved Leonard into the role of chairman and promoted Chuck Strobel to the position of president.

As Butch forged a path and developed his own company, Leonard stood in the distant shadows, willing to toss him a financial safety net if needed.

# 26

## First Key Milestone
## 1977

LEONARD ARRIVED EARLY, attending to last-minute details in the banquet hall at the Executive Inn in Sheboygan, Wisconsin.

Flipping open the large box he had set on the stage, he unpacked Dolores's candle centerpieces—three for each of the long tables. His daughter and three sons, each with their own preparty assignments, bustled about preparing the room.

It was the annual Christmas party, and by 1977, Larry, Lou, Lee, and his son-in-law, Ed Sturzl, held positions at Sargento, each somewhat independent of the other. By most indications, the company had become Leonard's long-sought-after family business.

Following his graduation from St. Norbert College—the first in the family to earn a college degree—his son Larry fought in the Vietnam War. Following that, he joined Sargento as head of the Purchasing Department. Leonard had immediately encouraged him to oversee the construction of a 37,000-square-foot addition to the Plymouth facility—the building that Jack Anton had helped Leonard acquire twelve years earlier.

Ron Begalke, their outside accountant, had joined Sargento in 1969.

Larry, Lee, Leonard, and Lou Gentine

Then, in 1973, following a degree at Notre Dame and then a three-year career at Price Waterhouse in Connecticut, Lou joined as an accountant reporting to Ron. Lou and Ron grew to become two strong financial pillars for Sargento.

Leonard's only daughter, Ann, married Ed Sturzl, and together they opened and managed a new Sargento warehouse in Stone Mountain, Georgia. After ten years, Leonard saw small advantages and large expenses in operating that building. He closed that warehouse, returning Eddie and Ann back to Plymouth. Eddie took a credit manager role until finally starting the Personnel Department at Sargento.

Ann and Ed Sturzl

Lee, Leonard's youngest, left an accounting firm in Chicago and became a salesman for Sargento in the Chicago market. Enamored of the potential of marketing, Lee enrolled at DePaul University to earn his second degree. Increasingly, he discussed the benefits of building a strong brand name for Sargento, an image that differentiated the company from competitors.

All four children were now plying their talents toward the organization of the annual Christmas party. As the first guests arrived, with the last-minute decorations scattered about the banquet hall, it was time for the Gentine family to form the reception line. Leonard wanted this night to be memorable—a reward for the year's efforts.

As every employee arrived, he shook their hands and chatted briefly as if each were a close friend of the family. Oftentimes, he referenced an incident, an inside joke, or a recent accomplishment, conjuring a smile or a laugh.

As the guest arrivals dwindled, all making their way into the dining hall, the reception line disbanded and Leonard escorted Dolores to their reserved spot at a banquet table. Laughter and chatter spiraled louder until the cacophony filled the room.

Leonard wagged his head in amazement. *How large the company had grown!* Over 150 employees and their spouses filled the banquet hall.

Seeking the secret to Leonard's good fortune, curious businessmen asked what he considered to be the most significant milestone for Sargento—the one thing that ultimately placed the company on its path to success. Leonard often thought the installation of peg bars gave the company its greatest traction. Since they began installing them, sales had increased nearly 700 percent.

Or perhaps the first milestone was not the peg bars but, instead, the day he met Chuck. Or his friendship with Joe. It's hard to measure the value of one individual and their long-term impact. What yardstick is used for that? Were there accurate measures to do so, thought Leonard, there was no doubt that either man—or both—would have been the linchpin for their success.

Sure, there were times when they failed to see eye to eye with him on matters, Leonard taking a more liberal view on some decisions, Chuck and Joe choosing to be more conservative. But in all, they balanced one another.

Chuck and Marge broke Leonard's train of thought. Lifting his wrist and tapping his watch, Chuck mouthed over the din, "Time to get this party started!"

Leonard nodded agreement and mounted the slightly elevated platform.

"I want to thank…" Leonard's voice failed to overcome the chatter and enthusiasm in the room even with the aid of a microphone. He waited a few seconds and tried again.

"I want to thank…" he began anew and pushed on as the crowd

quieted, "everyone for coming tonight. This is our fourth annual Christmas party. Those of you that are relatively new to the company may not know that our first holiday party in 1974 celebrated a special occasion—the twenty-fifth year after opening the Plymouth Cheese Counter. Although we sold that business to Jerry and Virgie Eigenberger, the day we started the Cheese Counter was the day we began our journey that led us to Sargento.

"Those here tonight, could you stand if you were part of the Cheese Counter?"

Leonard looked about the room. Five stood, one or two embarrassed by the attention.

"As many of you know," Leonard said, "one of the first employees of that business was my mother, Anna. Many knew her as Gramma Gentine. Although she is no longer with us, I like to think she is here tonight in spirit. Like I am, she was proud of her Sargento Family."

Leonard then named the four employees that were hired in the last year and asked each one to join him on the stage. Then, he invited Bob Gilles to the front of the room.

"As is our tradition, our new employees will sing 'Jingle Bells' for us tonight." Turning to his production manager, he said, "Bob, you have years of experience managing new employees. Let's see how well you direct these newest singers."

Amid laughter and a few hecklers, the four employees floundered through the verses but compensated for their stumbled words with a rousing chorus.

As the four employees returned to their seats, Leonard regained his solemnity.

"When our year ends in June next year, Sargento will have been shipping cheese to grocery stores for twenty-four years. It hasn't been easy, as many of you know. There are those here tonight that have felt our growing pains: a time when I've asked everyone to take a temporary pay cut, a time infrequent customer orders didn't keep everyone working, a time when we worked long hours to meet an unexpected customer order.

"We are here tonight because of you. We are here tonight because we stood as a family and faced each setback head on." Leonard paused momentarily in thought.

"Because of you, we merged Central Wrap and Sargento into one company without taking anyone off the payroll. Because of you, we now have our own fleet of semis. Because of you, a growing number of peg bars display our products in stores. And because of you and your determination to succeed, we are now a company that is so big, we run two shifts five days a week, providing more jobs for more people in our community.

"We continue to be leaders of innovation in the cheese category, being the first to blend spices with shredded cheese, being the first to blend two different types of cheese into one bag. These happened because you made them happen.

"There will be years ahead when Sargento will be profitable and the envy of many other companies. There will also be years when things will not be as good as we would like them. That's the way life is. But in those good times—and those that won't be—we will always rise to the top because of each other and what we believe.

"Tonight, this celebration is not only about a time when we reflect on the birth of Christ, it's also a celebration to honor all that you have done and continue to do. So after the meal, I hope you stay, dance, and enjoy each other's company."

Leonard held up a hand to signal a transition in thought. "Before we begin the meal, there is one individual here tonight that deserves special recognition. When I owned the funeral home, he occasionally drove the ambulance or served as a greeter. When I was involved in Genstrupp, he and his brother cooked cheese.

"At Sargento, he operated the cheese dryer, standing near the tremendous heat of that machine. And I'm sure his wife, Sylvia, would be more than happy to let you know what it was like to have a husband that smelled each night like aged Parmesan or Romano."

Twitters gave way to applause as Cletus and Sylvia Wieser took the stage to receive Leonard's praise and a plaque.

As they returned to their seats, Leonard nodded to the back of the room, cuing the servers. "It looks like they're ready to pass the food dishes around, so before that happens . . . Larry?" Leonard looked in the direction of his son. "Larry is making his way up here to offer grace."

After a prayer, dinner, and dessert, the waitstaff cleared away the dishes and then cleared the room of tables—just enough to provide a comfortable dance floor.

As the evening wore on, several employees drifted home. Bob Gilles, a man in love with life, flashed his infectious, boyish grin and spent most of the evening dancing with his wife, Angie. Unable to match her husband's high energy, she encouraged Bob to find another willing dance partner. "Go. Have fun. I'll just sit here and talk with friends."

Cupping his hands around his mouth to direct his request over the opening measures of music, Bob called out to Clarice Schneider, "Clarice, it's a polka! Come on, let's go!" Clarice smiled broadly and bounced up from her chair. Bob pointed in the direction of Geri Steiner. "Get ready, Geri. You're next."

Energized by the deep mellow tones of the tuba, Bob invested his full energy into the dance—the same vigor that fueled his life, the same energy he invested each day at Sargento.

Bob and Clarice whirled about, weaving in and out of other dancers that three-stepped to the music a bit slower. Heavy beads of perspiration formed and glistened on Bob's forehead, and discreetly, he mopped his brow with the sleeve of his white shirt. Then he took a sudden turn as his step gave way. Clarice, carried by Bob's weight, fell awkwardly over him on the floor. Heads jerked in their direction to see if either was injured in the tumble.

Clarice pushed herself from the floor, but Bob remained. Two men sitting at nearby tables rushed jovially onto the floor to help Bob back up and slap him on the back. As they approached, it was clear something was wrong. Bob remained prone, his face a chalky white, twisted in a contorted grimace, his eyes rolling upward as if in pain. Breaths came in quick gasps, and Bob unsuccessfully tried to sit.

In a rush, people gathered, encircling Bob's prone body. Larry pushed his way to him. Someone dragged over a chair. Another ran for water. Leonard and Chuck elbowed their way to the forefront. Confusion swept through the banquet hall. Larry's voice shouted above the frenzy, "Call an ambulance!"

Several rushed to the front desk to place the call as others continued to press around Bob. Many, faces etched with concern, stayed near to the walls. Stunned, the band watched from the raised platform, shifting uneasily, not knowing what, if anything, they should do.

"His pulse is weak," murmured Leonard after a cursory examination. "Several of you go out to the hotel lobby to direct the ambulance crew as soon as they get here. We don't want to lose any time while they try to find us."

The air in the room was thick and heavy, the wait for the ambulance unbearably long. People fidgeted. Others talked in hushed tones. Only a cough heard at the far end of the room broke the heart-sickened silence.

At last, a siren grew steadily louder as the ambulance rushed into the hotel parking lot. Then faint activity blossomed down the hall, and Leonard heard voices and quickening footsteps escalating as the first responders approached. In a whoosh of movement, two medics raced through the doorway with a portable gurney. In practiced movements, they supported Bob's body, lifted him onto the stretcher, and rolled him out the door, leaving behind a stunned room shrouded in silence.

All energy, all life, drained from the room. Leonard checked his watch. Ten o'clock. Although the Christmas party was planned to last closer to midnight, couples with muffled voices gathered coats to brace themselves against the December cold. Most left, praying there would be good news in the morning.

That would not be the case. Bob, the iconic production manager at Sargento, the man who kept life in order with his voluminous scrawled notes on his hat, apron, and arm, the man who gave his heart and his enthusiasm to Sargento and those who reported to him, had suffered a heart attack.

He didn't survive.

His love of life, his love of dancing, his love of people vanished—without warning. Bob's departure happened so quickly and in the presence of the entire company.

It threw Sargento into shock.

# 27

# A Near-Death Experience
# 1978

IT WAS AS if a torpedo had struck them broadside.

Leonard needed time to think, not react. As he strolled through the plant, packages filled, bumped down the conveyor, and then slid into cartons. Long ago, he had learned he found an emotional catharsis in watching the equipment run.

He waved at some employees. Talked with others. They would need to be told what happened, of course, but he would wait. He preferred to share the problem and the company's direction at the same time.

From the production floor, the typical route he traveled most days, he made his way to Shipping and Receiving. He walked among the rows of pallets stacked with cases of cheese, waiting their turn to be loaded onto one of the company-owned semis.

Unseen by the few that worked back here, he stopped to reflect. How far they had come in twenty-five years. A messy confluence of disappointment and pride stirred within him. And perhaps guilt. Had he been responsible—or rather irresponsible? He didn't think so.

Sargento lived on the financial edge, bailing out water as they sailed along. Thanks to their ever-expanding customer base, revenues were greater year after year. But as the money flowed in, Leonard subsequently invested the funds back into the company, investing in peg bar installations, upgrading equipment, and hiring new employees. As they shipped products to more stores, Sargento offered introductory deals, special discounts, and advertising support, each impairing the bottom line.

Spending had been aggressive but not indiscriminate. The money pushed them toward the vision Leonard held for a larger, more pervasive company. Perhaps they would never be a national company. Nevertheless, Sargento would be well respected in different pockets of the country.

The unexpected can happen to any start-up company, Leonard considered. Even Butch's company, World Wide Sales, had hit a bump in the road, requiring an unexpected influx of cash when a major customer—at the end of 1977—chose not to renew their contract. The lost volume and profits sent Butch's company into a tailspin. In July of the following year, Leonard loaned him money to stabilize that situation.

Now, by the end of 1978, it was Sargento experiencing a financial crisis. But Sargento was no start-up company. They were celebrating their twenty-fifth year in business.

Over the years, Leonard had built a strong personal relationship with their lender in Sheboygan, Wisconsin. He considered the Security First National Bank's chairman, Clarence Weber, a friend, a confidante, and a person he could trust. Meetings were frequent. As if possessing an insatiable appetite, Sargento continually needed working capital, and the bank offered what they could.

Although sales flourished, escalating each year, the margins remained paper-thin. As a result, the company struggled under the weight of a heavy debt-to-worth ratio. In numerous meetings, Clarence warned of the impending danger and the need to plow more cash reserves into the company.

What Leonard didn't foresee—what no one expected—unfavorably tipped the delicate balance of revenues and expenses. That blow arrived without warning.

Food Fair's October surprise announcement—their public notice that they were filing for bankruptcy—left Sargento management horrified. As a large grocery chain of over five hundred stores, one of the company's biggest customers, Food Fair may have appeared to Leonard as the lead horse pulling the Sargento business. He may have been too flexible, too trusting, allowing Food Fair to delay larger and larger payments owed to Sargento.

The turbulent news—the loss of that large sum of money—gravely threatened the viability of Sargento, sending Leonard, Lou, and Ron to Security Bank in hopes of securing a short-term loan. Jerry Thorne, a senior executive at the bank, escorted the three men into the conference room.

"Food Fair took with them over five hundred thousand dollars in receivables with their bankruptcy," Ron explained as he took a seat at the table and snapped open his briefcase.

Lou put a fine point to the purpose of their visit. "Jerry, we're going to need a loan to tide us over. A small one. Just until we can get on the other side of this."

Silence hung thick in the conference room.

Jerry furrowed his brow. "Your line of credit is fully drawn, and you've outgrown our bank's legal lending limit. And that debt ratio—the one you and Clarence have been discussing for years—won't qualify for financing from a money center bank."

"So...what do you suggest we do?" asked Leonard.

"To keep operational?" Jerry paused and then suggested, "Our best approach is a loan from a commercial finance company. But it's not ideal. It would be only a short-term solution, buying a little time. The main downside is that the interest rates are crushing."

The men shifted uncomfortably around the table.

"We're limited in our options at the moment," said Jerry, "but let me mull this over. We have a lot of able and creative people at the bank. Let's see what we can do."

All Leonard's past efforts—the struggle to start a small funeral home, the leap into the cheese world, and his drive to have Sargento wholly owned by his family—all those steps along the path were at risk. The loss would be devastating. Almost more than he could fathom.

At the age of sixty-four, would he have the years or the energy to start over one more time?

The three men returned to Sargento less encouraged than when they'd left. As Ron and Lou returned to their offices, Leonard slid behind his desk and tapped out a cigarette. Then he decided to walk through the plant in search of solace. So many families counted on him. So many families.

That afternoon, Leonard invited his sons and Ed Sturzl to his office.

"We met with the banker today," Leonard began. "Looks like it's going to be hard to overcome this Food Fair loss. They're trying to help us weather this mess."

He and Lou replayed the conversation with the loan officer.

"I'm sure there are things we can do," Larry suggested, "at least until the bank finds a way to give us another loan."

One of them suggested that they each take out personal loans to produce an emergency cash infusion. Leonard voiced opposition to that.

"If the company is going down," he said, "I'm not taking my children down with it."

"There's more at stake than just losing the company," Larry reminded his father. "All of our employees will lose their jobs. We need to consider that. What this will do to them and their families."

"Larry's right," added Lou. "We need to consider our options. They're going to trust us to make the right decisions."

Leonard lowered his eyes in thought. These were tough decisions. If Sargento were to take an objective approach, forfeiting the company, what did that say about his beliefs in the value of each individual? Should the business fold, how would he gain the trust of others in the future if he attempted to start another business?

"Here's what we can do, Dad." Lou laid out a proposal where each would contribute funds from personal loans in exchange for shares in the company. "You always wanted this to be a family-owned company. Here's our chance to do that. Each of us will own shares in Sargento, and if we're successful, it will be a good investment. If not... Well, if not, it won't be the end of the world. We're young. We'll recover."

It was a bitter pill to swallow. It's not what a father would choose for his children. Adamantly, they advocated their solution. Just as adamantly, Leonard opposed it. Finally, with reluctance, considering the broader group of people affected, he accepted, hoping there might be another option before they met again with the banker.

Later, as Leonard thought about it, he realized this was far more than children riding to the rescue of their father. It was a demonstration of the values instilled in them since childhood. Fairness. Respect. Honesty. And as it related to business, he frequently reminded them, running a company is never about greed. It's never about the accumulation of power. It's about serving. Serving consumers, serving employees, serving the community, and—in an odd way—serving competitors.

Not all companies followed that philosophy, he knew. But that was the way he wanted his business run. What good is a successful company if, in the end, you sell away your morals and your humanity?

Now, with a proposed direction, it was time for Leonard to talk to his Sargento Family—those working in the plant and in the office. At the end of the first shift and after the second shift arrived, Leonard broadly described the bankruptcy of their customer and the impact it had on Sargento. Then Leonard asked the hard question.

"I'm not asking for your answer today. I'm wondering if each of you would consider taking a temporary pay cut. Just for several months. I want you to know that I will be taking my salary to zero. I'm not asking you to do that. But perhaps you could consider a slight reduction in pay."

Leonard looked around the quiet production floor, watching employees shift from one foot to the other. Many dolefully stared at the floor.

"Think about it. Those that choose to work for a little less"—he paused, looking from person to person—"will be compensated when we turn this thing around. Let me know one way or the other. And what you personally decide will not alter my opinion of you. I know you need to think of your families."

With that, Leonard left the production floor.

By the following week, to Leonard's surprise, every employee agreed to a small reduction in pay.

When Lou, Ron, and Leonard again met with Jerry at Security Bank, they presented their short-term solution—one they hoped would buy additional time, allowing Sargento to recover.

"I've invited Russ Schuler to join us," said Jerry. "He's one of our experts on government lending programs. We've been talking about some options that might work for Sargento, specifically a Farmers Home Administration loan."

"So we can dump that high-interest finance-company loan?" asked Lou.

"No, you'll still need that," explained Russ. "That's your short-term solution. However, long term, we're suggesting an FmHA loan. It's ninety percent government guaranteed, designed to assist any rural business. And at a much lower interest rate. It's the obvious choice, if you qualify."

Leaving the sobering meeting, Leonard was certain that were it not for the friendships they developed with the bank, were it not for the willingness of those business friends to turn over every stone on their behalf, Sargento would have been forced to shutter its doors.

Within a few weeks, the financing with the commercial finance company began and it provided temporary financial relief for Sargento. The experience had been—and would be—painful. The lesson hard-learned.

Sargento was now in intensive care with improved hopes of surviving.

# 28

# Seeds Planted
## 1981

WITH THE PERSONAL family loans and the costly loans from a commercial finance company in place, eighteen stressful months passed. Yet the outcome could have been far worse.

With an approved twenty-year FmHA loan of $6 million, at half the interest rate of the commercial finance company, Russ Schuler and Jerry Thorne helped structure Sargento for a stronger future. With the capital provided through Security Bank, for perhaps the first time in the company's history Sargento had the necessary breathing room and an opportunity for stability.

As each family member shared in the financial stake in the company, tough decisions followed long hours of healthy debate, internal exploration, and strategic thinking.

In the years just prior to 1981, Lou Gentine, Larry Gentine, and Ron Begalke served as part of a three-headed presidency role—an evenly balanced tripartite. Each pursued a three-pronged imperative critical for the company's survival and growth: securing a solid financial foundation, continuing product expansion to other parts of the country, and driving innovation in the cheese category.

While each of the three presidents—and Leonard—offered a voice in each decision, primary accountabilities flowed from respective areas of responsibilities. Larry scrutinized the mix and margins of the company's products, Ron streamlined operations, and Lou held the line on administrative expenses. Slowly, painfully at times, Sargento began to evolve, shedding the competitive vulnerability of its adolescent years.

This encouraging progress at work was overshadowed only by the news that Lou's wife, Michele, had shared with him the previous summer. With two sons, Tony at age eleven and Louie at seven, Lou and Michele prepared the family and their home for another child. Early the following year, on a cold February 12, Michele gave birth to a third son, whom they named Joseph Leonard Gentine.

Unexpectedly, three days later, on the fifteenth of February, Joey was transferred to neonatal intensive care in a Milwaukee hospital. Hearing the turn of events, Leonard and Dolores flew back from their winter home in Florida to see and hold their newest grandson. The next day, four short days after arriving into this world, Joey would die from a heart anomaly. Fleeting days. Less than ninety hours. Not enough time to say *I love you* as many times as a parent would long to do. Not enough moments to hug and smile into the small face.

Joey's passing arced widening circles of grief over the entire Gentine family. It was the first personal loss for the family in recent years, and the whole family united in support.

In the evenings, Lou wrapped his arm around his wife and their two sons, each shedding tears, each praying for added strength and courage. As they held one another, through their profound faith, they came to understand that God now held their little angel in heaven.

In love and in faith, Michele chose that experience to help others—those who lost loved ones during their first year. She mailed cards to those bearing similar losses. Lou and Michele also sent notes of thanks to the hospital staff that cared for any lost infant despite their attempts to reverse the irreversible. And a year later, on the anniversary, they would mail another card of gratitude to those same people, sent to demonstrate that their caring could never be forgotten.

Lou Gentine pushed aside a manila folder to the corner of his desk as Ralph Platz and Ron Begalke laid their report squarely before him.

For three years, the Sargento sales force expanded availability of their products into additional parts of the country. At the same time, in stores that regularly sold Sargento cheese, the sales team increased the number of Sargento products each store stocked. The results of those dual efforts were phenomenal. Company sales dramatically increased each year.

Unfortunately, as sales rose, profits remained flat. For every dollar Sargento collected, they kept less than a penny. The remaining ninety-nine-plus cents covered their costs. Investing in a standard savings account in a bank would have offered greater profitability without all the effort.

Controlling costs was part of the solution, Lou knew. The other part of the equation was to sell products that offered greater profits. That said, knowing which products offered the greatest return was not easy to determine. Sargento needed better tracking tools. Earlier in 1981, he had asked Ralph to identify the cost of producing each of their items.

Lou fanned the pages of Ralph's report. "Are we getting a better handle on our product costs?"

"Ralph's been putting in some long days, Lou," said Ron. Then, turning to address Ralph, he added, "I think you've gathered information at each shift if I'm not mistaken."

Ralph nodded. "We did need to see if there were any variances incurred that could be attributed to the different shifts or the time of day."

"Gimme a sec to just glance at this," Lou said as he hunched over the numbers and dragged his finger down the report column, flipping the pages Ralph had prepared. Lou felt a comfort in his ability to quickly analyze figures, a skill developed during his employment at Price Waterhouse.

"How close are we coming to understand the company's true cost picture?" Lou questioned.

"There have been a number of assumptions that I have taken into account." Ralph leaned forward, resting his elbows on the arms of the chair. "Some costs, I've had to arbitrarily assign. Utilities were prorated, for example. But things like equipment repairs or other expenses not related to operations, I took some educated guesses."

"I think what we have to remember, Lou," Ron interjected, "getting costs for each SKU—each product we produce—is harder than one would expect."

"While not a hundred percent accurate," continued Ralph, "I think it's safe to say this gives us a better picture of our costs for producing each item."

As Ron and Ralph waited, Lou continued to study the numbers, written in Ralph's tightly etched figures. "Cost of cheese...film costs...scrap...line speed...labor...uh-huh. Looks like you are capturing everything. Overhead, the indirect costs. How did you arrive at these?"

"And that's the tricky part. A lot of assumptions went into those numbers. I think Ron will back me up on this. These are the best estimates we have so far."

As if talking to himself more than the two men before him, Lou brought the matter to its core. "We just don't make the amount of profit we should."

Lou stretched and pulled a black pen from his pencil holder. "I can't help but believe we're selling some products we have no business selling. Here, in the work you've done, it seems there's a number of products we're making that don't even make us enough money to pay for the coffee we made this morning in the office kitchenette. This one," he said, circling a line on the report, "when you add in the indirect costs you've estimated, we're actually losing money."

Lou tossed the pen on the report. "If we eliminate some products... what happens to those people in our plant that have a steady job because we're making those products? We can't be laying people off just because we're trying to get our house in order. But we can't go on losing money either."

"I think there's a way, Lou," said Ron. "Maybe as we introduce new items, we can discontinue those returning the least profit. The products losing us money..." Ron gestured with his hands in a way that said the solution to that was simple. "They should be eliminated quickly."

In thought, Lou tapped his finger on the desk. "Is this a copy I can keep?"

"Absolutely. That's yours," said Ralph.

"We're going to have Ralph keep refining these numbers," said Ron. "We thought the information was close enough to give us a clearer idea of our products. I think, even with these numbers, though, we can begin to make better decisions."

"I think you're right," said Lou, cocking his head to one side in brief thought. Then to Ron and Ralph, he said, "I want to look at these a little more. Then... sit down with Chuck, Larry, and Lee. Before we communicate anything to the sales group—before we even take this information to Leonard—let's make sure we have a high level of confidence in the accuracy of these numbers. Not that I'm questioning anything you have here, Ralph," he added, holding one palm out toward him. "I think you've done a great job. Let's just keep tracking everything to see how consistent they are."

Ralph nodded and then added, "I know the general belief in Sales is that every shredded cheese item we ship is profitable. I think that you'll see that's not necessarily the case."

Lou nodded and, with that, rose from his desk and ushered the two men out of his office, clasping his hand on Ralph's shoulder. "Again, nice job, Ralph."

Lou turned back to his desk and plucked the pen from the top of the report. He circled a product-cost line. Then another one and one more.

On the twenty-ninth of October, the board of directors had appointed him to the role of CEO, leaving his dad to serve as the company's chairman. October twenty-ninth, he had reflected at the time. Fifty-two years to the date of the stock market crash in 1929. In a way, that shared date inspired him. Though it was a once-ominous day for the nation, he would strive to make that date a positive turning point for Sargento. His father had carried an incredible load bringing the company along this far.

Now, it was his turn. He could not—would not—let his father down. Nor his family: his brothers, his sister. And yes, their children. What his father had started, the legacy he was leaving behind, needed... not to be preserved. Not that, he thought. His intent was not just to preserve. If a company isn't actively growing, then it's actively dying. He needed to expand the business. Make it less vulnerable to financial threats.

With a fresh idea, he grabbed a blue pen and marked lines that met a certain profit threshold. As he labored over the report, he could see a product-mix strategy forming.

There would be more tough decisions ahead. Some might even be moderately in opposition to the way his father had operated Sargento in the past. That was bound to happen, he guessed. He would address that as best he could when the time arrived.

For now, one step at a time.

# 29

# Persnickety
## 1982

THE PLANE HAD arrived late. Lou flipped his wrist to glance at his watch as he disembarked. Zigzagging between streams of people, he spotted the Sargento salesman, Pat Phillips, his shock of black hair bobbing between arriving passengers. Lou shot up a hand and smiled.

"Sorry," Lou said as he shook Pat's hand. "The plane sat nearly forty-five minutes on the tarmac before taking off in Milwaukee. Nothing I could do but sit and wait."

Pat shook his head then reached to take one of the bags that Lou had slung over his shoulder. "There's always some sort of delay." He tossed his head in the direction of the exit. "I'm parked out at the curb. We don't have our appointment with Kroger until one thirty."

The two slid into the car and wove through the airport traffic.

"I thought before lunch we'd hit a few places. Let you see what the dairy sections look like in different stores."

"Sounds good." Lou eased back into the passenger seat. "If we can see a Kroger store before we meet with the buyer, that would help."

"Actually, that was on my list, Lou."

Fifteen minutes out of the airport, Pat took an exit and followed the road to a small strip mall. "I'm going to pull in here first. We'll catch a Kroger next. This is an independent store. It carries more of our items than Kroger. More than most stores in Indianapolis. Besides getting our cheese from their warehouse, a distributor sells them a few of our items, too."

The store, not overly large, smelled of fresh-baked bread as they entered. They spent a few minutes at the deli department commenting on the different cheese varieties and then ambled back to the dairy department.

"What'd I tell ya. They have our shreds and our slices." Pat immediately began pulling the packages forward on the peg bar and checking the code dates.

"I see they even have Sargento Camembert, Gruyère, and fondue cheese. None of these items sell very well." Lou stepped back and took in the full scope of the department. "Oh, and they have our Finlandia and farmer cheese over here." Lou walked to the end of the shelf and picked up a package of farmer cheese.

"Yeah, this dairy case is a mess," the salesman grimaced. "It looks uglier than homemade soap. I've been talking to the owner, but he's been reluctant to let me group all our items together."

Uglier than homemade soap. Lou had to smile. Pat lived in Louisville, with deep Southern roots and a pocketful of colorful phrases. Those were his stock-in-trade. His charm and personality not only made him memorable but well liked.

Of all the Sargento salesmen that tried, only Pat—and his Southern charm—had been able to build a relationship with Kroger. He was the first to get Sargento products in any Kroger store. In three short years after Sargento hired him from Pepperidge Farm, he had built a reputation on the Sargento sales force. Leonard called him the Kroger Guy.

Lou studied the package of farmer cheese. "This item is going to be out of code in about four weeks." He dug deeper on the shelf, looking at each package. "They all have the same code date, all expiring the same time."

"Probably came out of the same case," Pat said with his head deep in the pegged cheese looking for code dates.

Lou counted the packages. Nine. If they came out of the same case, they had sold only three. The vacuum package allowed the product to remain fresh for over twenty-five weeks. Running that close to the better-if-used-before date was a sure sign there were few interested consumers.

"This is exactly what we've been talking about in Plymouth," Lou said. "This is what drives up our expenses. We sell an item like this to the distributor at our manufactured cost. He marks it up and sells it to the store at his distributor price. The store marks it up again and puts it on the shelf.

"We guarantee our products. If they don't sell, we buy them back from the store at the shelf price. The meager profits on the three items sold is more than washed away by the retail price we pay for the remaining nine.

"From what I can see from the reports that our cost accountant, Ralph Platz, shows me, we need to stop selling these items. Farmer cheese and other items are costing us money. We need to take them off our price list."

"That's easy to do with this distributor," said Pat. "But I got a buyer in Michigan that loves farmer cheese. I mean that guy really loves that kind of cheese. He buys it from us direct. Sells a bit better up there, but we still pick up some of that product."

"I think slow-moving items like that should be off our price list," suggested Lou.

"Well, I'll tell you what," Pat said. "The guy only agreed to carry our other items because we were the only cheese company that would sell him farmer cheese. If I tell him it's gone, I'll probably be gone. And they have thirty stores that order a bunch! I don't want to lose that business."

*That's the problem,* thought Lou. *There's a belief, unfounded or true, that if Sargento discontinues certain items, they will lose other profitable items.* He wasn't so sure that was the case. But once salesmen struggled for months—or years—to build a business in a market, they were reluctant to put that business in jeopardy.

"Well, let's see if we can remove the item from the distributors list," said Lou. "Who calls on that distributor?"

Lou made note of the salesman. Then he spotted a row each of Pot Cheese and Limburger Spread. He had discontinued these items in the past, but Leonard reintroduced them. Why his father insisted that JC Tupper make these items for Sargento was probably something only his father understood.

"OK, let's go see a Kroger store," Pat suggested. "It's better organized. They don't sell as many of our products but they turn over more quickly."

"That's fine," said Lou, "but—here—let's buy this farmer cheese to get it off the shelf. It's still good, but we don't need to be selling anything that old."

In the Kroger store, Pat led Lou back to the dairy department. Only a few Sargento products hung on the peg bar, but they were better organized. All the Sargento products were grouped together.

"Every Kroger store look like this," boasted Pat. "The buyer's a real nice guy. Wants to see Kraft have some competition so he added our products. They carry a few more items than the Kroger-Columbus Division. But it's about the same."

Lou had to agree that the section looked better, but standing back to study the entire peg bar, he furrowed his brow. "How come they carry our Shredded Taco but not our Shredded Cheddar? I would think our Cheddar would sell great in this market."

"I didn't ask that the buyer put Cheddar in his stores," Pat admitted. "He already has a Kraft Shredded Cheddar. I'm not out to start a cheese war with Kraft."

"Well, maybe Kraft would react and maybe it wouldn't. I think we owe it to the consumer to give them a choice. Why don't you see if we can get the buyer to buy our Shredded Cheddar? Shredded Taco is a good seller but our Cheddar sells even better. If he needs a place to put our Cheddar, maybe there's a slow-moving item it could replace."

"All right," Pat said in a long, drawn-out Southern drawl. "Tell you what. We'll stop at another independent store on the way to the buyer and purchase a couple of packages of Cheddar to show Kroger this afternoon."

As they sat in the Kroger lobby, Pat said, "Now, just so you know, I'm just going to show the Cheddar items to the buyer to start him thinking. I want to put together a presentation with rationale why his stores should be carrying the item. I'll do that on my next visit. This is just to lay the groundwork."

Pat introduced Lou as the CEO of Sargento. Lou, Pat, and the Kroger buyer chatted for an hour. Most of the conversation was only tangentially related to business, if at all. Early in the conversation, Pat had noticed a picture of the buyer's grade-school-aged daughter on the desk, commented on it, and said she was cuter than a speckled pup.

The buyer's smile stretched across his face and he thanked Pat. The remark set the tone for the remaining conversation. It occurred to Lou that a sort of kinship existed between this buyer and their Sargento salesman.

Pat did spread a few packages of Shredded Cheddar on the desk but didn't attempt to convince the buyer to put them in his stores. Instead, he explained how well the item was doing in different parts of the country and promised to talk more about it on his next visit. The buyer seemed open to hearing what Pat had to say.

After leaving the buyer's office, Lou and Pat stopped in a small café. Lou wanted to hear the salesman's thoughts on the company, the products, and the prospects for developing Sargento in his territory: Michigan, Indiana, and Ohio.

"I know I'm given a sales quota each year and a list of products that Marketing wants me to get in my stores." Pat took a sip of his coffee then left the table in search of a packet of sugar.

"It was a bit bitter," he explained when he returned. "I'm given a list of products Marketing wants me to sell, and sometimes it feels they believe all I have to do is walk in and put our products in the store. When you call on these customers, you gotta know where we're gonna put them. What should it be next to. Things like that.

"Putting the peg bar in stores got my foot in the door, but it's more than selling. It's building relationships, building trust. Being true to my word."

Lou listened, nodded, sought ideas he could take back to the home office to consider. After stopping in several more grocery stores along the way, Pat dropped Lou off at the airport in time to catch a flight back to Wisconsin.

On the plane, Lou reflected on the day.

On paper, it was clear that there were products that were losing money for Sargento. It was also clear that some of these odd products were instrumental in opening doors for Sargento, allowing them to place other, stronger-selling items in stores.

There was the morale of the sales force to consider. A rapid and sweeping discontinuation of slow-moving items just might throw a wrench into their growth momentum. No, they would need to strategically and systematically weed out the poor-performing products as they introduced new, innovative ones. That would take longer than Lou would have preferred, but no matter the length of the course, it had to be done.

Pat had been with the company for three years. Salesmen with more years of service would be more rigid in their thinking. Change rarely comes easy. Leonard and his sales team had been advancing the company in a specific manner: Sell whatever can be sold. Address the wants of the buyer.

There was nothing wrong with the way his father built Sargento. However, the retail business was changing. If Sargento failed to adapt, their old business model would eventually fail.

Lou would advocate for change, but he'd ruffle as few feathers as possible as he did. An airplane changes direction in increments. Small, almost imperceptible adjustments. That's the way he would do it as well.

In 1978, when Food Fair filed for bankruptcy, it did more than cripple an already cash-strained Sargento. More than an economic mental shift, it was a matter of seeing Sargento differently. Not as a small company offering an assortment of cheese products to retailers, but as a leader establishing category standards. Not the "big cheese" in the industry, just a better one.

With Sargento seemingly in its own self-imposed crucible, Leonard's children attempted to change the delicate chemistry of the company without damaging the legacy their father had built.

They would transform Sargento, not from the top down, but from the bottom up. If a company hires good people—and if they aren't good people, why were they hired?—then those people deserve the opportunity to shape the company. As a Sargento Family, they would be empowered to redesign Sargento in all its many facets.

As Larry, Lou, and Lee sharpened guidelines on spending and asset allocation, as corporate philosophy on product portfolio mix assumed greater importance, as quality overshadowed production speed, the

Sargento Family galvanized and became the active ingredient that triggered the transformation.

In search of adding greater value to their products, as self-subscribed leaders setting category standards, employees fussed and fretted over the tiniest details. Finished packages endured stricter scrutiny. If a package didn't convey quality, it was rejected. If the heating bar sealing the package left a crimp or wrinkle in the film, employees asked that that package not be shipped.

At the end of the production line, a Sargento employee carted cases of products to nearby water tanks, submerging each package under water—not statistical sampling, rather seal-testing *every* package, searching for those packages that weren't airtight. Products failing that "dunk test" were reworked. Airtight packages were hand-dried, recased, and placed in inventory.

Employees manifested an obsession with cheese quality—the way it was cut, the way it looked, its color, the way it was packaged, its shape, its meltability, and myriad other small details.

But the fussiness did not rest alone in product rejection. Just as fervently with each hint of imperfection, the Sargento Family organized into teams to restructure the manufacturing process so that the identified problem might be minimized or eradicated altogether.

At the same time, Sargento-empowered employees identified cost-saving initiatives. To further drive awareness and promote cost-consciousness, Larry began a "Bad Guy" campaign to deliver that message.

"There are no bad guys or bad ideas. Never hesitate to share your thoughts or worry what others may think," he had insisted. "One idea can stimulate a second idea, leading to a third invaluable suggestion." He challenged them to help uncover any dollars the company spent with little or no benefit. "Let's redirect those savings to improve the product or to make your jobs easier."

White coffee cups emblazoned with the words "I had a bad idea"—placed in break stations and lunchrooms—enticed employees to offer their cost-saving ideas, no matter how trivial. Those offering their "bad idea" were recognized.

It was into this burgeoning culture of corporate self-improvement that Steve Laughlin was asked to wade. His advertising firm, Frankenberry Laughlin Constable, had been assigned the responsibility of scripting a new television commercial for Sargento, and Steve vowed to accurately reflect the spirit of Leonard's growing cheese company.

Following weeks on the assignment, the new ad agency brought their idea from their Milwaukee office. Steve and Dick Papke, a short, energetic man the ad agency hired to work directly on the Sargento account, promised to present the agency's "big idea"—one they said would put Sargento on the map.

Dick Papke

Around the conference room table sat Leonard, Lee, Lou, Larry, Chuck, and Ron.

"Several weeks ago, as I toured your plant," began Steve, "I watched as employees tossed packages into water, checking for air leaks. Package panels inspected for appearance. Cheese rejected for the wrong shade of color. A minor shade difference undiscernible to me, I might add. It was all a sort of fussiness, fastidiousness, perfectionism that I'd not seen before from employees on any production floor."

"So Steve called me into his office," Dick jumped in. "He tells me what he saw and asked me what I thought of the advertising tag line, 'Sargento, the fussy cheese people from Plymouth, Wisconsin.'"

Steve lifted a stack of poster boards from the table, holding them in his direction, careful not to reveal the artwork they bore. "I thought that clearly described what I was seeing in the plant. Just a fussiness you don't normally see in a company at that level."

Dick reclaimed the dialogue looking as if he was unable to restrain his enthusiasm. "But there was something that bothered me about that, so after thinking about it overnight, I suggested we change the word *fussy*. Carnation cat food is using *fussy* in their advertising. We should have something that would set us apart—something that no one else is using. Instead of *fussy*—"

"Instead of *fussy*—" Steve flipped the poster boards around to display the artwork. "We are proposing that every commercial end with the tag, 'Sargento, the *persnickety* cheese people from Plymouth, Wisconsin.'"

The room fell silent. Lou watched as everyone's eyes darted from one to the other. Lee spoke first. "Persnickety? It sounds old-fashioned. Archaic. Who's gonna want to associate their products with a dusty old word like *persnickety*?"

Steve looked as if he was about to jump to the defense of their proposal, but Dick forged ahead.

"I have to agree with you that the word is old." Dick offered a cherubic grin. "Not sure if you could call it dusty, but I'll agree it's old-fashioned. Not many people use that word in conversation anymore. But that's the beauty of it. It's uniqueness. I think Sargento can 'own' that word."

"It is," Steve added, quick to follow up on Dick's comment, "a word that is old-fashioned. Old-fashioned ideas. Old-fashioned, time-worn principles. Craftsman care in producing products. This is what I saw when I walked through your building. This is what we will share with consumers in our ads."

Each voiced their thoughts on the television ads the agency proposed that day. Storyboards, hand-drawn and colored by the staff at Frankenberry Laughlin Constable, proposed three commercials depicting a master cheese maker and his apprentices. There was mutual agreement with the imagery. The tag line—and in particular the word *persnickety*—went unresolved.

"We'll give it thought and get back to you," Lou offered.

Sargento persnickety commercial

In the days following, the Gentine family granted approval for that proposed tag line. The ad agency scheduled the filming, and with the airing of the "Cheese Taster" commercial in the early part of 1982, the word *persnickety* began forging its link to Sargento.

Just as the word *persnickety* failed to meet immediate acceptance with the management team, its adoption within the Sargento Family required time. Yet slowly, among the employees, the odd word found its grounding.

That single word provided the rationale and corporate license to do what was right, to occasionally justify an inconvenient decision. In the beginning, employees uttered the word with an undercurrent of humor. Subtly, that changed. In its evolution, it finally found an attachment to the company's culture and its products.

Persnickety people didn't allow excessive cheese crumbs in the bottom of the package. A true persnickety employee was revered for voicing an objection and denying shipment of a product if the shreds of cheese were too short. Persnickety people refused to accept less than the best in product quality, packaging, or appearance.

In many ways, that single word succinctly encapsulated and outwardly embraced the culture of the company. Valuing and treating each other as members of one large Sargento Family, it overtly recognized consumers for their rightful membership in that family.

"If you wouldn't buy the package in the store," Leonard often cautioned employees as he watched the packages flow down the conveyor belt, "take it off the production line."

The company's persnickety mind-set also filtered into employee hiring. As Sargento attracted new employees, management measured each candidate's fit against the unique culture. Choosing to be persnickety in selecting a potential employee based on their personal skills and principles often left a position unfilled longer than at other companies. Yet it was that insistence for cultural fit that fostered record-low turnover rates with a heavy concentration of employees celebrating twenty- or thirty-year service anniversaries.

Endorsed, perhaps more heavily from the bottom up than from the top down, persnickety-ness, an employee badge of honor, soon took its rightful place in the company's firmament: stamped on internal communications, painted on company semis, referenced in meetings and memos. The company even changed its official mailing address to One Persnickety Place.

That single word galvanized the company, aptly describing the attitude of Sargento and the employees that produced its products. Unlike in the past, speed was no longer king, as it had been at Central Wrap. Quality now reigned. Being the best at responding to customers and consumers, being the best at producing and shipping quality products, forged a new sovereignty and authority.

# 30

# Reclosing the Opening
## 1987

AT TWENTY-TWO YEARS of age, seventy-two had seemed like an old man to Leonard: a wizened, doddering old duffer. But now that he was seventy-two and soon to have another birthday in September, he didn't feel any different inside than he had fifty years ago. He was as nimble and mentally alert as he was in his twenties. He was reminded of his age only when he looked in the mirror.

There was an annoying tremor in his right hand. He'd not had that before. Nothing to worry about really. It didn't happen all the time. Most likely, it was stress related. Or old age. Quirky things can happen with age. He was probably overtired. *Yes, most likely that*, he thought.

Leonard pushed away from his desk, grabbed his empty cup, and walked to the Sargento kitchenette in search of coffee. Just a half cup. If his hand jittered, he didn't want the embarrassment of spilling his coffee. It had happened before. Today, he would walk around the office and the plant, talking with others, taking stock of their progress. That was the easiest way for him to learn what was happening at Sargento. As the chairman, he needed to stay connected.

Rounding the corner with his partial cup of hot coffee, Leonard turned into Larry's office. Small stacks of papers fanned across his son's desk. A coat hung behind the open door. His son was in the building somewhere, just not in his office. Leonard would come back later.

Next door sat Dave Lorbecki, head down, writing notes on a large poster board covered with tissue paper. Leonard rapped on the door frame.

"Good morning, Dave." Leonard settled into the chair in front of the desk.

Leonard felt a certain connection with Dave. They shared similar pioneering spirits. Over nine years ago, Dave had gathered every food service account from each salesman, choosing to focus only on those types of customers. No one had known much about the food service industry or how to appeal to these customers and their unique needs. It was Dave who had built the foundation and direction for the company's food service business sector as if he were launching his own little company.

"Thought I would see how you're doing." Leonard rocked forward in the stiff office chair. "How's business?"

"Good. Real good. Just making a couple of notes for the ad agency. This is the ad they sent me to approve." Dave turned the poster board around and lifted the tissue paper, allowing Leonard to see it better.

"'Any Way You Want It.'" Leonard read the headline aloud. "What the hell is that supposed to mean?"

"That's it," said Dave. "That's our niche. Whatever the restaurant customer wants, we'll give it to them. They want shredded cheese in one-pound bags, we'll do it. They want twenty-four slices of cheese per package to match the number of buns per package delivered by their bakery supplier, we'll do it. Any way they want it, Sargento will do it."

"We can't do that!" Leonard shook his head. "That will drive our costs up."

Dave laid the ad back on his desk and explained how he and Larry were building the business. Anyone could supply a customer with slices of cheese or bags of cheese. What Sargento offered was quality cheese and *service*, matching the product with the needs of the customer to make the operations in their restaurants more efficient.

As Sargento employed dedicated salesmen to expand Sargento products in grocery stores, Dave and Larry had hired Bill Buranich, Tim Ross, and Pat Kennedy to expand sales of Sargento products into well-known restaurant chains. So large had that business sector grown that, three years earlier, Larry had been appointed to take the role of president of this new business—now a separate division under the Sargento umbrella— and the company recognized Dave with a vice president's title.

Leonard knew Dave could be single-mindedly passionate about an idea. For years, Dave had a burning desire. "We need to install a batter and breading line." Dave promoted that vision to anyone who would listen. "There's a great future for us if Sargento can offer breaded mozzarella sticks and breaded vegetables."

Investment money was tight as Sargento focused on stabilizing its financial base. Several years later, hearing Dave's pleas, Chuck Strobel stepped forward and championed the purchase of the equipment. When the machinery was installed in the Elkhart Lake plant, the products it produced quickly became some of the best-selling items for the Food Service Division.

" 'Any way you want it,' huh?" Leonard mused. "I understand the appeal that would have to a restaurant owner. I'm not sold on the idea but you seem to know this business better than me."

"It'll be fine, Leonard," Dave assured. "This ad campaign, our battered and breaded products—"

"Oh! I'm sorry, Dave. Can I come back later and talk with you about that?" Leonard flipped his wrist to check the time. "I just remembered they're running some equipment in the plant…or should be about now. There's a problem and I want to see the machinery running."

Leonard pushed up from the chair. "If you see Larry, tell him I'll be back."

As he swung by his office to drop off his empty cup, Leonard walked by Chuck's empty desk. It just didn't feel the same since Chuck retired. He and Marge would stop over at the house, of course, and sometimes Chuck would come into the office just to visit, see how things were going. The two years since he has been out of the business still felt odd.

Setting his cup on the corner of the desk, Leonard walked toward the production section of the building, stopping briefly to comment to employees along the way.

Recently, his son Lee had been working on a project that would really take Sargento in a new direction—one that none of the competitors had been contemplating. Lee had negotiated with Zip-Pak to gain exclusive rights to place a reclosable feature on packages of Sargento shredded cheese. The patent owners admitted, with very little attempt to conceal otherwise, that Sargento earned this opportunity only after Kraft had declined.

As Leonard pushed through the plant doorway and strolled onto the production floor, the thrum of the equipment surrounded him. Off to the right stood a knot of men studying a machine as it ran. He recognized Lee Schweitzer, the plant manager, and Jerry Kraus, the primary engineer on the project.

"Morning," Leonard shouted above the rhythm of the machine. "How's she running?"

"We're still having problems with cheese in the seal," Lee shouted back.

When bits of cheese were trapped in the seal of the package, not only did it detract from the package's appearance, it dramatically increased the chance for the package to leak and the cheese to mold.

Leonard stood mesmerized, watching the machine as it cycled through the process of making one package of shredded cheese, then another and another. Bill Salzwedel, a recently hired maintenance manager, Lee, and Jerry gathered around Leonard as he stood and studied the machine in motion.

Over the pulsating motor, Leonard shouted, "Do you see the problem?"

He stabbed his finger in the direction of the opening and closing jaws of the equipment. A long pause followed with no response, so Leonard turned toward the three men and shouted above the noise once again, "Did you see what just happened?"

Then Leonard looked directly at Bill and repeated the question. Bill pushed his nose closer to the cyclical, herky-jerky movement of the equipment as the drumming of the machine fought to penetrate the earplugs he wore. Apparently with nothing of value to offer, he remained mute.

As Leonard watched the equipment repeatedly fill packages of cheese, he logged each minute step of the process in his mind. Moments passed as he hovered motionlessly near the machine, with the intensity of a cat studying it prey. Then suddenly he jabbed his finger in the air again, pointing at the object of his attention.

"There!" he shouted. The equipment cycled and another bag filled. "There!" He pointed a second time. "Do you see it?"

Again, Bill peered intently, but in vain, as mechanical jaws opened, closed, sealed, opened, closed, sealed. Bill looked uneasy and bent still closer toward the machine. No one seemed to see anything but Leonard.

"Here's what's happening," Leonard explained, interpreting Bill's continued silence. "As the cheese drops, it's not catching on the top of the bag. It's settling in the bag properly. That's good. That's what we want."

Bill slowly bobbed his head in silent agreement.

Leonard continued punctuating each step as it happened. "Watch the sealing jaws. The cheese drops down. The jaws come together to seal the bag. The bag seals. The knife cuts the film. The bag drops to the conveyor belt. You gotta watch carefully!"

They waited, immersed in the thrumming beat of the machine. "OK, those packages are fine," Leonard said as he stood stiff, eyes locked on the equipment. "Sometimes, the cheese clears the sealing area and it... Wait! That's it. Right there. As the jaws come together and air is forced out of the bag, fine bits of cheese are whooshing up just as the bag is sealed, causing the problem. It's not the cheese falling into the bag. It's the cheese rising up! There's our problem!"

Leonard looked at the assembly of men around him. "So how do we fix this thing? We need to get the air out of the bag. So how do we do that and still keep the cheese in the bag?"

As the machine continued to cycle, each tossed out ideas, but little swayed Leonard from his belief that culpability rested in the foam padding on the jaws. The stiff texture exacerbated the problem at higher speeds.

"I have an idea," shouted Leonard, and he left, promising to return with a possible solution.

Sargento introduces Zip-Pak packaging

At the age of seventy-three, Leonard's life-long interest in problem solving, machinery, and innovation had not diminished. More than most individuals, he could rapidly assemble seemingly unrelated facts, mentally shuffle the pieces, and arrive at a solution. It was a rare talent.

One year prior, Sargento had negotiated and signed the agreement with Zip-Pak and begun applying the reclosable zipper to the side of its packages. Print and television ads began proclaiming another industry first. Leonard took pride that the honor fell to Sargento.

When the reclosable bags reached stores, demand had immediately increased. Not since the installation of peg bars had Sargento experienced such a sudden spike in customer orders. But there were problems.

"It's great that we have a new convenient package for the consumer," Lou had mentioned to Leonard, "but that new package is causing our lines to run slower. That means it takes us more time to produce the same number of packages. That's raising our costs. We need to get our line speeds up."

Given its importance, a team of employees had been assigned the task of increasing product output. Leonard jumped into the fray as well. This was just the type of challenge that appealed to him.

After watching the machinery in operation, Leonard felt confident he could fix the problem. Hours after leaving the production floor, he returned with two foam violins—props from an earlier sales meeting. With a pocketknife, he scraped the stiff foam from the jaws of the sealing unit, replacing it with strips of foam he had sheared from the violin.

Confident that the test material would adhere long enough for a trial, Leonard signaled Jerry to restart the machine. The number of poor seals dropped immediately, but not to the level Leonard had hoped. "We need something that has some gaps in it. Kinda like an egg carton. You know...that kind of configuration."

Leonard stared in thought, mentally reviewing things he might own that fit the shape he held in his mind. Finally, he said, "I'll be back in a little while. Maybe tomorrow." And with that, Leonard left again.

The afternoon of the following day, Leonard returned with a section of foam and threw it on Lee Schweitzer's desk. "Let's give this a try," he said with enthusiasm. "Dolores is probably gonna be mad as hell when she finds out. I cut a section out of the middle of the mattress pad in the guest bedroom."

They walked out to the production line, shut it down, and replaced the foam on the jaws with a section of Leonard's mattress pad. To the amazement of everyone but Leonard, the padding immediately solved the cheese-in-the-seal problem. A section of a mattress pad! It was exactly the right firmness with the needed cavities to flush oxygen out of the package without stirring up the small pieces of cheese.

Just to be sure, Leonard lingered close to the line, watching as package after package traveled down the line for case packing. He wiggled his finger, drawing Bill over to the equipment. "Bill, I'm glad to have you at Sargento." Leonard leaned down to better communicate over the noise of the equipment. "Your mechanical education is just what we need around here." Leonard tapped his finger to his head. "Just remember, attention to the small details is just as important. Sometimes more important."

Finally satisfied the production line would consistently run at higher speeds without incurring product rejects, Leonard left in haste. Another pressing issue needed resolution. Before Dolores returned home, a new mattress pad would need to be purchased at the local Kmart.

Later that year, Leonard and Dolores sat in the waiting room of the hospital. He reached and grabbed his wife's hand to comfort her. Their firstborn, Butch, had suffered a second heart attack. This time far more severe than the one he had experienced three years earlier.

It had been a rough year for the Sargento Family. While on the road working, one of the salesmen, Len Grzeca, had also suffered a heart attack. Rushed to a nearby hospital, Len never walked back out of that building. He left behind a loving wife and fifteen children.

Out of respect for Len, Leonard and the Gentine family provided financial and moral support. Either Leonard or one of the Gentine family stopped by periodically to ensure Len's family had the resources to meet the challenges that lay ahead of them.

Now Butch lay in the hospital and the family prayed for a better outcome. Their interminable wait for the doctor's report kept them on edge.

Even when the doctor provided Butch's status and ushered the family into the recovery room, the emotional anguish failed to subside. Leonard threw his arm around Dolores as they stood at his bedside. Butch was weak, but he would recover.

This had been his second warning.

# 31

# A Day in a Life
# 1990

IN OCTOBER 1989, with Father Wayne Bittner presiding, Leonard and Dolores celebrated their fiftieth wedding anniversary. Friends, family, employees, and a few members of the original wedding party attended the services.

Not only did Leonard set an example for business protocol, but he and Dolores were living examples of a great marriage. Despite his fervent interest in Sargento, he left little question that his main love, first and foremost, was Dolores.

Just prior to the close of Mass that Sunday, Father Wayne invited Leonard and Dolores to the front of the altar. After they each renewed their vows, a lull settled over the service as the reverend waited.

"Leonard?" prompted Father.

Responding, Leonard arched his snow-white eyebrows and slowly lifted his head until his eyes met those of the priest.

Father Wayne smiled. "You may kiss the bride, Leonard."

As the couple embraced, a burst of applause and camera flashes filled the church proper, giving testament to the love Leonard and Dolores held for each other and their family.

Leonard and Dolores Gentine's fiftieth anniversary, Father Wayne
Bittner presiding

Even with the passage of fifty years, Leonard could recall the first
time he drove Dolores to his grandmother's farm. What an amazing
road they had traveled since then—a journey of trials, tears, and tri-
umphs. At that moment, surrounded by friends and family, he felt God
had kindly favored them with His blessings.

As long-term residents of Plymouth, Dolores earned the friendship of
many in town and Leonard earned a reputation as a venerable and experienced businessman—esteemed among his peers in the community
and the food industry. Presented with a vision, it was widely known,
Leonard could find a means to achieve nearly any goal, most frequently
through his talents and the talents of others.

He and those around him designed new products, new equipment, and new processes. Just recently, he'd overcome the hurdles of applying a reclosable zipper to a package of cheese. But there was one thing that stymied him: the tremor in his hand.

It had gotten worse. Recently, and more disturbing, other parts of his body had begun to present similar problems, forcing him to realize he was losing control of himself and his daily life.

Dr. Scott Peschke, Leonard's physician, confirmed that Leonard was suffering from the early stages of Parkinson's. It was nothing to mutter and complain about, Leonard thought. It was a disease. And what good would anger or resentment do? None.

As he did with anything in life, Leonard asked questions, undertook his own research on the subject, read about the disease, learned what he would expect in the months ahead. He understood how the disease would progress, eventually consuming him. As he prayed for a medical breakthrough, he contributed to Parkinson's research and, through his neurologist, Dr. Paul Nausieda, was the focus of a wildly successful fundraiser. But above all, he persevered. Each day was just another day in his life, doing what he loved best until he could no longer do so.

Leonard looked at his hands in his lap. Unconsciously, his index finger and thumb rubbed together. How odd, how strange to lose control, as if another force guided them. He could see the difference in the mirror and tried not to dwell on it. The muscles in his face had gone slack. He had a stooped appearance and a slower gait.

Family meant more to him than ever before, as if the disease had sharpened its importance. His wife, his children, his grandchildren, and his Sargento Family grew all the more valuable.

Instead of the varied activities of the past, life had evolved into a routine, a script to be followed. The restrictions were not that difficult to accept, he thought. In many ways, the routine brought a sense of comfort.

Each morning began with a warm breakfast, just him and Dolores. He'd pull a chair from the table and stiffly ease into it.

He looked at the plate of food and the cup of coffee before him, and it occurred to him that, while he'd spent his life watching over Dolores, she had always done the same for him. How fortunate he felt to have her in his life. Now, it was her habit to thoughtfully arrange each meal in a fashion to make it easier for him to eat. The coffee cup half full so it wouldn't slosh.

Looking up from the table, he could see the sorrow in Dolores's eyes. And yet she never fussed over his growing limitations. Never offered pity. Without seeking praise for doing so, she shouldered the small things to make his life easier.

It was more than serving soup in a cup so he wouldn't struggle transporting a spoon of liquid to his mouth. It was more than suggesting shoes or clothing that projected a professional appearance but offered ease in dressing. It was more than her thoughtfulness in supplying him with clean handkerchiefs, kept in his pants pocket to occasionally dab at the corner of his mouth when facial muscles failed him. These were selfless acts of love.

In every sense of the phrase, they were life partners. Best friends, husband and wife, confidantes. They both shouldered the joy and sorrow life unapologetically dished out. In so many ways, Dolores was his foundation and, indirectly, the foundation of Sargento. In the quiet of one of their breakfasts, over a cup of coffee and conversation, it occurred to him. It had been Dolores. It had been her unwavering support that had allowed him to achieve what he wanted out of life.

Following one leisurely breakfast, Leonard drove the short distance to work, swinging his Lincoln Town Car next to the cheese sculpture at the entrance of Sargento. He lifted his briefcase from the seat of the car and slowly walked into the building.

Off to the side of his desk, but still near his chair, Leonard kept a reminder of his days in the funeral business: a sturdy blue metal sign with white letters that said *Funeral Space*. Those days seemed so long ago and, at the same time, so recent.

Since his last visit to the office, a neat stack of papers had taken residency on one corner of his desk. Dominating the primary workspace, front and center, rested a freshly typed letter for his signature. Sandy Mahlich, the executive secretary, had prepared it for him that morning, expecting his eight thirty arrival.

Uneasy, Leonard shifted in his chair. He penned his name on the letter in a script that, he noticed, had grown smaller and tighter in recent years. As his tremoring hand fluttered the paper before him, he read several memos and an executive summary.

He grew restless. All that interested him lay outside the four walls of his office. The need to connect with others in the company tugged at him.

Reaching over, he grabbed his empty coffee mug and the signed letter. Slow but determined, he walked to the end of the short hallway to visit Lou. After handing the signed letter to Sandy and wishing her a good morning, he walked into Lou's office to find him and Larry engaged in conversation.

"Good morning, Dad," Larry said as he turned his head toward the office doorway.

"Larry was on the road with Dave Lorbecki," Lou said, "and was just telling me some of the opportunities we could have with one or more of our food service customers. Grab a seat." Lou pointed to the other empty chair in front of the desk. Leonard took it, carefully sliding his coffee cup on the edge of the desk.

Larry, slumped nonchalantly in his chair, threw one leg over the other and continued summarizing a few of the highlights from his customer visits. Leonard listened. As the conversation drew down, Leonard offered a suggestion. Then, using both hands on the arms of the chair, he pushed himself up, grabbed his empty coffee cup, and indicated his need to talk to Lee.

After launching Sargento Shredded Cheese in Zip-Pak packaging, Karl Linck—director of engineering—and his staff began development of an easy-open tear strip. Not only would Sargento packages be easy to close, they would be equally easy to open. No scissors needed. Leonard hadn't seen the new package design and believed it was important that he approve the look of the package.

Leonard's gait—not quite a shuffle—slowed his ability to move from office to office. Although he would celebrate his seventy-sixth birthday this year, he knew it was not age influencing his footsteps.

Only from word of mouth did most employees learn of Leonard's personal challenge. Long-term employees probably noted the decline, the increasing tremors, the way he crossed his arms tight across his chest or thrust his hands in his pockets to still them. Out of respect, he knew, they rarely made mention of it.

When Leonard arrived at Lee's office, he found it empty. So many offices seemed to be vacant, he thought. Back in the days when they worked out of the carriage house—even when they operated out of the tiny building in Elkhart Lake—he could find anyone he wanted. Talk with them. Find out everything that was happening.

Now everything was so complex. *Lee's probably in a meeting*, he imagined. He could stop by another time. Then he thought of Bob Peiffer in Creative Services. After all, Leonard reasoned, Bob would have designed the package graphics. His office was a short distance away.

With Bob also absent from his office, Leonard moved along to another opportunity. He would join the meeting in progress behind the closed Marketing conference room door. He had no inkling of the meeting's purpose, of course, but what better way to learn what was going on than to sit in a meeting?

As he entered the room, heads turned and smiled, but no one seemed surprised to see him come in. The conversation continued uninterrupted as Leonard found a seat along the lengthy conference table. He listened.

Dorothy Farrell, one of the new product managers, was delving into the details of a new line of children's snacks Sargento would be introducing. MooTown Snackers, the creative offspring of Lee Gentine, promoted cheese as a better nutritional choice for children. They offered refrigerated and nonrefrigerated cheese snacks—products that centered around the fictitious location of MooTown, USA, in advertising. Now, Sargento would provide a light version of those products, Dorothy explained.

Around the table, representing the Consumer Products Division, sat Bob Peiffer, Lee Gentine, Randy Winker, and Mike Gordy. That explained why many of the offices were empty, thought Leonard.

Without interrupting, Leonard lingered for twenty minutes, absorbing the gist of the details. Never speaking. Then, as discreetly as he'd entered the conference room, he left.

Sargento had recently negotiated the purchase of two companies with the intent of expanding the company's presence in grocery stores. Hernke Foods, located thirty-two miles north of Plymouth in Hilbert, Wisconsin, manufactured salsas, guacamole, and cheese sauces under the brand names Pablo's and Sonora Valley. The second company, located in Florida, also manufactured a broad line of ethnic foods—frozen and refrigerated.

Tom Needles—tall, with finely spun white hair—had served on the board of directors for Sargento over the past ten years. With the

Sargento nutritional snack cheese

acquisition of these two new companies, Tom agreed to serve as president of Sargento Specialty Foods Group, a new division at the company. His goal was to introduce these acquisitioned items into the deli department of grocery stores, giving Sargento presence in the dairy department and the deli.

As he left the conference room, Leonard decided to ask Tom for a brief business update.

"I thought I would stop by to see how you're doing," said Leonard as he set his empty cup on the desk and lowered into the office chair. "Getting the new division in shape?"

"It's taking some time," Tom admitted. "I keep reminding myself, Leonard, that success doesn't happen by luck. It's a result of hard work and insightful thinking."

Tom pulled a small collection of 3-by-5 index cards from his pocket. Never was Tom without his notes. In a way, it reminded Leonard of Bob Gilles, who, years before, wrote notes to himself on his apron and hat. The old ways were still the best.

"After adding Ron Richards as vice president of finance," began Tom, "I've been hiring salesmen. As my senior VP of sales, Dick Williamson has helped in filling out the team. We were fortunate enough to have offers accepted by"—Tom shuffled his dog-eared index cards— "John Bottomley and Steve Foerstner. A couple of guys I think will do a good job for us."

Leonard nodded. He would be sure to meet them both when they were in town and welcome them to the company.

"I brought Mark Donlan over from the New Products Department." Tom slid the index cards back in his pocket. "Already, he's working on product concepts for us."

Leonard looked at his watch. "Can you join me for lunch? You can tell me about the product ideas and what you're planning to get this business off the ground."

"I would but I have a meeting over lunch. Perhaps tomorrow or later this week?"

Leonard nodded agreement and went in search of another common lunch partner. This time he asked Tom Faley, one of the product managers.

Lunch was at their usual location, Silver Springs, a restaurant that Leonard's son Larry owned. Topics over the meal were predictable: one asking about Leonard's background and the history of the company, the other hoping to better understand the mechanics of marketing.

At the close of their lunch, Leonard suggested a short visit to a cheese company.

Rows of glass jars spun, bumping and thumping against each other as they traveled down the conveyor at the Tupper Cheese Company. Located behind the old A&P store, now the Piggly Wiggly, in Plymouth, JC's sons—Tom and Steve Tupper—carried on the family business.

"I've been thinking," Leonard said to Steve, quickly addressing the purpose of his visit. "You produced a line of cooked cheese for us a few years back. For some reason, we discontinued those items. We hired a couple of new marketing people." Waving to the person beside him, he continued, "Tom's one of the three we now have in the company. The market is probably right to reintroduce Sargento cooked cheese. Would you be interested in being our supplier again?"

"Absolutely," Steve replied as he grabbed an empty carton and filled it with a variety of samples. Handing the case of samples to Tom, he said, "These are a few of our best sellers. Let me know which ones you'd want to add. We'll work with you on label design."

As the two drove back to Sargento, Leonard turned and said, "Tom, I think some of those items would make a great addition to our price list. Talk to Lee. See what you can do."

Returning to Sargento, Leonard continued his routine, walking from office to office, finally catching up with Lee to study the easy-open package graphics. Leonard carefully read the wording, then reflected a moment. "I think the instructions should be bigger on the package. When you're standing in the cheese section of the store, you should be able to read it."

Lee studied the package artwork. "I can have them make it a little bigger. I'll ask for a couple of different sizes to see how that looks."

The day continued, meeting one person and then another until midafternoon when he would return home, tired. In the morning, if his body allowed, he would do it all again. Refusing to retire. Refusing to separate from what he held most dear: his family and Sargento.

# 32

# Recognitions and Honors Earned
## 1991

David Rufenacht presenting Leonard Gentine with the NCI Laureate Award

AT THE END of 1990, the National Cheese Institute (NCI) requested nominations for individuals who had significantly contributed to the cheese industry. Annually, at the Dairy Forum, that person would be honored with the industry's highest tribute—the NCI Laureate Award.

Well in advance of that April conference, the National Cheese Institute phoned Leonard. "A panel of industry professionals reviewed all the nominees, Leonard. They have chosen you, recognizing your long-term service to the industry."

Leonard was speechless.

Months later, at the Dairy Forum luncheon, Leonard sat with Dolores at his side, their children joining them at the table. The waitstaff took great pains to present the meal as conveniently as possible for Leonard. The water glass stood half full. The soup arrived in a coffee cup.

As the meal began, Leonard sipped the soup and quickly returned the cup to the table to avoid watching it vibrate. It occurred to him, perhaps not for the first time, but more clearly than in the past, that he had achieved what he set out to do. That this recognition was proof he was approaching the finish line. Success had extracted a stiff price from him. Decades of his life in exchange for a business—his long-sought-after generational business.

He thought of his grandfather and his grandmother. How proud they would have been. Of his father's pride and of his mother, who labored to make his businesses a success. How he would have loved to see their faces this day. To share the moment with them, too.

He speared cooked vegetables onto his fork from his plate as he studied his children around the table. From his oldest to his youngest, they were here: each in a sanguine mood; each laughing, sharing stories; each beaming with pride. Together, they sat as a family, united. A deep sense of satisfaction rose from that thought.

Across the table, he watched Butch throw back his head and laugh. Leonard had always regretted the moment Butch left the company. Not that he would force any of his children to be a part of Sargento. His decision to leave hadn't bothered him. It was the circumstances that had led to his leaving.

He and Butch shared a history of seeing life just a bit differently. More times, it ended in verbal blows, blows that scarred them both. It had always bothered him. When he had mentioned the consultant's recommendation for succession, could he have presented it to him differently? Made an alternative suggestion, perhaps, or arrived at a compromise?

It's one thing when a child has no interest in the business. It's another when they have a driving passion to be a part and still they leave. He had always looked back at that moment, second-guessing what he should have done, what he should have said. He blamed himself for what had happened.

Butch helped build Sargento from its early beginnings. Perhaps, in the future, Butch would reconsider. Even today, Butch directed business to Sargento. Just as he had merged Central Wrap and Sargento, could there be another merger in the years ahead?

As the waitstaff cleared their plates and distributed the dessert, David Rufenacht, representing the NCI, approached the podium. From a prepared speech, he read through the litany of innovations and industry firsts stemming from Leonard's passion for the cheese industry.

He made note of Leonard's leadership in forming the Wisconsin Cheese Seminar, now called the International Dairy Deli Bakery Association. In 1965, David noted, Leonard and ten other "dairy apostles" visited cheese countries in other parts of the world, hoping to extend American products abroad.

Then David spoke of the qualities of the man honored: his personal values and his loyalty to his employees, his community, his suppliers, and his customers. This year's recipient, David affirmed, was a strong family man with sons following his footsteps into the cheese industry.

At the conclusion of David's introduction, a gaunt and unpretentious Leonard Gentine walked to the podium to accept the wood-carved award and share his prepared remarks. Looking about the room, he recognized nearly everyone. Men from other cheese companies he had grown to know. Men who now were lifelong friends. He felt humbled. Below at the front table sat his children—his family. Among them, smiling up at him, sat Dolores. Emotions pulled at him as a lump formed in his throat.

"Thank you for this honor," he said, his voice faltering. "I want to especially thank my friends here today and the many others that made so many achievements possible over the years."

Again, he looked at his family and then spoke from his heart. "I've always believed one man cannot start and continue a business alone. It took the support of my family...my children and my wife, Dolores...who always believed in me. Who shared my vision. And it took people—people willing to remain year after year. To do that, to have people support you for years...for decades...you must treat them as if they are your own sons and daughters...because, in a real sense, that's exactly who they are."

Leonard reminisced with a story from his past, thanked the National Cheese Institute for this recognition, and slowly left the podium, returning to his seat with his family. As the audience extended a second standing ovation, David carried the wood-carved recognition for Leonard from the podium and placed it on his table.

It was an appropriate keystone to a life dedicated to cheese—a product about which he humorously admitted when recalling the company's start in 1953, "I knew very little about cheese, except that I liked to

Butch, Larry, Ann, Lou, Lee, Dolores, and Leonard Gentine

eat it." His passion for cheese and, of greater note, his passion for people drove innovation and convenience in an otherwise commodity-driven category.

Following the ceremony, a photographer memorialized the occasion, gathering Leonard, Dolores, and their family in a corner of the room for a photo. This photo would later be remembered as one of the last formal pictures of the family. Before the year would end, health issues and a sudden death would leave the family with a sizable void.

Leonard woke up early the next morning, before the sun rose, before Dolores awoke. For an hour, he lay in bed. At first, he listened to the slow steady rhythm of Dolores sleeping. It comforted him. But soon afterward, he listened to the thoughts as they formed in the predawn darkness of the bedroom.

It was that fragile moment between sleeping and waking—that diaphanous border—which Leonard had always enjoyed and had learned to prolong. A malleable, flexible—yet fleeting—time when thoughts were clearer and ideas freely approached him.

Once again, he reflected on the path he had taken in life—that part of the race between the starting line and the finish line. Crossing the line, ending the race, promised a feeling of exhilaration, yet the ending point was so elusive. What is a finish line if not just a marker on an ever-lengthening path? Who can say they ever reach the end far before they take their last breath? New things pop up on the horizon, and there's always the urge to go see what they are all about, where they will lead.

More important than the end, he realized, was the space between the two lines. It's the experiences in the middle that subtly carve away the detritus, as a sculptor might do, leaving behind the true character of the person. It's those events along the way that define who we are and who we become.

Now, in the dark silence of the bedroom, he wondered if, with the passage of years, his long-term goal had somehow been recast. Did his long-term vision change?

No, he considered, leaving behind a family-owned company remained important. He would have to say that was still true. But the trials, the successes, the failures shaped far more than a company in the end. Those experiences, he realized, shaped *him*. He was different today. Not just physically, but inside there had been a change, too.

Treating others like family, that's not just a way of doing business. It's being human. It's always been the right thing to do. To respect others. To hear their thoughts. To recognize their individual worth. Not for the sake of making money, not for the purpose of building a business, but for the sake of acting with humanity.

Any company could voice a belief that everybody matters. But if the intent isn't sincere, there's no credibility, no trust. It's just the wind blowing in one direction, shifting over time with everyone shoving an index finger skyward to see which way the current is flowing that day.

The true test is not found in the *promise* of a culture of mutual respect and inclusion. It begins to manifest itself only when everyone in the company sincerely, consistently *experiences* it. And yet it occurred to him as he lay in bed that this was not the complete level of success. The true strength is when others exhibit the same sense of honest appreciation and respect in return.

When the admiration flows in *both* direction, when there is an *inter*dependency, a wind blows back in equal force, scribing a circular motion that feeds upon itself. It is then that the impossible becomes possible. It is then that any hurdle in the path is vanquished. It is then that a company gives birth to a sustained, intergenerational culture.

His life's greatest achievement, he thought, was not just a cheese company. Rather, his legacy was a corporate culture, one in which *he* was treated like family in return. He was the familial head, but his inverted role was to serve others, not the other way around. It was that that had made all the difference.

He felt a warm sense of peace and pride rush over him.

In his youth, his parents and grandparents had instilled a deeply ingrained belief: Live your life in such a way that others would be glad you were born. They spoke of their faith in God, of principles and values—not just venerated weekly in church, but lived in the moment as a testimony of character. The same spiritual values he'd infused in Sargento.

He thought—he believed—he had lived up to those expectations. Yet there was more. More things he could do. More things he wanted to do. And he would, he vowed to himself.

He closed his eyes, comforted, and fell back asleep.

# 33

# The Cheese Industry Mourns a Loss
## 1991

MANY, HEARING THE news of his death, flew in from all parts of the country and the globe. Industry leaders and business associates, people he'd met while traveling, converged on Plymouth, Wisconsin. The prior night, at the funeral home, a line of mourners extended a block down the street as each waited in the snowstorm to enter the building and pay their respects.

The next day, St. John the Baptist Church, perched atop a large hill overlooking Plymouth, offered enough pews for twelve hundred people.

Despite the blustery day in December, the church—and even its large-windowed "crying room"—sandwiched people shoulder to shoulder, crammed into solemn pews, compressing thick winter coats between them. Before the funeral Mass began, people unable to squeeze into a pew stood along the walls and at the back, as if proud to demonstrate their respect in this manner.

As a few of the designated pallbearers, the Gentine brothers gathered along the burnished wood casket in the church vestibule. Then, at the appointed hour, Father Wayne Bittner began the procession as the pallbearers wheeled the casket to the nave of the church. Following the sprinkling of holy water, a white pall draped the casket as a heavy silence draped the congregation.

On the altar stood an enormous flocked Christmas tree—the tree that had decorated his home for the upcoming season. The family had lugged it into the church earlier that day for the service. Symbolically, its sheer mass represented the man who had loomed larger than life as well.

Seated in the front pew was Dolores, stoically holding Leonard's arm. Through the years in which Leonard had served as the director of the Gentine funeral home in Plymouth, he witnessed, and was moved by, many emotional funerals—deaths of friends and those who had worked with him at Sargento. Even the death of his father, Louis, and his mother, Anna, failed to prepare him for the deep loss he felt this day.

Butch's death and its finality fell hard on Leonard, and its impact frequently drove him into a catatonic silence so profound that neither Dolores nor his family could fully shake him from its depth. It left him empty, and he had crawled into that lonely emptiness.

No longer could be seen that spark of energy he held in the past for those things that defined him, that fueled his passion. No longer did Leonard choose to go into the office, talk with his Sargento Family, or wander among the equipment that fascinated him.

He felt numb. The loss so deep, so painful. All he could hear were the arguments, the past disagreements, the head-butting between him and his son. He would give anything—anything—to take back those moments.

As the loss of his son tore at his heart, he now wished for the opportunity to tell Butch so many things. He had always believed that Butch's indefatigable drive stemmed from his son's need to prove himself to his family, to show he could be a success on his own without the shadow of Sargento, no longer under the wing of his father. Leonard longed for the ability to tell Butch how proud he was of his son's success. Of what he had accomplished.

Now everything was irreversible. He had lost a son from his business and yet held hope that Butch would one day return. Now he had lost his son. Again. This time, forever. With the onslaught of his crippling Parkinson's, this was just…too…much…to shoulder.

At one point, Larry tried to reach him, to make him see the positive, perhaps. "Dad, you lost a son. We will all miss him. Just remember, you still have four other children. Try to focus on them."

Dolores and the other children encouraged him to see the blessings that remained. But they didn't understand. How could they ever understand what losing Butch meant? The finality. The unresolved issues.

The chill of the December weather, even though just a few days into the month, did little to lift the severity of the loss. Butch had suffered his third heart attack. News of his critical condition had driven the entire Gentine family into the hospital room.

Leonard and Dolores were wintering in Florida when they received the phone call. Hours later, via a private plane arranged by their children, they joined the rest of the family in the intensive care room with their unconscious son.

Although Butch was in a coma—one that he would never come out of—the family took turns sitting at his bedside, talking to him. Since the brain is the last organ to shut down, each member poured out their love for him, spoke of the influence he had on their life. Tears traced down faces. Each poured out their love for the man who touched their lives and left an indelible print.

Perhaps it was the stress from the life Butch preferred to live, pushing his heart beyond its limit, burning the candle at both ends and in the middle as well.

Some suggested it was the stress of business. Over the years, Butch had leveraged his bulk cheese–trading business into a new company, renaming it Masters Gallery Foods—a company that packaged cheese products for a variety of retailers under the store's name. Building on Leonard's original idea behind Central Wrap, Butch had pushed the opportunity further and wider with Masters Gallery.

In addition, Masters Gallery supplied cheese to Healthy Choice, Beatrice Cheese, Land O'Lakes, and other large manufacturers.

Butch Gentine

Butch had just invested in a plant expansion to accommodate the anticipated growth of his customers and spent another million dollars for additional manufacturing equipment. But shortly after Butch's company poured cash into those investments, a couple of his larger customers started sourcing their cheese from a competitor.

That business loss layered stress onto an already stressful life. It was the confluence of those ill-timed events married to a detrimental life-style that drowned Butch in their wake.

Father Wayne looked over the standing-room-only crowd, as if struck by the volume of people. He bowed his head as he began the opening prayer. The solemnity was palpable.

Butch left behind his own legacy. Unique unto himself, he filled any room he entered. His home was filled with the souvenirs from countries he'd visited, including a table made from a hollowed tree with carved vines and leaves, a set of wooden carousel horses—three of them—complete with their poles reaching floor to ceiling, canvas art, and other treasures enough to accent his substantial home on the lake. But more than filling a room with his presence or his home with interesting objects, Butch had filled the lives of everyone he met.

As the Mass concluded, Lou delivered a eulogy, honoring the life of his brother. Spatters of humor lightened the somber mood. These stories shared by Lou, of course, were small fragments of the joy Butch unabashedly added to the lives of those he met. As the congregation listened to Lou's anecdotes, each one seated that day could have contributed their own individual stories—experiences that would layer one over the other, capturing the depth of Butch's humor never fully defining his character.

There was the time Butch pretended to have a peg leg, asking those around him to help him move his leg as he walked. Or the frequent times that he claimed that there was so little room in the house when he was born that his father, the funeral director in town, put him to bed each night in a small casket. Or the time Butch, lofting a drum major's baton high into the air, led a marching band through a hotel lobby. Butch's humor was boundless.

As a fitting honor to Butch, at the end of the Mass Father Wayne stretched his arms to the heavens and, looking up as if speaking humorously to the Creator, said, "Lord…here comes Butch! Heaven will never be the same!"

So large the life he led. So large the shadow he cast. So large the void he left behind.

For those whom Butch would never befriend—who would never know his personality—his family commissioned the following quote inscribed on his tombstone:

I am of the opinion that my life belongs to the whole community and as long as I live, it is my privilege to do for it whatever I can. I want to be thoroughly used up when I die. For the harder I work, the more I live. I rejoice in life for its own sake. Life is no brief candle to me. It is a sort of splendid torch which I have got hold of for the moment, and I want to make it burn as brightly as I can before handing it on to future generations.

—George Bernard Shaw

# 34

## Giving Back
### 1992–1993

The SECAP Singers

THE BEARD WAS scraggly. Near Saint Nick's ears, small elastic bands offered evidence that the real Santa Claus still labored at the North Pole, preparing for his delivery on Christmas Eve.

The nursing home residents easily looked past the charade.

As Santa gave each resident a small stocking containing a minia-ture flashlight, a candy cane, and a stick of Sargento String Cheese, he struck up short conversations. To one resident, he bemoaned the cold weather at the North Pole. To another, he glibly mentioned the challenges related to the care and feeding of reindeer, and to still another, he pointed out the difficulty in balancing his sleigh on pointed roofs.

It was all part of a corporate outreach program Ron Begalke had proposed earlier that year. He called it SECAP: **S**argento **E**mployees **C**aring **A**bout **P**eople.

"Actually, Kathy Arbuckle in Food Service suggested the name," he told Lou. "There will be two SECAP groups. One will focus on feeding the poor in Milwaukee at St. Ben's Meal Program. The second group will sing for local nursing homes. It's all volunteer. All after-work hours."

Sheboygan County nursing homes warmed to Ron's idea, with residents welcoming the entertainment, the holiday spirit, and—especially—the attention given to them. Confined to wheelchairs, over forty residents of the Rocky Knoll Health Care Center sang "Rudolph the Red-Nosed Reindeer" with the Sargento SECAP Singers as Santa distributed those stockings and each smiled into his face as if they were a small child again.

Sporting the SECAP white sweater and red turtleneck, Lou and his wife, Michele, as well as Eddie Sturzl and his wife, Ann, joined the other singers that night in December. They had also attended other performances as their schedules permitted. Between Thanksgiving and Christmas, the SECAP Singers brought the Christmas spirit to nine nursing homes in the county.

The eyes of most residents followed Santa as he walked through the audience. President of the Consumer Products Division, Mike Gordy, infused his gregarious personality into Santa. Without question, his arrival at each performance climaxed the entertainment.

Announcing that everyone in the room—apart from a couple of

SECAP Singers, he humorously added—was on his good list, Santa left to rescue his sleigh from being double parked.

As Santa and his chorus of seventy-five employees and their family members offered presents at nursing homes, Sargento had been gifted with a successful year as they approached the end of December. Sales had broken the $300 million mark for the first time in the company's history. Of greater significance, profits had widened, adding to the financial stability of the company.

But it was not all about the bottom line. When a company is blessed with good fortune, its character is revealed by the stewardship of that blessing. Many of the dollars would find their way into the development of innovative products for consumers. Other funds would be spent to improve their equipment, hire additional employees, and reward existing ones. Just as important, their success would be shared with the community as well—giving back.

St. Ben's had been a successful outreach. Sargento supplied the ingredients for the sloppy joes—including the cheese, naturally. Employees cooked the meals and contributed desserts they made at home. Once a month, a different department in the company placed the meal on trays for those less fortunate as they walked through the food line.

Lou had signaled his approval to pursue the SECAP initiative, and the results had been rewarding its first year.

Following in his father's footsteps, Lou continued to see that Sargento also supported the community in other ways: sponsoring cancer drives and local festivals and donating to local food pantries. The previous summer, trying something new, he announced the company's first year of participation in Habitat for Humanity. The homes Sargento helped build were in Milwaukee—a nod to the community where Leonard lived as a boy.

For four days, Sargento executives swung hammers, operated circular saws, and hoisted exterior walls into place. They hung drywall, laid plywood, and built rooms. They were the first southeastern Wisconsin corporation to "blitz build" two new Habitat homes.

The experience not only built two homes, giving a family a hand up, but also built camaraderie and strengthened the executive team. Lou vowed to build another home the following year. However, next time, he would offer the opportunity to all employees.

Even in the earlier years of the company, before Sargento could afford to do so, Leonard had made it his responsibility to give back, playing a highly active role in both the church and the community. A philosophy, a fervent belief that if a company and its employees have the ability, they have the responsibility to lend muscle and heart to others.

As the company's CEO, Lou had every intention of maintaining that philosophy.

# 35

# Sargento Mourns Once More
# 1993

A PARENT NEVER recovers from the death of a child. Leonard continued to bear the burden of that loss as best he could, fighting back against the emotional anguish, focusing more on the future and less on that which had passed.

With the passing of an additional two years, with the slow erosion of health, Leonard realized that age—he would be turning seventy-nine this year—coupled with his degenerative disease limited his presence at Sargento. Slowly, he foresaw life as a growing dependency, relying heavily on his children.

Understanding the looming downside of the progressive disease, his sons asked Leonard to consider recording an oral history of Sargento. Leonard promised to give the idea some thought. Several weeks later, donning his light blue sports coat, he sat, unscripted, before a video camera in his Sargento office.

Parkinson's made the filming uncomfortable, forcing him to shift in his chair at frequent intervals. He felt his upper body quiver, not dramatically, he thought, but a continual, slightly noticeable vibration. Pushing aside any self-consciousness, he focused on telling the story until it all became so overwhelming, at one point, that he put his hand to his forehead and requested a break. With an occasional retake and editing, the film became the only historical video with Leonard documenting the birth of Sargento.

Life grew more challenging each day. His memory, while still sharp, was not what it used to be. Ideas didn't flow to him as fluidly. More than in the past, he found it difficult to sleep at night or stay asleep. During the day, it was the opposite. If he remained inactive for too long, drowsiness overtook him. He adjusted the best he could.

Normally, over the winter, Leonard and Dolores vacationed in their condo in Florida. But in February, a phone call changed that. Reminiscent of two years earlier, when they returned to be at Butch's side, they flew back to attend another funeral for a close member of the family.

Chuck Strobel had retired from Sargento in 1985 and, since that time, had served on the company's board of directors, providing direction for the company. As Chuck began experiencing health issues, his doctor advised bypass heart surgery. After discussing it with his family, Chuck scheduled the operation for Saturday, February 13.

The operation went as expected. The recovery did not. Following the surgery, Chuck suffered a stroke. He never recovered.

When Leonard and Dolores arrived at the funeral home, they found a long line of grieving friends. *What a nice tribute to Chuck*, Leonard thought. Out of the kindness of others waiting at the front of the line, they were able to quickly talk to the family. Dolores hugged her sister, Marge, and promised to help her through this in any way she could.

For Leonard's benefit, Dolores found nearby empty chairs, relieving them from a long stretch of standing. Their proximity also allowed them the benefit of remaining somewhat close. Dolores wanted the ability to be emotionally supportive.

Chuck Strobel

Although little compares to the loss of a child, Chuck's death was yet another blow. Leonard grew up as an only child. But if he could have had his pick for a brother, he would have requested Chuck.

Almost from the beginning, Chuck had served at Leonard's side. He shared the rare fortunes and many disappointments as the two of them struggled through a string of businesses, starting with the funeral home and ending with Sargento. For every business in between, Chuck remained an advisor, a business partner, a friend.

He'd first met Chuck as a shy young man just out of high school. His former teacher brought Chuck to him because she thought Chuck would end up like so many others in the community, working for a cheese company. Ironically, that's what had happened despite her best effort. Chuck did have his heart set on being a mortician like his grandfather, Leonard remembered.

Still, were it not for his brother-in-law, Sargento may have turned out slightly different. On occasion, it was Chuck who opposed some of Leonard's decisions. It was Chuck, most likely due to his comfortable relationship, who had the strength to say "No" when Leonard adamantly said "Yes." And it was Leonard who said "No" on occasions when Chuck firmly said "Yes." They balanced each other.

"It's very sad," came a voice breaking Leonard's thoughts. He had not noticed that Bob Unger had taken the seat next to him.

Leonard turned and merely nodded. Leonard didn't have the heart for a lengthy conversation.

Bob leaned around Leonard to better see Dolores. "My condolences to both of you."

Dolores offered a faint smile with her thanks.

"Chuck's interest in antiques gave us plenty of things to talk about when he regularly stopped by my shop for a haircut. We both collected shaving mugs and shaving brushes. He liked the collection I have on display."

"He loved antiques," Leonard agreed.

Bob looked straight ahead as if seeing events of the past. Then he lowered his head and sighed. "Chuck was a good friend."

Lacing his fingers and dropping them to his lap, Bob continued talking, as much to himself as to Leonard and Dolores. "Last Friday, the day before his surgery, Chuck stopped by and asked me to give him a haircut. Just a trim. Said he just came from Sargento and talked with all of his old friends there. People in the office. People in the plant. Spent a good part of the day there, he told me."

"Chuck had a lot of friends in town and at the company," Dolores offered. "He was well liked."

"Yes." Bob nodded his head, still staring straight ahead. "People liked him. As I'm giving him his haircut, he tells me that he is nervous about the heart surgery." He shook his head as if he were trying to wave away the memory. "Nothing to worry about, I told him. This day and age, bypass surgery is a routine procedure. Now, a couple of decades ago, it would be serious. But today's medicine...they got things figured out."

Bob turned and looked at Leonard and Dolores. "Told him I expected him back in a couple of weeks for his next haircut. I could use the business. I made him smile."

"No one could have expected this," said Dolores as she reached over and patted his arm.

"All the same, his family lost a great husband and father." Bob paused, pressed his lips into a straight line as if they could hold back the emotions inside. "And we lost a good friend."

With that, Bob stood and left with his wife, Elizabeth.

Leonard shifted in his seat to find a more comfortable position, watching the line of people pass before the Strobel family. Dennis and Joan Butters smiled in his direction as they drew closer. Dennis, Leonard remembered, was one of the Sargento employees who helped him organize a team of men each spring for the controlled fire at La Ferme—farmland he had purchased years ago. Since then, they had been subdividing that land and building homes.

The annual field burning killed the old growth and weeds, allowing the new seeds to better take root. In a few months, Lee would be coordinating that burn again. Clearing the land. The old making way for the new.

He thought of the many people he had known and who had now passed away. The old making way for the new. The next generation was taking root as the prior generation faded away.

Chuck was seventy. *Too young*, thought Leonard. Then he wondered how many years he had remaining.

# 36

# Industry Leadership
# 1994–1996

PARKINSON'S DISEASE EVENTUALLY reduced, and then eliminated, Leonard's ability to visit the company he loved. With the inexorable onslaught of his physical affliction, muscles and functions regressed, slowly at first, then at a disheartening pace. He remained home, or in earlier years, if he could tolerate the travel, he wintered at his condo in Florida. Captive inside his shrinking world.

Following his father's earlier example for keeping life in balance, and in lockstep with his brothers and sister, Lou adroitly pursued two lives: a public life as he presided over the growth of Sargento and a private life with family and an ailing father.

By 1994, Lou reorganized the company, changing it from Sargento Cheese Company to Sargento Foods Inc. with only two divisions: the Consumer Products Division and the Food Service Division. Salsas, guacamole, and other ethnic foods, along with the focus to uncover a foothold in the deli departments in grocery stores, diminished in importance as the Specialty Foods Division was dissolved.

That same year, a more visible, outward change also occurred: the company logo.

In Lou's office, Lee Gentine shared the top line results from a recent consumer research study. "Consumers are seeing Sargento as a different type of cheese company than our competitors." Lee slid the report's summary page to Lou. "Here are some of the ways they describe us. A company that has European roots. Better-quality products. A company most likely to pay attention to details."

Lou didn't respond at first, taking the time to consider the ramifications of the research study. "Interesting," he said at last. "European roots? Well, our heritage does go back to France. Maybe this is one more indication that we need to refresh our logo and packaging. Use them to better communicate how consumers actually see our products."

Toward that end, by the close of 1994, packages appearing in stores replaced the old logo depicting a small farm scene and the words *of Wisconsin* with a sleeker logo, bearing a pair of golden swooshes that graced—top and bottom—the name *Sargento*.

The somewhat surprising consumer research in 1994 could be traced back, in part, to the efforts of many, but in particular, Don Cripe, a man the company hired in 1989 to head the small Quality Assurance Department.

Not one to languish behind a desk, Don would tuck his stack of overhead slides, mounted in white plastic frames, under his arm and, with the fervent passion of an evangelist, attend department and plant meetings, proposing his culture of quality. Presentation after presentation, repeating the same message, he outlined the tools, an unfamiliar language, and a vision for every department and production team.

"Quality is not a department," Don Cripe asserted. "Quality is everyone's responsibility, not just the responsibility of a select few. You and everything you do affect the quality of our products."

Slowly, Don introduced new terms—and sometimes abstract ideas—into the daily conversation: GMPs (Good Manufacturing Practices),

HACCP (Hazard Analysis/Critical Control Points), SPC (Statistical Process Control), competitive benchmarking, Pareto charting, histograms, x-bar and R charts, scatter diagrams, attribute charts, six-sigma quality, and QC (Quality Circles).

It was enough to cause heads to swim! Not only did Don conduct recurring meetings to define these concepts—describing their underlying value in commonplace language, explaining how to implement them—he published articles in the company newsletter and invested hours—and years—in follow-up meetings and training.

Department by department, Don led his crusade in favor of ever higher levels of performance—an upward spiral on the way to an unreachable perfection. His battle cry was clear: "Our goal is to allow only 3.4 defective packages for every million packages produced."

It was a lofty goal. Even the most recognized companies rarely reached that level of quality.

Karl Linck, vice president of engineering, and Lee McCollum, plant manager, also contributed to Don's aspiring target. Stealthily, after months of manufacturing trials and tweaking, they walked deep into the new Fond du Lac, Wisconsin, facility to witness the start-up of the new state-of-the-art equipment. Lou joined them that day.

Garbed in white protective lab coats and wearing white netting on their heads, the three men stood before the equipment that, for so long, had been deemed a highly confidential project. In a rhythm bearing the cadence of a rapid heartbeat, film cycled below the throat of the equipment as a precisely timed shower of shredded cheese filled each open package.

"The speed is amazing," shouted Lee over the syncopated beat of the machine. "We're getting ten times the number of packages produced per hour as we do on the current equipment."

"No other major cheese company is doing this," Karl pointed out to

Lou. "We've tinkered with this idea and then with the equipment for years. But now, you can see, we're ready to phase in this new version of machinery."

Lou gave his approval. Methodically, they would decommission all the current package-filling equipment, replacing them with the new machines that moved packages through the filling area horizontally instead of vertically. That change not only increased output, but also increased the package quality, substantially reducing zipper and packaging film waste.

As Sargento rolled out its new equipment and new package, the entire shredded cheese industry took immediate notice. Although competitors longed to equally benefit from this innovation, the custom-designed machines were proprietary to Sargento. Eventually, other shredded cheese companies engineered similar equipment, resulting in a near 100 percent replacement of the old shredded cheese packaging technology across all major cheese companies.

Although Sargento remained short of market-share leadership in shredded cheese, judging by the reaction of other cheese companies to the new package redesign and manufacturing process that occurred at Sargento, it was now becoming obvious which company was leading the industry and which companies were followers.

By 1995, Leonard's Parkinson's disease was unrelenting. In the middle of the night, in response to involuntary muscle control, he would toss himself to the floor, unable to return to the bed on his own or with Dolores's aid.

Their daughter, Ann, lived near and was called at odd hours of the night to stop over to help her father. Fortunately, Dr. Peschke also lived close by and would drive to the Gentine home, at any hour, to help. At one point, the doctor fashioned a railing from his child's bed to prevent Leonard from tumbling to the floor.

However, the Sargento Family was sheltered from many, if not all, of these distressful occurrences.

True to Leonard's values, he dealt with his affliction each day with the courage he had shown his entire life. That courage and his unflagging determination inspired his children, his grandchildren, and those close friends who consistently inquired after his health.

A hospital bed with side rails eventually replaced his bed. Twenty-four-hour care watched over Leonard, helping him with his medicine and daily needs. The stress on Dolores grew as her life and her relationship with her husband changed. The presence of other individuals in her home providing round-the-clock aid became a source of stress for her. Feelings of helplessness filled her as she watched Leonard struggle with sundown syndrome, causing him restlessness, disorientation, and agitation in the evenings.

Eventually, it became apparent to the family that Leonard would no longer be able to remain at home. The local nursing home, Rocky Knoll, found a room for him, and faithfully, Dolores visited him every day.

As Leonard continued his decline, the Gentine family sheltered the Sargento Family from Leonard's weakening condition. True to the way Leonard, and now his sons, chose to separate business from home life, each was able to compartmentalize life, respectfully balancing the concerns of both worlds.

As best they could, they kept Leonard comfortable and pain-free. With family gathered around his hospital bed one weekend afternoon, the television in Leonard's room aired a championship golf game, providing a soft backdrop to their visit. As the golfers attempted to finish their round, a sudden cloudburst rolled in, causing spectator umbrellas to pop open and the golfers to scamper for temporary shelter.

Noticing that activity, Leonard turned to Larry. "Bring the car around for your mother. It's starting to rain outside."

"Dad," Larry assured him, "that's on TV. Look outside. The sun is shining."

With more conviction in his voice, Leonard repeated, "I said bring the car around. I don't want your mother to get wet."

Larry looked at his mother and then back at his dad. "OK, Dad. I'll bring the car around."

Unsympathetic to the number of lives one man affected, uncaring for the impact he had on the food industry, unaffected by the means by which a man lives his life based on principles, Parkinson's first stole Leonard's ability to walk and build a better world with his hands.

Now, it chose to strip away the brilliant mind that had forever changed the trajectory of the lives around him.

Leonard resided at Rocky Knoll for six months before being transferred to Plymouth Hospital. He would speak in whispers of the family, of the grandchildren he loved. And in those six months, his family shared their love in many forms. When the need arose, Dolores gently wiped his brow with a cool washcloth. His daughter spooned pudding into his mouth. They held his hand; they shared their favorite memories. They helped him remember or understand the small things that confused him.

One day, Tony, Lou's oldest son, and his wife, Mary, brought Maggie to the nursing home. Their daughter was nine days old. As in other visits, Leonard was conscious but somewhat disconnected from his world.

"Dad," Lou said to his father lying in his bed, "Tony and Mary are here."

Shallow breaths followed but no response.

Gently, Mary laid Maggie on Leonard's shoulder. Leonard stared ahead, unmoving, and took another shallow breath.

"This is your great-granddaughter," Mary said. "Your first great-grandchild."

A small tear formed in the corner of his eye. He offered only a faint smile followed by a slight sigh.

In the early hours the next morning, Leonard passed away in peace.

# 37

# An Era Ends, a Future Defined
## 1996

THE BONE-WHITE church crowning one of the town's highest elevations stood like a beacon under the late-morning sun, its August beams reflecting from the building.

More than an hour before Mass—with the three overburdened parking lots—drivers not anticipating the large attendance at St. John the Baptist Church framed curbs for several blocks in all directions. Those fortunate to find parking on level ground enjoyed a comfortable walk. The remaining traffic claimed less-desirable spots two blocks away at the base of the steep hill.

Flanking the nave, men and women, wearing somber tones of brown, black, and gray, were uncomfortably wedged shoulder to shoulder, maximizing seating in the pews. Ushers, unprepared for the exceptional turnout, hastily unfolded chairs in the back corners and along the wall fronting the "crying room." Those arriving minutes before the funeral—those that may have parked their cars at some distance—stood along the side walls.

In his violet vestments, Celebrant Father Wayne Bittner stood in solemn posture as he greeted those walking into the church vestibule.

Pallbearers, awaiting the beginning of the ceremony, wore placid faces, a few shifting from foot to foot or unconsciously buttoning and unbuttoning their suit coats. Gathered in small clusters of soft-spoken voices, they occasionally splintered from their group to greet a friend or relative.

The family chose six men from Sargento (Dick Staples, Norman "Bud" Dick, Jerry Kraus, Mike Gordy, George Hoff, and Ron Begalke) to serve as pallbearers. Ten other individuals, drawn from friendships, held the honorary title. Included in the latter was Leonard's closest friend, Joe Sartori.

At the appointed hour, Father Wayne led the casket and pallbearers toward the altar. The celebration of his life involved his children and grandchildren. Lou and Larry read the first and second readings, respectively, from Leonard's 1938 missalette. Grandchildren read prayer petitions.

Recognizing his friendship as well as his vocal abilities, the family asked Father Wayne to sing, toward the end of Mass, the verses from "Here I Am, Lord." In doing so, he couldn't help but look upon the sea of faces that painted the congregation before him—a dappled pointillism of emotions, coalescing into a single longing for the man they had lost in their lives. Tears welled in the eyes of burly men. Others bore their loss as ponds of still water, breathing slowly, not wishing to agitate the surface.

Funerals are for the living, to console and support the family, Leonard frequently advised. They are not to bemoan the loss of a loved one. Honoring that belief, at the end of Mass, Lee painted his reflections of his father with splashes of humor.

It was, after all, a celebration of an amazing life. Because he chose to pass this way, because he was willing to take life's blows, to suffer defeats and to dismiss all setbacks, because he refused to offer less than his full self, Leonard made a difference in the lives of people who knew him. The momentum he fostered in others would rush onward, unhindered by his passing. A wave of influence that would wash, unchecked, across decades following his death.

Concluding the Mass, the family trailed the pallbearers and casket from the church, followed by the congregation as it formed a languid stream of soft murmurs. An aromatic film of incense hung thick in the air as the church bell tolled its loud sonorous *bong* for each year of Leonard's life. A reverent interconnection of sight, sound, and smell.

As the disquieting tone of the bell pierced the silent community, it underscored the close of an era, the finish line at the end of Leonard's journey. Each mournful tone wafted from the steeple, drifting downward, blanketing Plymouth, as if offering comfort to the town he'd left behind.

With the casket sealed in the hearse, a long rope of cars dragged behind in a short winding tour of Plymouth, taking Leonard where he could lie in peace near his mother, his father, Butch, and baby Joey.

An hour before even the most ardent employee arrived, the office building was quiet. Lou set his briefcase on his desk but chose not to open it. Not yet. Instead, he walked down the hallway to his father's office. Weeks had passed since his father's funeral. Some of his father's personal effects had been removed by the family. Many still remained.

Flipping on the light switch, Lou was immediately struck by its surreal state of suspended animation, an office that had hovered near dormancy for months following the final stage of Parkinson's. To the side of his desk, the metal funeral sign—a remnant Leonard cherished— stood as a sentinel. His desk calendar lay open to a long-forgotten day. Even the chair seemed to patiently wait for his return.

In thought, Lou tapped his knuckles on the top of the desk then turned toward the bookcase. Faces smiled back at him, photos nestled within books and other materials on the shelves. The office spoke of family more than of cheese. That was logical, thought Lou. Relationships meant everything to Leonard.

Lou took an empty chair in front of the desk, threw an ankle over his knee, and rested his chin on his laced fingers as he pondered the desk before him. He imagined the timeless nights when Leonard sat there, long after the others had returned to their homes. Too often, his father bore the yoke of worries, disappointments, and uncertainty in the earlier years, trudging onward, propelled by his unwavering belief in himself and others.

On the road his father had traveled, Chuck Strobel had remained his staunch confidante. Now, with both of them gone, only their wives remained, sisters sharing a common destiny. How unfair that some entrepreneurs enjoy their success only during a small band of time at the end, after grueling years of sacrifice and naysayers.

In his later years, Leonard had not agreed with every board decision and, in one particular hard-fought defiance, stood solitarily against the selling of their Mitchell cheese plant. Yet, on the other hand, Lou knew that his father took pride in knowing Sargento had pulled itself from the edge of bankruptcy to an enviable financial position. The company was now, for all intents and purposes, debt-free. They owned the land, the buildings, the equipment, and the vehicles. But that, Lou knew, didn't happen without some hardship, without sacrifice.

After Leonard's funeral, the board of directors had elevated Lou's title to that of company chairman, replacing the role his father had held. Following that announcement, others assumed Lou would automatically move into Leonard's office. In the quiet of the morning, Lou studied the space his father had occupied, absorbing the details. Lou had considered moving into these quarters, but quickly dismissed the thought. It seemed appropriate that his father's office should remain as is for a while.

Lou looked once more at the metal funeral sign standing guard, protector at the side of the desk—an icon of Leonard's past. More intrinsically, it represented his father's drive, his optimism, and his unyielding desire to build a business for Dolores and their children. No, he would not move into his father's office, but he would bring with him a few things that were meaningful to his dad.

Clicking the light switch off, he carried the sentry to his office, placing it next to his desk. Save for that funeral home keepsake's new location, all else in Leonard's office would remain for now.

Lou opened his briefcase and reviewed his notes for the morning's meeting. He would meet his brothers in the board room to discuss what he believed to be a potential, long-term threat to Sargento. In the days following the funeral, the topic was mentioned several times. This meeting was to formally put those conversations into motion.

For the next hour, Lou scrawled, scribbled, and scratched notes on a pad of paper. Then, noting the time, he grabbed the pad of ideas and walked across the hallway to the board room. Around the corner of the long table sat Larry, Lee, and his brother-in-law, Eddie Sturzl.

Lou tossed his notepad on the table and slid into the chair behind it. After a brief round of bantering, he led the discussion. "Innovation was important to our father," he began. "We have every intention of continuing that. This year, we're launching a line of reduced-fat cheese. New Product Development has four different items that look like they'll be ready to introduce next year."

"They're part of some consumer research studies," Lee confirmed.

"So the new product pipeline is filling with innovative products," said Lou. "Lots of ideas. Lots of opportunities. Innovation drove the company for our dad, and it has to be the driver for the company in the future. But what we can't lose sight of is the company culture. The corporate values that made Sargento what it is today."

"Surrounding yourself with good people," interjected Larry. "Treating them like family."

"I don't see too much of a risk in losing that feel in the company," said Eddie. "In HR...when we're talking to our people...we mention it all the time."

"I know that, Eddie," said Lou. "We need to do more. Find a way to institutionalize...and I mean that in a positive way...institutionalize our culture. In a way that we reduce the risk of losing it. It's what sets us apart. It means something to each employee to—"

"And I don't want this taken out of context," Larry jumped in. "Just now, Eddie, you said 'our people' when you were referring to our employees. You don't normally phrase it that way. I know. But Leonard considered Sargento as his family. Acted, in many ways, as if each employee was a member of a large family. We should make it a practice of referring to them that way. The way Leonard said it...the way we all feel...I know each of you do because we all tend to say Sargento Family as a synonym for employees."

"Because they are family," agreed Eddie. "And yes, that 'our people' comment was not intended to be as it sounded." He looked from one brother-in-law to the next. "Everyone is family."

"All this is nice," Lou added, "but the issue is more than that. It's the whole belief system that Leonard had. And this is the hardest part. He never sat down and described his beliefs to us. To anyone that I know of. You just knew what he believed by the way he acted. How he treated people."

"In some ways, they were expectations," said Lee. "Expectations of our employees. Our employees' expectations of us."

"And that's what I want us to do." Lou leaned back in his chair.

"Capture those things that have become our culture. Those expectations, I guess as you put it, that Leonard had. The ones he expressed. The ones he never expressed but you knew he believed in.

"I've asked each of you to jot down what you think our culture is. This isn't an easy thing to do. But not having a clear definition of who we are as a company could eventually cause us to drift. So that's what I want to do this morning. Compare our ideas and see if we can capture all this while it's fresh in our minds."

It proved not to be a one-day assignment, not that anyone's expectations saw it that way. The meeting blossomed into many similar conversations over the weeks and months ahead. At first, the Gentine family assembled a list of attributes and values portraying the company as they saw them. In turn, they presented their list to the company officers for validation. Not surprisingly, additional ideas surfaced. The list grew. Principles that came naturally to Leonard proved hard to condense, hard to crystallize.

Through some consolidation and elimination, the corporate officers then compiled and presented to the Gentine family the first round of Sargento principles—forty attributes in all.

"Too many," Lou said as he shook his head. "Too cumbersome to communicate generation to generation. And far too complex for an individual to subscribe to as a set of guiding principles."

As a means of filtering and fine-tuning the unwieldy list of tenets, the company officers solicited the opinions of the Sargento Family through employee surveys, exploring each of the forty attributes, asking that each corporate value be ranked and rated based on importance.

The process proved more arduous than anyone had imagined.

Through more consolidation and soul-searching, the forty values were pared to twenty. Lou assigned a team of three individuals noted for their skill in written communication—Barbara Gannon (VP of consumer and public affairs), Bob Leverenz (a member of the board) and Lee Gentine—to word-smith and succinctly describe each tenet. In turn, that three-person team categorized each value under three different pillars: *People*, *Pride*, and *Progress*.

A few years earlier, under the leadership of Bob Leverenz, the company drafted its *Code of Business and Personal Ethics* and the company's *Statement of Values and Purpose*.

Complementing the cultural tenets, the *Statement of Values and Purpose* in many ways defined the "soul" of Sargento: guided by a faith in God, an insatiable winning spirit, dedicated to enhancing long-term stakeholder value and sharing the results of success with those who contributed to it.

Now, through the efforts of the entire Sargento Family, the company offered clear expectations in retaining its greatest asset: its culture. Sargento would remain an employee-driven company. That would not alter, but now the rules of the road were clearly defined. Like points on a compass, the corporate values could remain fixed despite the inevitability of change in the industry and the world.

# 38

# The Wizards of ROZ
## 2001

THE FIVE YEARS following Leonard's death witnessed a proliferation of ideas, projects, and activities, all threading in the same direction but on slightly divergent paths, like a rapidly growing plant branching in different ways to reach the same sun.

It was a time when Joe Sartori, one of the last to witness the company's beginning in 1953, died in a medical center in Jupiter, Florida. Since Joe's early involvement, the second generation of the Gentine family had taken full ownership of the future of Sargento.

It was a time when the *third* generation of the Gentine family considered careers at Sargento as the second generation considered other life options. Lee, the youngest brother, left his position as president of the Consumer Products Division (CPD) to focus on real estate development. He had fulfilled his mission, redirecting Sargento from a sales-driven company to a marketing-driven company. Eddie Sturzl retired to spend more time with his family. Larry, Leonard's oldest son at Sargento, also began eyeing a not-too-distant retirement.

It was a time when the entire company took up Leonard's mantle of growth through innovation, with teams, departments, and divisions pursuing advancements in manufacturing efficiencies, new product development, and quality improvement. Capital investments ballooned. Department expenditures escalated.

Sales surged skyward at an exhilarating pace, but like a rocket that expends the majority of its fuel during the launch, Sargento found its profits depleted. No other time in the history of the company had Sargento posted so much red ink.

In a focused effort by the Sales Department, Sargento pushed product distribution to all grocers in all states of the country—to become, at last, a national company. With that, Marketing focused on driving consumer awareness, investing dollars to make the name Sargento increasingly recognizable to consumers.

These broad, bold brushstrokes of activity arced over the canvas of a weakened economy in the country. The dot-com bubble burst, shaking the financial world, and by 2001, the economy found itself in a full-blown recession. The cheese-block market pricing—the primary measure of raw material costs at Sargento—whipsawed year over year, challenging the company's ability to stabilize pricing.

In the end, there came a time in 2001 that Sargento found itself at a critical juncture, choosing one of three possible outcomes: to follow the current path, in turn shrinking the company's importance in the cheese category; to seek marginal growth, forgoing its innovative heritage; or to pursue the painful path to reinvent itself, redefining its targets and success measures. Each of the alternatives and their attendant pressures and discomfort would stress the company's structure. As chief financial officer of Sargento, George Hoff took the lead role.

"We are plowing through cash at an alarming rate," said George. "The path we are on is failing us big time!"

Together in Lou's office behind a closed door sat the executive team, the small group of advisory officers representing the key functional areas within the company. The financial picture George painted was not unexpected, but that didn't make it any more palatable.

Following Leonard's death, the company had suffered a small loss. An aberration, Lou had thought, as the company switched accounting cycles from a fiscal year to one aligned with the calendar.

But the next year, Sargento posted the largest loss in the company's history. And the year following that, the losses sank into an inexorable decline, pushing Sargento deep into debt.

"We are out of balance," continued George. "We've lost money in three of the last five years, and the two years of profits were not enough to offset our total losses. And this is not a reflection on our Sargento Family."

George leaned forward, barely sitting on the edge of the office couch. "Our employees are doing more projects than anytime in our history. They're running harder. We couldn't ask for a more supportive, dedicated group of people. But we are posting monthly operating losses and ballooning capital investments."

Except for the rustling of paper, the office was still.

"I believe we need to call a time-out," George said, breaking the silence. "The cost of cheese…our raw material costs…accelerating expenses. Mushrooming capital spending. We're working on too many projects. Everyone's heart and mind is invested in our success. I could not be more proud of our employees. But we need to shove a stick in the spinning wheel. Use industry benchmarks for growth, expenses, and profitability. Recalibrate. Reset our scale to zero."

George's words hung in the air as Lou—sitting in the overstuffed chair, his legs crossed and George's stack of papers tapping at his knee—weighed his thoughts. Many sleepless nights had plagued him over the past few months, and he could see that his brother Larry shared his insomnia. The livelihoods of eight hundred employees were in jeopardy. The worry, more for the fate of the Sargento Family than for the fate of the company, kept him awake.

Lou looked from person to person—his executive staff, his top advisors: CFO George Hoff; Mark Rhyan, executive VP of operations; Karri Neils, executive director of human resources; his brother Larry, president of the Food Service Division; and Bob Clouston, president of the Consumer Products Division.

"I'm recommending some very dramatic cost cutting," George said at last.

"How dramatic is dramatic?" asked Larry.

George looked at his notes. "I would say we are looking at cutting total company expenses a million dollars...or even a million and a half dollars...each month."

Mark studied the faces in the room. "And," George continued, "it will most likely take us two years to fully get us back on track."

*Two years! At that cost-reduction level!* Lou felt as if he had just taken a blow, knocking the wind from him.

Bob Clouston had suggested downsizing, a proven way to quickly reduce expenses.

Lou thought of the inked sketches of Leonard and Chuck in the board room. Never in the company's history had Leonard chosen to downsize. Quite the opposite, he and Chuck Strobel sacrificed—personally if necessary—to keep the Sargento Family intact, employed, and paid. How could Sargento be so duplicitous as to preach the importance of people and then, when in a financial corner—a temporary one, Lou believed—lay off a large part of its workforce, forcing families to face their own financial crisis?

An uneasiness, borne out of a desire to do what was right, stirred a sickening churn, a hollowness in his stomach as he struggled with the implications. "OK, let's not abandon our values as part of the fix. Let's be creative!" Lou urged. "I want to have as little impact on our employees as possible."

He raised his index finger. "Plus, I don't want to cut contributions to retirement funds. Health care. Things like that. We need to keep in mind the good of the company as well as the good of those working here."

Over the course of several meetings, Lou's staff drafted a master plan reviewing every project, every process, every department, and sadly, every employee. In the end, and much to the dismay of the Gentine family, there seemed no other alternative but to reduce some headcount.

Lou reluctantly accepted the possibility. He made it clear that, if downsizing proved inevitable, it would be the company's *last* resort, affecting as few employees as possible—no more than two people per department.

Like shoving a stick in a spinning wheel, the recovery plan abruptly jarred multiple departments in the company.

Over the previous two years, Sargento had invested $34 million in capital spending: upgrading buildings and equipment, developing new technology. The revised, dramatically reduced budget now diminished future spending. Only projects that reduced product costs or enhanced capacity on key items survived the budget cut.

Marketing and Sales trimmed its planned spending, following a focused path in the recovery plan. Only specific product lines offered a price reduction to spur sales. Advertising and promotion spending were shifted to best accent short-term gains, with advertising highly targeted in those markets that represented the company's strongest base.

Management charged each department with cost-savings goals, asking them to identify unnecessary spending. Small savings were not to be overlooked. Simply turning off lights when leaving a room offered only a small contribution to the total picture, but played a significant role in reminding employees to be attentive to financial leaks.

Human Resources shared unpleasant conversations with employees as officer compensation, salaries, and hourly wages were immediately frozen. Portions of the profit-sharing contribution were held back as well as a portion of the annual bonus.

New product development had in the past maintained an expansive list of projects in the queue. Each month, those projects were coded based on prioritization. Just the management of so many projects in motion drained resources. Now that project list was dramatically trimmed to the select few that offered the greatest opportunity in the shortest amount of time with the least amount of investment.

It was an all-out war against an invisible enemy.

In company-wide presentations, George painted a common image easy for all to understand. "Just as a scientist resets the scale to zero before weighing, Sargento will reset its zero by benchmarking other similar-sized businesses." ROZ (Resetting Our Zero) became the rallying cry. "We're establishing clear, simple criteria for steering the ship."

Over the ensuing weeks, the employees rallied around ROZ. One day Larry stopped by Lou's office. "I'm scrapping my plans for retirement. For now. This is a very stressful period for the company and everyone involved. I'm going to push out my retirement a couple more years. It's not fair to you that you take on this problem alone.

"Besides," he added, "we are asking people to sacrifice and make personal changes to get the company back on the right path. I'm sticking around to do my part."

The next twelve months were stressful. "Communicate! Communicate! Communicate! Involve the Sargento Family," urged Lou. "Ask for their ideas. This is our family. Everyone should have a voice, have the right to be heard."

Each member of the executive team traveled from department to department, plant to plant, covering all shifts, extolling the message of ROZ. Although wages and salaries were frozen, Lou committed to making up any loss in take-home pay at some point in the future if they quickly executed a turnaround.

It became the most comprehensive financial restructuring the company had ever witnessed. ROZ would be the focus, the primary focus, for the next two years. In a surprising way, the concept of ROZ married well with the "persnickety" attitude. Not settling for less than the best in safeguarding the financial base.

By the end of 2001, the response of every employee to the company's plea amazed top management. Even the most ardent doubter in the Sargento Family converted. George's two-year vision to turn the company around completely underestimated the passion of every employee.

In only one year, Sargento reset its zero and charted a stronger course. The Sargento Family—the true wizards of ROZ—turned the company on its ear and on a path to lead them successfully through the new century. It had been painful, but Sargento had, indeed, reinvented itself. In half the projected time.

# 39

# Milestones and Modest Mastery
## 2012

JANUARY 19, 2012, marked an important day for Lou, an honor at lunch that would overarch his career. Twenty-one years earlier, his father received the same lifetime recognition, and Lou could only imagine the thoughts that ran through Leonard's head then.

But as Lou prepared for this day, he thought of the many paths he and Sargento had traveled. In a rush of memories, he could recall the good times as well as the unpleasant ones. And he thought of the tenacity, the unwillingness of the Sargento Family to relent, despite the occasional hurdles in their path.

Some days required that he face complex business issues, leaving him wondering if he had considered all the options, if he had made the right decisions for the benefit of all.

On the other hand, there were times—and fortunately, there were plenty that he could recall—when he injected fun and humor into his job. In 2004, he directed all Sargento semis to be repainted with Swiss cheese holes. After the first few cabs and trailers were redesigned, he drove his mother to the company parking lot. Dolores, ninety-five years old at the time, sat in the passenger's seat and studied the parked Sargento semi.

He recalled looking at his mother, noticing how she had grown so frail over the years, that her mind wasn't as sharp as it had once been. Nevertheless, Sargento was her company as much as it was Leonard's. Her opinions mattered. There was a time when she voiced her belief that young men should wear shirts with a collar and a tie. "That's the way a businessman should look," she had told him. For longer than at other companies, shirts and ties remained the dress code at Sargento. Bringing his mother to see the new truck design was more than just a courtesy. It was a respect for her opinion, a respect Lou felt she deserved.

"I need to get the boss's approval," he told his mother that afternoon with a grin. "This will be the way all our trucks will look."

"Very nice," Dolores said. She paused for a moment and then added, "They're bright!"

A Sargento semi with swiss cheese holes

That was confirmation enough for Lou.

Repainting all the Sargento trucks was one of the fun projects that offset the more serious, intense issues he navigated. Sargento had its fair share of those: a near bankruptcy in 1978, ROZ in 2001. Then, under the weight of the Great Recession in 2009, Sargento struggled initially but, unlike other companies in the category, finished the year strong.

In each instance, it was the Sargento Family that rallied—sometimes temporarily sacrificing wages—making it possible to cross each chasm in the road. It was that same family that explored and proposed solutions, then trudged through the daily effort of achieving those solutions, growing stronger in the process.

At noon, the National Cheese Institute would be honoring him—and the Sargento Family, he reflected—at the Dairy Forum luncheon, presenting him with the NCI Laureate Award, the industry's highest honor, just as they had given his father.

He glanced at his wife, Michele. As she looked back, he could clearly discern all that he admired in her. Warmhearted, accommodating. Her transparent pride in the way he led Sargento. Her faith, knowing that God's hand guided him and the company.

What man can become successful without a supportive wife, a supportive family? Her patience on the many nights he came home late from the office. Her understanding when he told her he needed to fly out, unexpectedly, to see a customer. Her faithful attendance at a child's sporting event—ones he occasionally missed. All an outward sign of her love for him and their family.

As often as he could, he dedicated time to his family. But because of Michele, he had achieved so much more. He was suddenly filled with a rush of love and gratitude.

"Ready?" Louie's voice sounded from behind him. As he turned, Lou saw his son approaching, checking his watch. "We're still in good shape. Plenty of time."

Lou patted his pants pockets, pulled out the room key, and deposited it at the front desk.

"Checking out?" asked the woman behind the counter. "Shall I leave everything on the card?" Then, looking up, the woman spotted the pin on Lou's lapel and squinted as if attempting to better read the name embossed on it. "Sargento? Is that where you work?"

Lou nodded.

She seemed to be puzzling out some connection to the name. "Isn't that the company where all the employees won the lottery?"

"That's right," said Lou. "You have a great memory. That was six years ago." Like others who worked at the company, he had grown used to this association. It surprised him how quickly the story spread and how long people remembered it. "Not everyone won the Powerball," he explained. "But a hundred employees on second shift were surprised to learn they picked the right six numbers."

"I thought it was Sargento that had the lottery winners. I bet a lot of employees left the company that day."

"Well, no," said Lou. "Everyone but one or two showed up for work. At least three-quarters of them still work there today."

The woman gave a furtive glance from side to side as if assuring herself that her boss was not within earshot. "If I ever won the lottery," she said, adopting a confidential tone as she handed him his paid bill, "I'd be calling in my resignation over the phone."

He guessed nearly everyone pledges to abandon their jobs after winning the lottery, choosing what they believe to be a path of worry-free living. But that had not been the case in 2006. After investing weekly in the lottery, a hundred employees split a jackpot that had swollen to $206,600,000. After taxes, each was awarded $670,000, enough to pay off their mortgage and add the remainder to their retirement fund.

Concerned for their safety around the equipment, their minds on the excitement of winning, Lou had offered them the day off at full pay. He organized a cadre of trusted financial advisors, support, and guidance for each employee. Sargento picked up the tab for that.

"You weren't one of the lottery winners, were you?" asked the woman at the hotel desk as Lou began to walk away.

"What?" He turned back to face her. "No, but I did tell them that the next time they took up a collection for the lottery to be sure and ask for my dollar." With that, Lou smiled and left.

Sargento lottery winners

A hundred employees—the Miracle 100, as the employees called themselves—became the center of national media and the local press. NBC sent a camera crew to the Sargento campus for a remote interview.

Mark Rhyan, executive vice president of operations, arranged a suitable location in the truck yard—a space large enough to gather every lottery winner. Powerful flood lamps burned, bleaching the predawn darkness into day. Wearing the same cheese-colored shirts, the Powerball winners waited for the cue, signaling the start of a live interview.

"By any standard, this is a life-changing amount of money," said one of the hosts of *The Today Show*. "How about a show of hands? How many are still going to work here?"

Every hand shot into the air. Mark Rhyan smiled as if enjoying the shocked expression at NBC.

"You're kidding, right?" the broadcast journalist pushed. "That's a lot of money. There must be a few of you thinking of quitting."

"Nope," one of the employees responded. "We'll be going into Sargento every day. We won a lot of money. But we still have a job to do."

Those unrehearsed, off-the-cuff remarks from the Sargento Family to the media had made Lou proud that day. Proud that the nation could see his family—Leonard's family—demonstrate what company pride meant. What dedication meant. How a company acts when employees know they are valued, that they matter. It was such a fine testimony to Leonard and the type of company he struggled so hard to build. And that day, on NBC, the entire nation saw the legacy Leonard left behind.

As Lou walked into the Dairy Forum luncheon, he was struck more by the accomplishments of the Sargento employees than by his own. It was nice to receive the recognition from his peers, but he knew where most of the credit lay.

As the lunch ended and attendees reached for the dessert at their tables, Mike Reidy, serving as vice chairman for the association, approached the podium. He shuffled a few of his notes and paused until the volume in the room receded.

"Today," Mike began, "it is my distinct honor to present this year's NCI Laureate Award."

As the room quieted, Lou relaxed in his chair and laid both arms on the table before him. Michele smiled at him and placed her hand on his arm.

Mike looked around the room and then gazed down at Lou and his family. "This year's NCI Laureate is a family man, leading a family-owned business that understands the nutritional needs of the modern family. Lou Gentine has built a remarkable reputation for delivering groundbreaking products in the cheese industry—reduced-fat cheeses, the Slide-Rite freshness seal, and specialty cheese blends, just to name a few from a long list of contributions.

"Lou began his career at Sargento in 1973, and for nearly four decades—most of which he served as CEO and leader of the company— Lou led Sargento as sales grew from ninety-one million dollars in 1981 to just shy of a billion dollars. By 2012, Sargento employed more than fifteen hundred employees.

"Recognitions have been numerous for Lou. Just in the four years leading up to the Laureate Award, Sargento was named Business of the Year by the Plymouth Chamber of Commerce. It was named Dairy Processor of the Year by *Dairy Foods* magazine and Manufacturer of the Year by Wisconsin Manufacturers & Commerce.

Louie, Michele, and Lou Gentine

"Sargento has repeatedly been named Top Workplace in Southeastern Wisconsin."

Mike walked the audience through an ever-expanding list of accomplishments. Then, as Lou took his place behind the podium, the attendees rose to their feet. He thanked the industry for the honor, Michele for her unflagging support, and the Sargento Family. "I can't think of any greater tribute to our employees' efforts," he added, "than to display this award in our lobby."

It would be one of Lou's final recognitions as CEO of Sargento.

Seven months later, death's shadow once again swept over the Gentine family.

In somber rooms, filling with hushed conversations and hugs between family members, easels sprouted, bearing an assortment of old photographs.

In 1991, they had lost Butch, Chuck two years later, and Leonard in 1996. Now they lost Dolores. Although she had lived to the age of 103, death always comes too quickly, so unexpectedly.

The hot August afternoon offered little promise of cooling. Cars, glaring in the punishing sunlight, filled the parking lot as employees, friends, and neighbors offered their condolences. As vehicles continued to stream in—overflow parking available on empty lots adjacent to the funeral home—the line of friends and Sargento employees snaked into one room, then through another, constantly lengthening in the process. Another loop became necessary, then another. Finally, unable to be contained within the air-conditioned building, the line spilled out into the heat of the day.

In the viewing room stood her family: Larry and Kathy, Lou and Michele, Ann and Eddie Sturzl, Lee, the grandchildren, and the great-grandchildren.

The next day, those attending the funeral filled St. John the Baptist. Like that at the funeral home, the family's mood at the funeral Mass was celebratory and Larry gave an upbeat eulogy at the conclusion of the service.

Dolores joined Leonard, their son Butch, and their grandson Joey. Anita Malone, Dolores's younger cousin who first arranged the blind date between Dolores and Leonard, attended the funeral, comforting Marge Strobel. Marge, now eighty-eight years of age, stared in somber reflection as the sister she idolized was laid to rest.

Of those involved in the very beginning, witnessing firsthand the string of businesses Leonard started—the funeral home, the mink farm, the ambulance service, the start-up of the Plymouth Cheese Counter, Genstrupp, and Sargento—of those that had been a party to it all, only Marge Strobel now remained.

Dolores had seen Leonard's vision grow, stabilize, and finally become a formidable cheese competitor—a huge milestone for a small company to achieve. She had seen her family take the reins of what Leonard had started and build upon that foundation. Now, what she and Leonard had built—Sargento, and most notably, her family—would carry on without her.

Four months later, in December, at the end of the business year 2012, Sargento reached a major milestone. It closed the year posting sales that exceeded a billion dollars.

Dolores never saw that achievement, but Lou doubted that it mattered. He knew that Leonard, Dolores, Butch, and baby Joey all witnessed the accomplishment from above and smiled at what had been achieved. And he knew that his mother had experienced the long saga firsthand: Leonard's long-sought family business take root and grow. She had been proud enough of that accomplishment, of what they had achieved in their lifetime.

With equal pride, she had been proud of her children for taking Leonard's dream, keeping it alive, allowing it to thrive. And she had known in her heart that, of the many grandchildren, there would be a few who would continue to make Sargento a family business.

The road had not been straight nor the sign markers along the way clear. Nevertheless, the two families—the Gentine family and the Sargento Family—had never given up.

# 40

# The Torch Is Passed
## 2013

Louie Gentine, CEO

OUT OF FEAR, most people would rather face their own death than do what Louie Gentine planned that morning.

Louie, at the age of thirty-nine, had been a full-time employee of Sargento for over thirteen years, proving his competence as he worked through the corporate ranks. Today, as president of Sargento, he would stand before fifteen hundred people—the entire Sargento workforce—and orchestrate a four-hour presentation.

Public speaking was not new to him. He'd spoken—scripted and unscripted—countless times. With so many occasions afforded in the past, he had developed a poised, conversational speaking style as well as a command of the stage—characteristics of a charismatic leader. This blustery February morning, he would not only inform but also overlay snippets of humor and entertainment to soften the duration of the morning.

For the past two decades, his father, Lou, had presided over the content, composition, and character of the annual All-Employee Meeting in the Plymouth High School auditorium. This year, Louie assumed that responsibility.

New employees to Sargento oftentimes referenced the upper-management communication style of their former employer—a tendency to keep employees at arm's length, spoon-feeding select information, giving the impression of "inner circle" accessibility. In contrast, Sargento made it a practice, numerous times a year, to provide honest, candid communication, revealing the company's strategic thinking; detailed descriptions of product and process innovations; and full financial disclosure on profitability and expenditures.

As CEO of Sargento, Lou opened the meeting with an affirmation of the company's commitment to its *Statement of Values and Purpose*. It laid the foundation for everything to follow. As Lou turned the stage back to his son, Louie offered his opening remarks, centered around the company's sixtieth anniversary.

George Hoff, the company's chief financial officer, then presented the previous year's financial results but, in view of the anniversary, also provided a retrospect of the entire financial trail leading to 2013.

Lou Gentine, George Hoff, and Louie Gentine

"After twenty-five years of near-zero revenue growth," he explained as the slide behind him portrayed a flat, green line lumbering along the bottom of the graph, "the second generation joined Sargento and focused on developing the Sargento brand."

The green line began rising.

"It took thirty years for Sargento to break the one hundred million net revenue threshold. That's half of the corporate history just to get that far!"

George advanced the slide, and the sales line lifted as it stretched to 2004.

"It took another twenty-one years for our revenue to reach five hundred million. Then"—the slide expanded to 2012—"it took a mere seven years to double what we achieved in 2004 and break the billion-dollar threshold. That's compressed accelerated growth.

"Sixty years ago," George said in summary, "Leonard planted a small mustard seed of our culture—his idea of Sargento. Today, that plant has developed into something that is unbelievably large and strong. All of this could not have been possible without the dedication of those that have come before us, your efforts, and through the grace of God."

Spanning the course of the morning, Michael Pellegrino, president and chief growth officer, presented a recap on new products in development and marketing support. Other presentations included planned capital investments and changes to employee benefits. As the last speaker left the stage, the meeting prepared for its closing.

Karri Neils, the executive vice president of human resources, unexpectedly walked onto the stage. "Lou and Louie, would you be kind enough to come up here with me?"

Louie, expecting to be introduced to offer his final remarks, felt a sudden uncertainty sweep over him.

It was not unusual for the executive team to interject ad hoc material, in the name of fun. Whatever they had up their sleeve, Louie thought, he was up to the task. He felt confident he could respond in kind, with grace and with his own brand of wit.

As Lou and Louie stood to one side of the stage, hands tucked behind their backs, Karri explained.

"Over the past sixty years, the Gentine family has touched so many of us in so many ways that the employees...your Sargento Family"— Karri looked at the two men at the corner of the stage—"decided to show you their appreciation. Cindy Spradau in our HR Department suggested the idea and worked with every one of our employees to give you this..."

The house lights dimmed. A video played.

Visual expressions of thanks wheeled on and off the screen over a bed of music. Employees gave thanks for a stable job, for personal development, for the company's generosity, for company-paid tuition, for the company's way of giving them a second chance in life, for the friendships they developed in the family, for the on-site health care, for the personal recognition—the reasons for the gratitude were as numerous as the employees. The nine-minute video poured out their authentic appreciation.

The screen darkened and the house lights returned.

Employee thank-you video

Louie felt a well of emotions rise within him. His breathing grew labored and shallow. He knew many of the faces in the video and understood their sincerity.

This was not just an entertaining recognition of the past sixty years. It was an outpouring of love. A visible tribute to the culture of Sargento. A demonstration of loyalty to Leonard, Dolores, his father, and his uncles.

Unspoken, it was also an implicit message to him and the third generation. The employees were offering their loyalty—their trust. "Thanks for all you do for us!"—the last image on the screen burned fresh in his memory.

He felt compelled to respond, to speak ahead of his father, but knew he had to first face down his emotions, take control of the moment. Louie blew out a deep breath and grabbed the microphone.

The words struggled to form. His mind raced as another wave of emotions threatened to choke his comments.

"Thank you very much for that. That was great. The creativity in doing that!"

Louie took a quick breath. "Sargento is not about the Gentine family…" His voice cracked. He paused. Pushed back the wellspring.

"You guys are just amazing! What you do every…every single day for the entire stakeholder family is really…really remarkable.

"And…" He felt the undercurrent rise and overtake him once more. He paused. *Breathe*, he told himself, and emotionally bound, he felt the vulnerability of standing before the entire company. To his surprise, the audience clapped. This was not applause earned, but something else, Louie thought. It was a visceral connection, an acceptance. They were treating him as if he were one of *their* family members.

"I really thank you," Louie said, and then could say no more.

Taking the microphone, Lou smiled at his son. "And I thought I was the schmaltzy one in the family." Lou clapped his son on the shoulder as everyone laughed.

"You know," Lou began, "I usually jump up in front of Louie and say everything he wants to say. Then he doesn't have anything to say. So I guess he just showed me how that really works!" A small wave of chuckles rose and died away.

"But that video," Lou went on, "was very nice, and from my standpoint, I can't imagine anything more important than your appreciation. We do our best to follow the guidelines set by my father and then together—everyone in this auditorium and those that couldn't be with us today—just contribute to the success of the company."

Lou paused as if pivoting to drive home a thought. "You know…

it's wonderful to be successful. But there's going to be times…there have been times…and there'll be times in the future when things don't work out quite as well as they have in the last couple of years.

"But the one thing that carries us forward and it gets us through some of those zigzags—George pointed it out in his graph earlier—we've got you. We've always considered it our highest honor that you are a part of our family."

With the conclusion of the meeting, Louie watched as the employees gathered their winter coats, left the auditorium, and started their weekend. His future, the future of his entire family—the Sargento Family—suddenly shrank, he realized, to their ability to maintain trust and work as one. It was all they had—all they ever had in the past—but it would be enough. More than enough.

Later that year, Lou announced his retirement and the board of directors approved Louie as the company's next CEO. The torch passed on October 29, the anniversary of Leonard passing the torch to Lou in 1981.

Just as Lou and his brothers transformed Sargento in ways Leonard never would have considered possible, Louie and his generation would transform the company in ways unimaginable to Lou. But despite the changes ahead, the corporate culture would remain an immutable cornerstone.

Louie would continue to lead Sargento in his own unique style but with his family's same brand of leadership: *one that serves the employees of Sargento and not the other way around.*

# Epilogue

## 2016–2018

Louie Gentine and Jessica Schultz

AS IF THREATENING to unleash an icy spring rain, thick, leaden clouds choked the sky, chilling the Sargento campus on April 1, 2016.

Atop the metal cheese sculpture in the parking lot stretched Louie Gentine and Jessica Schultz, a production employee from first shift, hands pressed against the cold steel as they planked. Jessica's fitness boot camp requested photographs in unusual locations while holding that rigid, core-strengthening position. Louie eagerly participated.

"Although I had never actually spoken to him before, everyone knows Louie is such a down-to-earth CEO, that I felt comfortable asking if he would be in the picture with me," Jessica said afterward as the two of them rested on the large images of cheese.

Purposefully, that April photo never found its way into the local newspaper or any trade magazine. As a CEO—at least a CEO at Sargento—Louie gets out-of-the-norm requests with surprising frequency. His employee involvement is never for any self-aggrandizing, self-important purpose, but always for the benefit of the employee.

Three years earlier at the All-Employee Meeting, the empathy Louie projected on stage—his heart open to the employees—signaled a clear emotional attachment to the Sargento Family. It was the same rapport employees once shared with Leonard and then with Lou.

From the time the torch passed to Louie in 2013, Sargento posted a string of record sales years—additional years of sharing the results with those that contributed to those successes.

Under the direction of Mike McEvoy—vice president of operations and a third-generation Gentine family member—robots and high-speed equipment were installed in the production facility without displacing a single employee. Those replaced by a machine were retrained, at the company's expense, for new positions. The company expanded into new strategic job responsibilities, attracting some of the industry's smartest with new ideas, innovative approaches, and an indefatigable passion to succeed.

Company loyalty permeated Sargento. By 2018, nearly 40 percent of those winning the lottery twelve years prior still reported to work as usual. Employee turnover rate hovered around 1 percent—outlandishly low by any standards. Few companies could boast as many long-term employees as Sargento, many with forty and fifty years of service. An unparalleled depth of loyalty and experience.

Leaders were found everywhere, Louie believed. Not just at the top of an organization. Assemble a team of passionate, experienced employees—ones found at all levels of the company—give them the air to breathe, and they will outperform even the best "superstar."

Unimpeded, Louie and the Sargento Family continued to drive corporate growth through innovation—the foundational imperative first established by Leonard over sixty years ago. New products such as Ultra Thin Slices and Balance Breaks cheese snacks garnered the spotlight in national publications and earned industry awards.

Years reshaped buildings and manufacturing processes, but the tenets of the culture remain intact. SECAP celebrated its twenty-fifth year of service, feeding the poor and comforting those in nursing homes. Sargento remains committed to building homes in Milwaukee and Plymouth with Habitat for Humanity. Louie continues to recognize employee contributions at all levels, and employees pursue balanced-life careers peppered with humor and fun.

With corporate culture so defining, so critical to the success of Sargento, Louie had unrolled the blueprint for one of the company's greatest objectives in the years ahead: laying the foundation for the fourth generation. In a complex and protracted exploration, he and the Sargento Family prepare for the future: the anticipated changes in automation, technology, and food innovation, understanding how these inevitable changes will affect the fourth-generation Sargento Family, community, consumers, and customers. As a visionary, Leonard looked beyond the moment. Louie has chosen to do no less.

One of the company's retired sales representatives, Steve Foerstner, was known to say, "A family united in a single purpose with the right culture is unstoppable."

*How true that was*, thought Louie. *It's that simple. It's that complex.* Yet there's a certain exhilaration felt as an issue—once onerous at the outset—finds its resolution at the hands of a team of employees.

Regularly, like his grandfather before him, Louie walks a familiar route through the company hallways and then back to his office. With multiple locations and nearly five times the employees that Leonard knew, the task to personally interact daily with the full Sargento Family pushes beyond the realm of physical capability. Nevertheless, personal interaction remains critical, and Louie leaps at every opportunity along the way.

Funeral sign

Although products change, equipment grows more complex, and interpersonal communication often relies on technology, unaltered are the principles and values that Leonard cherished.

The corporate walls tastefully display memorabilia, awards, and employee recognitions. The past is never meant to remain in the past. It must endure. It demands a role in the present, and as the company's crucial infrastructure, it gives service to the future.

Returning from one of the innumerable meetings filling his calendar, Louie glanced at the blue and white funeral sign tucked to the side of his desk. That same sign had stood sentry at Leonard's desk, then at Lou's. Now it took up residence near Louie.

Its sturdy frame had taken the blows of time: a scarred base, a bent corner. To Louie, it was a reassuring reminder of those who had walked before him. It spoke of tenacity, perseverance, a steadfast belief in a vision.

A faint smile crossed his face as he walked by, brushing his hand along its top edge. His grandfather would be proud. Not only of the company but of the people who still pursued his mission.

*Leonard would be proud of one more thing*, Louie thought. It had been commonly believed that Joseph's vineyard—and the Gentine farm in Brookfield, Wisconsin—had fallen victim to a bulldozer. In the late 1940s, the family homestead had been sold and subdivided for housing.

Out of curiosity, two members of the Sargento Family had sought permission from the current homeowners on that property to explore the sanctuary land behind their homes. There, in a thicket of scrub brush, weeds, and undergrowth—there, struggling to survive in a copse of trees with arching branches and spreading leaves prohibiting the sun to enter—were the faltering remains of six ancient grapevines. Only six remained of the once-proud Gentine vineyard.

Cuttings from those Gentine vines had been given to the care of a local nursery, where they rooted and pushed forth new shoots and leaves. In the fall of 2017 and spring of 2018, Louie transplanted the family arbor onto the Sargento campus.

The vineyard his great-great grandparents, Joseph and Josephine, brought with them from Chavannes-les-Grands, France, returned to the Gentine family. The vineyard Leonard had hoped to one day own was introduced to the business he eventually built, shared with his Sargento Family. The disrupted French legacy now restored.

Louie dropped into his chair and began preparing for his next meeting.

The story of a successful company has no ending, no finish line, no last chapter. The horizon always looms just ahead and it beckons. It promises an enviable future. It offers the capability to achieve things not yet imagined. To accomplish more together as a company than one could ever hope to achieve alone.

As days follow days, the present becomes the next generation's history. But for now, the pages of that future remain blank, its story yet untold.

As the past can never be forgotten, neither are lost the individual sacrifices leading to the present. Joseph, Leonard, Lou—each seeing a broader horizon, forgoing short-term gains for long-term benefits. Each measuring success less by the dollars summed on the profit line and more by the sum of the humanity each one brought to others.

Louie and his Sargento Family will be no different. They won't succeed because each employee is treated *like* family. They will succeed because they *are* family.

# APPENDIX A

## *The Sargento Corporate Culture*
### *People, Pride, and Progress*

## People

*Ethics*: Our code of business and personal ethics calls upon us to be legal, moral, honest, respectful, responsible and fair.

*Trust*: Fellow employees share a mutual faith in each other that the overall good of the company is paramount in the suggestions offered, decisions made and actions taken. We are also confident that when properly informed and prepared, they can be counted on to carry out their responsibilities.

*Balance in Life*: At Sargento, we support our fellow employees' efforts to balance the physical, social, emotional, intellectual, financial and spiritual dimensions of their lives, as each of these contribute to overall personal wellness.

*Employee Equality*: Each employee has an integral role to play in the success of the company. While the amount of responsibility may differ, the importance of each job or the person performing it is not diminished.

*Creativity*: We need to foster creative thinking, not only in the products and services we provide, but also in the organization and processes used to provide them.

*Humor and Fun*: An appropriate level of lightness, providing opportunities to smile or laugh, brings enjoyment to work while reliev-ing stress. If we consider our place of work and the work we do to be fun, we will be more satisfied and successful.

*Accountability*: Employees have a personal responsibility to the com-pany and their fellow employees to perform their jobs as expected. They should remember that their behavior, within and outside of the workplace, has implications for the company.

## Pride

*Excellence*: All employees should do their best to provide a quality product or service. Continuous improvement of work processes is pos-sible through team or individual initiatives and training.

*Effective Communication*: The ability to convey an understandable message with appropriately delivered feedback helps others assess their performance. To be truly effective, communication must be "two-way." In a trusting environment, that not only allows for, but encourages, candor.

*Mutual Support*: Fellow employees should expect that they can depend on each other for support of and cooperation with their best efforts to perform their jobs.

*Sense of Ownership*: All employees should protect the assets of the company and use their best efforts to achieve the highest level of return for the company's investment in these assets, just as if they were their own.

*Recognition*: Achievement, whether great or small, is worthy of cel-ebration and is encouraged as part of the feedback process.

*Community Outreach*: Sargento believes that our community is not narrowly defined by our residences and encourages every employee to return time, talent, and treasury to the local community and the broader remote communities. The company is also financially support-ive of many community-based causes.

*Fair Compensation*: All employees are entitled to compensation commensurate with their job responsibilities within the industry in which we compete.

## Progress

*Career and Personal Development*: Sargento encourages all employees to seek personal and professional growth through a variety of lifelong learning opportunities offered by the company. Each employee must also accept responsibility to remain professionally or technically proficient to meet the changing demands of our dynamic industry.

*Customer Focus*: Every employee, regardless of responsibility, must always focus on meeting the needs of our customers when those needs are aligned with our strategic vision and corporate objectives.

*Innovation*: The willingness to innovate in all aspects of our business is essential, as it recognizes one of the most important reasons for our past success and sources for our future success.

*Risk-Taking*: The entrepreneurial "spirit" at Sargento requires a willingness of employees to take thoughtful risks when making decisions. Failure at times is inevitable, but should be viewed as beneficial if the employee and the company learn from the experience.

*Profitability and Growth*: Sargento seeks to rank among the premier companies within our industry relative to profitability and shares the results of such success with the employees who contribute to it. Continued growth is also important to maintain the credibility of our position as a leader within our industry.

*Enlightened Leadership*: Sargento believes that leadership which dedicates its attention to the positive aspects of what we accomplish, concentrates on solutions instead of problems, is focused on the future instead of the past, and encourages both team and individual initiative will be capable of greater challenges lending to heightened levels of success.

# APPENDIX B

## *The Sargento Corporate Culture*

### Statement of Values and Purpose

Sargento is a family-owned cheese company dedicated to enhancing long-term stakeholder value. Sustained by an insatiable winning spirit, we are guided by our faith in God. Our central purpose is to be the best at responding to customer and consumer needs for cheese and cheese-based solutions.

We will achieve this goal by exceeding expectations for innovation, service, quality, value, taste and convenience. We share the results of our success with those who contribute to our success.

### Stakeholder Value

At Sargento, we believe in a concept of ownership that goes beyond our stockholders to include the other important contributors to our success. We include as stakeholders not only our stockholders, but also our employees, customers, community, and suppliers. Although clearly different from that of a stockholder, they each have a meaningful stake in our company. Because of this, we recognize the importance of evaluating the impact of our decisions on each of our stakeholders.

## Corporate Objectives

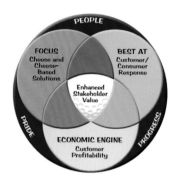

## Code of Business and Personal Ethics

*We Will Be Legal*: We recognize the authority of legal constraints and our obligation to be in conformance with both the spirit and the letter of the law.

*We Will Be Moral*: In our public and private lives, we will strive to give precedence to that which is right over that which is merely expedient or convenient.

*We Will Be Honest*: To warrant the trust of all with whom we come in contact, we must ourselves be unflinchingly honorable in whatever we think, do or say.

*We Will Be Respectful*: Whatever our station in life may be, we will respect in others of all ranks those virtues and strengths of character which we collectively and individually endeavor to exemplify.

*We Will Be Responsible*: To each other and to those outside Sargento, we will strive to fulfill both the obvious and the unenforceable obligations we owe to all whom we serve and with whom we work.

*We Will Be Fair*: In regard to decision-making at all levels, we will strive for maximum objectivity and evenhandedness with all those whose lives we touch.

# ACKNOWLEDGMENTS

*Treated Like Family* had an unexpected beginning. It was not a desire to write a book. It was a longing to share Leonard Gentine's sense of humanity and unflagging dedication to others.

It was my good fortune to know the company founder. In 1996, when Leonard lost his battle with Parkinson's, the world lost a visionary with an innovative mind and a benevolent heart.

In 2010, during a company-sponsored photo scavenger hunt, several new employees noted on their tally sheet that they had found a picture of an old man who parted his hair on the left side. *My God!* I thought. *Some of these new employees don't even know the founder of Sargento.* How could a man who impacted the lives of so many be forgotten so quickly?

At my request, Lou Gentine, then CEO of Sargento, agreed to let me write his father's story. For his confidence in my ability, for his patient coaching along the way, I am most grateful.

A round of sincere thanks goes out equally to others in the Gentine family—Larry, Ann and Eddie Sturzl, Lee, and the Butch Gentine family—as they opened their hearts to this project, sharing memories and stories of the past. To Kristin Strehlow, Leonard's granddaughter, thanks for sharing multiple shoe boxes crammed with family photos.

Special thanks go out also to Louie Gentine. How honored I am to be employed by him, witnessing the third generation–led Sargento. Louie is a remarkable man with a strategic mind equal to his father and his grandfather, and he provided a fresh perspective during the writing of this book.

For my two supervisors over the past seven years—Karen Lepisto and Barbara Gannon—I thank each for their flexibility as I attempted to balance my job responsibilities with my need to write the manuscript. Each offered a sense of quiet forbearance as I tackled the largest project of my career.

Nor can I fail to extend my thanks to their supervisor, Karri Neils, who believed in me and this project from the start, never asking for regular status updates but, instead, allowing me to find my own path at my own pace.

For teaching me the dynamics of different disciplines, I'm indebted to many. In particular, I thank George Hoff for his corporate financial insights and Dr. Scott Peschke for his medical knowledge of Parkinson's disease. Jerry Thorne and Russ Schuler dedicated hours sharing their insights on corporate financing. Ron Begalke, my friend and a key employee in the early history of the company, volunteered to be my historical advisor. Ron read the early drafts of the chapters and provided comments until his unexpected death. I miss you, Ron!

Regarding the pre-Sargento years described in the book, I'm forever indebted to Marge Strobel. As she and her husband, Chuck, played pivotal roles in the success of Sargento, so, too, was Marge's contribution to the success of this book. Without her recall of early events, *Treated Like Family* would not have been as engaging.

Getting the story on paper, keeping all the facts in chronological order, and adhering to individual personalities referenced proved to be a greater challenge than originally anticipated. My endless gratitude goes to Katie Kotchman and Cara Bellucci at Don Congdon Associates, Inc., for their writing insights and their innate ability to tactfully nudge me in the right direction. I've learned so much about the craft from them!

Equally, I extend a sincere, heartfelt appreciation to Keren Baltzer and Grace Tweedy Johnson of Hachette Book Group and the team at

Center Street: Patsy Jones, Laini Brown, and Katie Connors. Thanks for believing in this story and for being the catalyst, allowing so many readers across the country to know Leonard, the Gentine family, and the Sargento Family.

To Jeff Holt and Joan Matthews at Center Street, your attention to detail and fact-checking is amazing. Thanks for tightening the narrative and helping to clarify the communication for those reading this book.

To Chip Schuman, Bill Jacob, Mark Gumm, Heidi Haack, Sarah Ninmer, Meaghan Daly, Gabriella Ferroni, Damon Mooren, Ben Rackl, and Katie Wesch, thanks for developing the marketing and sales platform for this book, raising it above the clutter and noise so prevalent in this world today.

To all my Sargento Family members—too many to mention, but indispensable in their willingness to help in any way—your kindness and friendships will never be forgotten.

To Sue Faley, whose belief in me began in 1970.

For the ability to travel when I needed without shirking my responsibilities at home, I thank Tricia Casady, Kurt Casady, Cindy Spradau, and Keith Abler.

While the development of *Treated Like Family* was supported by talented friends and coworkers, I owe a great deal of thanks to my personal family. It was my mother, Maxine, who taught me to read despite my slight undiagnosed dyslexia. It was my father, Frank, who taught me to love words and encouraged me to write—a passion he shared, writing two books of his own.

To my sisters and brothers—Ann Rex, my departed sister Sue Schaver, Jolene Schaver, Tim Faley, Terry Faley, and Lisa Balk—for their early belief in me and their constant encouragement. I don't think I would have made it without their confidence.

And finally, my unending love goes out to my canary-winged

parakeet and three cockatiels that live with me (Banana, Jack, Hope, and Frosty, who has since passed on). They are my companions in this world. Though they will never read these words, I thank them for tolerating my early-morning departures and my late arrivals in the evening, seven days a week.

But all the above appreciation pales in comparison to the profound love and gratitude I have for my daughter and son, Linda Hopson and Mike Faley. Each offers me their unconditional love despite my constant obsession and conversations about writing. The two of them mean more to me than life itself.

It is only when a family pulls together and unites behind a common cause that the seemingly impossible becomes possible. Each of the above played a significant role and each, in their own way, allowed this book to happen. It has been my luck to be given the opportunity to serve as their spokesperson, voicing their love of Sargento and the Gentine family.

Tom Faley
2018

# ABOUT THE AUTHOR

Tom Faley, born and raised in the Midwest, attended Northern Illinois University and earned his MBA at Western Michigan University. Given his lifelong passion for writing, he worked in sales, marketing, and management positions for forty-five years, writing advertising and promotional copy as well as corporate communication articles. Still employed by Sargento, Tom has celebrated his thirtieth year with the company. He currently lives in the Plymouth, Wisconsin, area and can be found at TomFaley.com. *Treated Like Family* is Tom's first business memoir.